ADVENTURES IN EATING

ADVENTURES in Eating

ANTHROPOLOGICAL EXPERIENCES IN DINING
FROM AROUND THE WORLD

EDITED BY
HELEN R. HAINES and **CLARE A. SAMMELLS**

UNIVERSITY PRESS OF COLORADO

© 2010 by the University Press of Colorado

Published by the University Press of Colorado
5589 Arapahoe Avenue, Suite 206C
Boulder, Colorado 80303

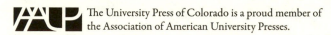 The University Press of Colorado is a proud member of
the Association of American University Presses.

The University Press of Colorado is a cooperative publishing enterprise supported, in part, by
Adams State College, Colorado State University, Fort Lewis College, Mesa State College, Metropolitan State College of Denver, University of Colorado, University of Northern Colorado,
and Western State College of Colorado.

∞ The paper used in this publication meets the minimum requirements of the American
National Standard for Information Sciences—Permanence of Paper for Printed Library Materials. ANSI Z39.48-1992

Library of Congress Cataloging-in-Publication Data

Adventures in eating : anthropological experiences of dining from around the world / edited by
Helen R. Haines and Clare A. Sammells.
    p. cm.
  Includes bibliographical references and index.
  ISBN 978-1-60732-037-1 (hardcover : alk. paper) — ISBN 978-1-60732-014-2 (pbk. : alk.
paper) — ISBN 978-1-60732-015-9 (e-book) 1. Food habits. 2. Food preferences. 3. Dinners
and dining. I. Haines, Helen R. II. Sammells, Clare A., 1973–
  GT2850.A48 2010
  394.1'209—dc22
                                    2010028346
Design by Daniel Pratt

19 18 17 16 15 14 13 12 11 10   10 9 8 7 6 5 4 3 2 1

To my comadre Paulina, for feeding a hungry anthropologist,
and to Chris, for always sharing meals with me.

CLARE A. SAMMELLS

To my father who encouraged me to travel,
my godparents, Rita and George,
who gave me my first taste of "other" foods,
and my mother, who always enjoyed a good meal

HELEN R. HAINES

CONTENTS

List of Figures | **ix**

List of Contributors | **xiii**

1. The Importance of Food and Feasting around the World | **1**
   Helen R. Haines and Clare A. Sammells

SECTION I—THE MAIN COURSE

2. Boiled Eggs with Chicks Inside, or What Commensality Means | **21**
   Roger Ivar Lohmann

3. A Rat by Any Other Name: Conflicting Definitions of "Dinner" in
   Belize, Central America | **43**
   Helen R. Haines

4. The Delicacy of Raising and Eating Guinea Pig | **59**
   David John Goldstein

5. Termites Tell the Tale: Globalization of an Indigenous Food System
   among Abaluyia of Western Kenya | **79**
   Maria G. Cattell

SECTION II—SIDE DISHES AND ACCOMPANIMENTS

6. Ode to a Chuño: Learning to Love Freeze-Dried Potatoes in Highland Bolivia | **101**
Clare A. Sammells

7. Durian: The King of Fruits or an Acquired Taste? | **127**
Maxine E. McBrinn

8. MSG and Sugar: Dilemmas and Tribulations of a "Native" Ethnographer | **145**
Lidia Marte

SECTION III—TABLE MANNERS AND OTHER RULES TO EAT BY

9. Eating Incorrectly in Japan | **167**
James J. Aimers

10. No Heads, No Feet, No Monkeys, No Dogs: The Evolution of Personal Food Taboos | **181**
Miriam S. Chaiken

11. *Buona Forchetta*: Overeating in Italy | **191**
Rachel Black

12. "No Thanks, I Don't Eat Meat": Vegetarian Adventures in Beef-centric Argentina | **203**
Ariela Zycherman

13. Eating with the Blackfeet: Who's Been Eating Whose Food? | **223**
Susan L. Johnston

SECTION IV—BEVERAGES

14. Drinking Ethiopia | **243**
Ronald Reminick

15. You Are What You Drink in Honduras | **263**
Joel Palka

SECTION V—THE LAST COURSE

Epilogue: Edibles and Ethnic Boundaries, Globalization and Guinea Pigs | **277**
Miriam S. Chaiken

Index | **281**

0.1 World map showing research areas of authors | **xvi**

1.1 Plate of chapulines | **3**

1.2 Haines washing chapulines down with liberal amounts of gin and tonic | **4**

2.1 Map of Papua New Guinea showing research location | **22**

2.2 Sago grubs in 1994 | **23**

2.3 Eating boiled sweet potatoes from a common pot in 2005 | **27**

2.4 The already-hatched brush turkey chick in 2005 | **28**

2.5 Eating "Papua New Guinea pizza" in 2007 | **29**

2.6 Sablaio holding a steamed *kuyamodu* (terrestrial phalanger), formerly taboo to non-initiates, in 2007 | **33**

2.7 Sago pudding and a pot of boiled greens in 2007 | **37**

2.8 Rex unpacking eleven brush turkey eggs for the egg and sago bread in 2005 | **39**

2.9 Laurie taking the baked egg and sago bread out of the leaf oven in 2005 | **40**

3.1 Map of the program for Belize National Park | **44**

3.2 The road through the program for Belize Biosphere in 1990 | **48**

3.3 Photo of an agouti in the Belize National Zoo | **49**

4.1 Guaman Poma's representation of *cuy* offering, seventeenth century | **61**

4.2 Fried cuy (cuy chaktado) in Moquegua, Peru | **63**

4.3 Traditional Highland Andean kitchen, Urubamba, Cuzco, Peru | **65**

4.4 Author's nephews and their classroom guinea pig in Lexington, Massachusetts | **66**

4.5 Vendor displays seven-toed cuy in Moquegan market | **70**

4.6 Cuy as sporting club mascot, Moquegua, Peru | **73**

4.7 Cuy graffiti depicted with political aspirations behind the Faculty of Social Sciences, National Major University of San Marcos, Lima, Peru | **74**

6.1 Preparing to plant potatoes on the Bolivian altiplano, November 2002 | **107**

6.2 A woman and her two children dine with other family members at a fiambre with chuño, papa, mote, and a spicy sauce in the center, November 2003 | **108**

7.1 Durian tree | **130**

7.2 Durian fruit | **131**

7.3 Map of Malaysia | **136**

8.1 Views of Dominican food ready to eat (*left*) and coffee greeting (*right*), the Bronx, New York City | **148**

8.2 View of environment in Dominican Republic; New York and Dominican Republic maps and produce; view of New York City subway | **150**

8.3 Dominican woman preparing fresh seasoning in Brooklyn | **152**

8.4 View of R.'s *sancocho* prepared in Brooklyn | **157**

8.5 MSG clean-up day in R.'s kitchen, Brooklyn | **158**

11.1 Moroccan women buying chickens at the Porta Palazzo market in Turin, Italy | **197**

11.2 Culatello di Zibello, a dop product, curing in a cellar near Parma, Italy. The damp, humid fog in this area helps produce the mold that covers the salami and gives it a complex and unique taste | **199**

12.1 An entire side of beef for sale in the butcher shop, a typical sight in Tucumán | **211**

13.1 Montana tribal areas | **225**

13.2 Reservation land with a view toward Glacier National Park | **226**

13.3 Lone reservation supermarket and local restaurant, ca. 1996 | **231**

13.4 Crowd at the annual Browning powwow (North American Indian Days) | **232**

13.5 Assorted food dishes at a potluck | **233**

14.1 Reminick journaling in the mountains | **246**

14.2 Asqala pouring batter for sourdough flat bread | **247**

14.3 Amhara woman preparing coffee | **251**

14.4 Rahel pouring coffee | **252**

14.5 Women with t'ej | **257**

14.6 Reminick and Yismaw with Johnny Walker Black Label Scotch whisky | **259**

CONTRIBUTORS

James J. Aimers
Assistant Professor
Department of Anthropology
SUNY Geneseo
Geneseo, New York

Rachel Black
Lecturer
Food Systems, Culture, and Society
Graduate Institute
Universitat Oberta de Catalunya
Barcelona, Spain

Maria G. Cattell
Research Associate
The Field Museum of Natural
    History
Chicago, Illinois

Miriam S. Chaiken
Academic Department Head and
    Professor
Department of Anthropology
New Mexico State University
Las Cruces, New Mexico

David John Goldstein
Visiting Professor, Facultad de
    Ciencias
Universidad Peruana Cayetano
    Heredia
Lima, Peru

Helen R. Haines
Assistant Professor
Department of Anthropology
Trent University
Peterborough, Ontario

Susan L. Johnston
Professor
Department of Anthropology and
    Sociology
West Chester University
West Chester, Pennsylvania

Roger Ivar Lohmann
Associate Professor
Department of Anthropology
Trent University
Peterborough, Ontario

Lidia Marte
Adjunct Instructor
Cultural Foundations / University
    Programs
St. Edwards University
Austin, Texas

Maxine E. McBrinn
Research Associate
Paleo Cultural Research Group
Broomfield, Colorado

Joel Palka
Associate Professor
Departments of Anthropology
    and Latin American and Latino
    Studies
University of Illinois, Chicago
Chicago, Illinois

Ronald Reminick
Associate Professor
Anthropology Department
Cleveland State University
Cleveland, Ohio

Clare A. Sammells
Assistant Professor of Anthropology
Department of Sociology and
    Anthropology
Bucknell University
Lewisburg, Pennsylvania

Ariela Zycherman
ABD Doctoral Candidate
Department of Applied
    Anthropology
Teachers College, Columbia
    University
New York, New York

ADVENTURES IN EATING

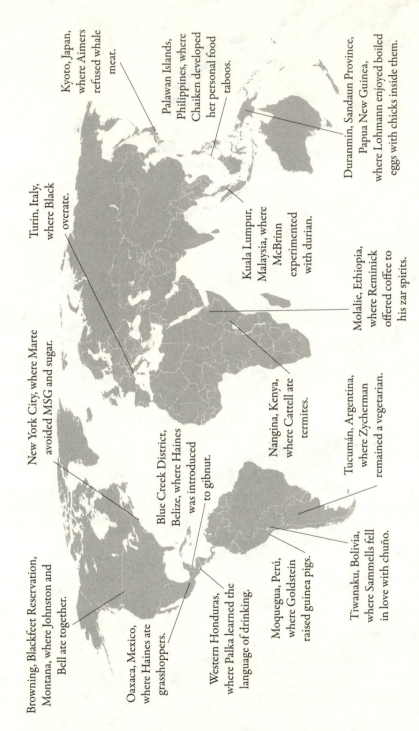

Kyoto, Japan, where Aimers refused whale meat.

Palawan Islands, Philippines, where Chaiken developed her personal food taboos.

Duranmin, Sandaun Province, Papua New Guinea, where Lohmann enjoyed boiled eggs with chicks inside them.

Turin, Italy, where Black overate.

New York City, where Marre avoided MSG and sugar.

Kuala Lumpur, Malaysia, where McBrinn experimented with durian.

Molalie, Ethiopia, where Reminick offered coffee to his zar spirits.

Browning, Blackfeet Reservation, Montana, where Johnston and Bell ate together.

Blue Creek District, Belize, where Haines was introduced to gibnut.

Nangina, Kenya, where Cattell ate termites.

Tucumán, Argentina, where Zycherman remained a vegetarian.

Oaxaca, Mexico, where Haines ate grasshoppers.

Western Honduras, where Palka learned the language of drinking.

Moquegua, Perú, where Goldstein raised guinea pigs.

Tiwanaku, Bolivia, where Sammells fell in love with chuño.

0.1. World map showing research areas of authors. (TEXT BY CLARE SAMMELLS)

CHAPTER ONE

The Importance of Food and Feasting around the World

Helen R. Haines and Clare A. Sammells

When I (Haines) first got the idea for this book, I was part of an archaeological field project living in Mitla, a modest-sized town in the western part of the Tlacolula Valley in Oaxaca, Mexico. It was late in the afternoon on a hot Saturday and my colleagues and I had just finished visiting the ruins of Cuilapan in the Valley Grande and were on our way back to the Tlacolula Valley. We had been living in Mitla for almost three months and were wrapping up a somewhat long and arduous field season. Consequently, we decided to extend our day off and stop in the capital city of Oaxaca for a drink and something to eat. Although Mitla boasted a lovely ruin that attracted many visitors, the alcoholic beverages offered to both tourists and locals alike were limited to mezcal,[1] beer, and the occasional bottle of surprisingly good Chilean red wine. While I was generally quite happy with the wine, it was not in regular supply and there is only so much beer I can drink. Mezcal, I discovered, was an acquired taste—one I never quite managed to master.

Tired of our usual fare, I was convinced that *somewhere* in Oaxaca City I could get a gin and tonic. I will readily admit that I have a weakness for gin, specifically gin and tonics. While I do not consume them often or in excess, I must confess to a fondness for unwinding over a lovely lowboy filled with a shot of

Tanqueray,[2] topped with tonic water, two cubes of ice, and a double twist of lime. Although I was raised in a British-Canadian household, it was not until I studied for my doctoral degree in "London over home" (as my grandfather called it[3]) that I truly developed my passion for gin. Gin and tonics were the quintessential drink of the British Empire in the nineteenth century. Not only was it "medicinal," in that the tonic water contained quinine powder (a malarial prophylaxis[4]), but gin and tonic water is also amazingly relaxing and refreshing on a hot afternoon. The late Queen Mum (the mother of Queen Elizabeth II of England) was famous for her fondness for a good gin and tonic. As for myself, I have since gone to great lengths, incurred large expense, and suffered through some truly awful beverages to satisfy my occasional craving for a gin and tonic during my travels.

On that particular day I was quite ruthless as I dragged my colleagues up and down the streets of Oaxaca City, obsessed with finding a place that could make me a gin and tonic. I finally found a place on the north side of the main plaza, a bar in the lower level of a hotel that catered to tourists. The bartender assured me they had gin (*ginebra*) and tonic (*amarillo lata*[6]) and that he could fashion me the drink I so ardently craved. The gin turned out to be a local Mexican brand called Oso Negro (Black Bear). While a bit strong, it was quite palatable, and as the bartender had no trouble supplying us with plenty of lime to "take the edge off," it turned out to be quite a pleasant concoction.

We sat basking in the warmth of a bright and sunny afternoon, enjoying the glories of a refreshing gin and tonic, and looking out over the colonial construction of the *zocalo*. It was there we were spotted by a colleague from another archaeological project. After he joined our merry band, our minds (and stomachs) turned to thoughts of food to accompany our drinks. Our colleague, a long-time researcher in Oaxaca, was shocked to discover we had yet to try the local delicacy *chapulines*. These are small grasshoppers dry-roasted with salt, chilies, and lime that are commonly available in the zocalo. Women carry large platter-like bowls filled with them around the plaza. They scoop them into little bags much like chestnut vendors do, and happy patrons pop them into their mouths as they walk, in a manner reminiscent of people consuming popcorn at a fair.

As insects are not normally on the menu in Belize, where I conduct most of my research, let alone in Canada, where I live, I was quite happy to avoid this dish. I had (naively perhaps?) believed I could make it through my postdoctoral tenure without consuming it. Needless to say, before I could stop him, my colleague called one of the women over and purchased a large bag of chapulines for us to share. This involved him shouting out across the street and then haggling for them over the patio railing, so it was not long before all the patrons in the bar knew that I was about to try my first chapulines. The local patrons

1.1. Plate of chapulines. (PHOTO BY H. R. HAINES)

and staff cheerfully gathered around, exuding the open hospitality and friendliness that is a hallmark of public drinking in Latin America (see Palka, this volume). Others, who judging by their clothing and reticence were tourists, merely turned to watch the goings-on. Based on the joking and smiles, I was guessing they all thought I would refuse, or perhaps gag on the insects.

Had my colleagues been the only witnesses I quite likely would have refused to eat the chapulines. Despite being an anthropologist and knowing that insects are a great source of protein consumed by many people around the world, the idea of consuming them myself was something at which I balked. However, I was not given the luxury of refusing. Surrounded by the staff of the restaurant who had oh-so-helpfully brought us a plate on which to spread the delicacies (Figure 1.1) and watched by the women who were selling them, my only option was to eat. If I refused, I risked not only loosing face in front of my colleagues but, more importantly to me, insulting the local people. Fortunately, the anthropologist in me rose to the occasion and, following my friends' instructions, I poked through the plate, picked a plump one up by the leg, and tossed it into my mouth.

A long time ago my finishing-school teacher taught me the importance of always being gracious and to smile regardless of how you feel. That lesson

1.2. Haines washing chapulines down with liberal amounts of gin and tonic. (PHOTO BY JILL SEGARD)

has served me well as an anthropologist. Sitting on that patio, surrounded by expectant faces, her lessons came flooding back me. While I am positive she had not envisioned me eating insects, I was grateful nonetheless for her instructions. A smile firmly fixed to my face, I chewed and swallowed the chapuline and then quite confidently pronounced it "delicious"—a declaration that met with laughter and applause from the crowd.

Once the crowds dissipated, however, so did my smile. In truth I found chapulines to be even more of an "acquired taste" than mezcal, and I did not hesitate to tell my Oaxacan colleague so in no uncertain terms. I remember very little about the actual taste. What I do remember was a distinct crunch followed by a wet squishy sensation that shot across my tongue. I did try a few more (each hastily washed down with liberal amounts of gin and tonic [Figure 1.2]), but I could not get past the crunch *then* squish. I think perhaps if it had been one or the other sensation, I might have fared better.

It was my confession that chapulines were perhaps the worst thing I had ever eaten that led to a discussion comparing food horror stories. Competing for the most nauseating, exotic, or unbelievable eating experience is a popular sport among tourists and anthropologists alike, but our discussion focused on how our positions as anthropologists obligate us to accept any hospitality offered, no matter how shocking or unappealing, lest we seem to be criticizing or passing judgment. We all noted that while our courses taught us to be culturally sensitive, nothing in our training ever addressed the reality that we might have to eat things that we would not normally expect or, in some cases, not even think of as food. Despite being trained anthropologists, we were like any other tourists arriving in a new country unprepared to deal with the most basic and necessary requirement: food. But unlike tourists, we frequently lack the freedom to refuse something we find unappetizing. It was from this realization, and a desire to share our unexpected and often humbling experiences with new anthropology students, that this book was born.

As the dawning of the twenty-first century has seen the Western world proclaim the idea of its own multiculturality, it seems oddly appropriate that this book was born over British gin and tonics and Mexican chapulines on the side of the Oaxacan zocalo replete with Spanish colonial architecture. The inhabitants of North America see themselves as living in the ultimate global village, one that is not solely the result of technologically enabled instantaneous global communication, as envisioned by Marshall McLuhan (1967), but also a very real cultural microcosm of the world. On a personal level, this means that we believe that we are now exposed to more "cultures" than our grandparents, and possibly even our parents, ever dreamed possible. For those of us who live in North America, this seems self-evident from our own daily experiences. The United Nations estimates that in 2005, 3 percent of all people in the world lived in a nation other than where they were born, but in the United States that number was closer to 10 percent.

Even beyond interactions with people from elsewhere, residents of the North Atlantic have access to technologies that bridge physical distances. More than half of U.S. households have at least one personal computer, and access to the Internet is widespread, allowing individuals to interact with others around the world. The Zapatistas' declaration of war against the Mexican state in 1994 was the first political movement to seek international allies through the Internet. Web pages, blogs, Facebook, and Twitter are commonly used to show support for social movements across national boundaries, while e-mail, instant messaging, and Skype allow people to communicate cheaply on a global scale.

This multicultural milieu is also apparent in the food we eat. In Chicago one can purchase Thai sauces from California-based Trader Joe's (distributed from their Massachusetts warehouse). Hanukkah holiday crackers, modeled after English Christmas crackers, are sold in Crate and Barrel stores throughout the United States. Both items would have required some searching to find in the United States in the 1980s. Chinese and Thai have become synonymous with take-out food, and virtually every North American home has been exposed to Italian cuisine, courtesy of the local pasta aisle at the grocery store. Tortilla chips sit comfortably beside bags of potato chips at the corner store, and the appetizer menus of many bars and pubs list Indian samosas or Mediterranean calamari alongside American buffalo wings.

This is not new, of course. People have long indulged in luxury foods from faraway places, combining the exotic with the local and purchased imports with homegrown staples. Exchange networks have long brought goods far from where they were produced for consumption. Sidney Mintz (1985) shows how the industrial revolution in England, supported by slave labor on Caribbean plantations, made sugar the mainstay of the masses in both locations and linked diverse populations together through the movements of goods and capital. Chocolate was brought from Mexico to colonial Spain, where it quickly transitioned from a medicine to an elite drink and acceptable pre-Mass beverage and then to a childhood snack, while simultaneously shifting from a beverage to a solid (Coe and Coe 1996). Coffee moved from Africa, to Brazil, to Starbucks. None of these trajectories are singular; following the movements of global products like sugar, chocolate, or coffee would create weblike networks covering much of the globe.

This multiplicity of conversations about food and food networks has allowed our dinner plates to acquire the veneer of global cosmopolitanism. It has also led anthropologists to consider globalization and how world systems are created and reproduced not only through the movements of people but also by foods-turned-commodities. Plantation cropping as an agricultural system allowed for foods to become commodities on a global scale. Colonial powers often went to great lengths to move crops from their places of origins in order to capitalize on their economic value; botanic gardens arose for economic, not aesthetic, reasons and were intimately connected to structures of power (Brockway 1978). Mintz's seminal work on sugar (1985) gave rise to a large corpus of literature on systems that link people through agriculture and the processing, transporting, and distributing of food (for a literature review, see Phillips 2006).

Despite the interconnectedness of our food, global cuisine remains delightfully diverse. Nevertheless, anthropologists have found that even the most powerful symbols of the supposed homogenization of global food, such as the "meta-commodities" of Coca-Cola and McDonald's, turn out to be not so uniform after all when considered within specific local contexts and quotidian patterns of eating (Miller 2005; Watson 1997). The culinary patterns of individual households are themselves flexible, accommodating new knowledge from friends, cookbooks, and TV shows. All these media and networks of culinary knowledge can expand food horizons, even while sometimes simultaneously serving to delineate the boundaries of regional, national, or ethnic cuisines (Appadurai 1988).

These global movements are not uncontested. In the twenty-first century, environmentalists encourage people to think of "food miles" in terms of the fossil fuels needed to stock their refrigerators, leading to a new category of "locavores," who privilege the consumption of locally grown, in-season foods. North Atlantic consumers worry about the slave or child labor that may have produced their candy bars. Meanwhile, farmers exoticize the familiar and invoke visions of an authentic rural United States by selling heirloom-variety tomato plants to aspiring urban gardeners. These counter-discourses about food, while largely about taste, also revolve around issues of forms of production and use of resources, claiming a certain kind of relationship to food and expressing specific lifestyles through eating. These discourses are framed within a global context where consumers can choose between Washington State or Chilean apples, between cheap candy or fair-trade chocolate based on geography and economics. Seasonality at many North Atlantic supermarkets is often expressed (if at all) more through price than availability, since fruits and vegetables can be transported from other regions when not available locally. Modern locavores find that simply discovering where their food comes from is often a lengthy research process.

What is perhaps more surprising is that we increasingly travel to our food rather than the other way around. Secure in a sense of worldliness and aided by increased disposable incomes and the ease of international travel, North Americans are traveling to more, and more far-flung, locations around the globe than ever before. The anthropology of tourism talks about the "democratization of travel" after World War II, but North Atlantic citizens have been traveling since the end of the 1800s. At the close of the nineteenth century, mass travel became both possible and more accessible. Companies, such as Thomas Cook's, offered travel opportunities to groups previously excluded from this activity by virtue of either their economic position or the social morals of the day, such as single women and the middle class (Ingle 1991; Hamilton 2005; Urry 1990:24).

Today, tourism is not only a common pastime of the North Atlantic middle class but is also increasingly linked specifically to the experience of food. A brief glance at any tour book will show how important eating well is to tourists while traveling; nearly a third of most travel books are dedicated to dining options, restaurant descriptions, and culinary vocabulary. An increasing number of tours focus specifically on experiencing local food by touring farms and marketplaces, tasting wine, and taking cooking lessons in places like Italy, Thailand, and France. Such tours bring to mind Thorstein Veblen's classic work *The Theory of the Leisure Class*, where he noted:

The quasi-peaceable gentleman of leisure, then, not only consumes of the staff of life beyond the minimum required for subsistence and physical efficiency, but his consumption also undergoes a specialization as regards the quality of the goods consumed. He consumes freely and of the best, in food, drink, narcotics, [etc.]. . . . In the process of gradual amelioration which takes place in the articles of his consumption, the motive principle and proximate aim of innovation is no doubt the higher efficiency of the improved and more elaborate products for personal comfort and well-being. But that does not remain the sole purpose of their consumption. The canon of reputability is at hand and seizes upon such innovations as are, according to its standard, fit to survive. Since the consumption of these more excellent goods is an evidence of wealth, it becomes honorific; and conversely, the failure to consume in due quantity and quality becomes a mark of inferiority and demerit. (Veblen 1899:73)

Today it is the mark of a well-educated, middle-class North Atlantic citizen to know how to eat with chopsticks, where to pour soy sauce for sushi, how to pronounce the names of Italian dishes, and how to properly consume a taco.[5] This is not to say that all people know all these things but that such types of knowledge mark a level of sophistication in North Atlantic cultures, one that indicates the wealth to dine out and perhaps even to travel to distant locations. Eating is not just about sustenance but also about indicating one's position in society. Dining therefore forms an important marker of class (Bourdieu 1984; Goody 1982).

For many in the North Atlantic (who we suspect make up the majority of our readers), international culinary knowledge demonstrates world citizenship. As tourists, they are sure of their own cosmopolitanism, confident that wherever they go they will gain weight on foods either familiar or exotic, but (almost) always palatable. But this veneer of global cosmopolitanism is often superficial. It is rare to find a dish on North American restaurant menus that is unpalatable to Western culinary tastes, such as fried scorpions, durian fruit, and freeze-dried potatoes. Most ethnic dishes pass a series of unannounced tests of cultural acceptability before becoming widely served in their new homelands. Consequently, the shock of being served food that we have never seen before, let alone even imagined, can be a challenge for even the most daring traveler. Even the most extreme guidebooks lack answers to such questions as, What do you do if asked to kill your own dinner? They usually fail to say how to relish a dish that is a considered a rare delicacy in its own country but for which most North American health inspectors would arrest the cook. Most travelers have the option of saying "no thanks" when presented with unappealing culinary offerings. But what does one do when saying no is not the best option?

Food and feasting, as many anthropologists will tell you, forms an important part of social integration (see Dietler and Hayden 2001). It is used to create and cement alliances among the living, assure a peaceful transition into the afterlife for the dead, and induce the gods into bestowing their blessings. People in many cultures consider offering food to a guest the most fundamental form of hospitality, and the refusal of food may be considered a grave insult to the host (Sahlins 1972). Food can even be used by the cook to send important messages to diners about their interpersonal relationships (Stoller and Olkes 1989).

Yet for all anthropologists' awareness of the importance of food and their extensive training in the cultures in which they specialize, they are frequently presented with unexpected dishes and faced with unfamiliar dining customs. For anthropologists, refusing to partake is often not an option, and even when it is possible, such refusals must be negotiated with care. This book is a collection of stories from anthropologists and archaeologists who have come up against these finer points of culinary differences. The chapters in this volume span many years of anthropological research and encompass much of the globe. They are intended not only to demonstrate the importance of food and feasting activities in cultures around the world but also to show that perhaps the world is not as small as we sometimes like to think.

METHODOLOGIES, OR WHAT FOOD CAN TELL US

This volume is not just about food. It is also concerned with anthropological method, and not just for those anthropologists specializing in foodways. Eating is one of the basic things that anthropologists do in the field and one of the major ways of interacting with informants. Mintz and DuBois (2002), in their review of the subdiscipline of the anthropology of food, point out that food has long been important to anthropologists not only because it is central to human existence but also because of the larger methodological questions it illuminates. And Holtzman (2006) demonstrates that food is often integrally linked to memory—something that is as true for anthropologists as it is for the peoples they meet in the field. Food memories are often linked to important realizations, relationships, moments, and fond (and not so fond) memories during fieldwork. The chapters here explore those kinds of events and their importance in the production of anthropological literature.

We have to learn to listen with our taste buds and our stomachs. Stoller and Olkes (1989), in the first chapter of *The Taste of Ethnographic Things*, give a wonderful example of how food can speak. As guests, they put the household where they stay in the spotlight as neighbors come to partake in the hospitality offered to them. This becomes the stage for the cook of the house—a daughter-in-law who married into the family against the wishes of all but her young husband—to serve bad sauce. This bad sauce is not a reflection of her skills as a cook (she has already proven she *can* cook delicious sauces if she chooses to) but a deliberate message sent to the authors and the other members of the household about her frustrations. Stoller and Olkes use this example as a call to a "tasteful ethnography":

> In tasteful fieldwork, anthropologists would not only investigate kinship, exchange, and symbolism, but also describe with literary vividness the smells, tastes, and textures of the land, the people, and the food. . . . In this way, seemingly insignificant incidents as being served bad sauce become as important as sitting with a nameless informant and recording genealogies—data—that eventually become components in a system of kinship. . . . A tasteful ethnographic discourse that takes the notion of mélange as its foundation would encourage writers to blend the ingredients of a world so that bad sauces might be transformed into delicious prose. (Stoller and Olkes 1989:29, 32)

Holtzman (2006:364), in his discussion of Stoller's book (1989), notes that it is unusual in that it focuses on unpleasant eating experiences rather than the more common "ethnography of tasty things—food-centered analysis that feeds on Western epicurean sensibilities, popular culture notions concerning how foods serve as markers for immigrant communities, the nostalgia that wafts from home-cooked broths, and the connections forged between mothers and daughters through food." Our volume is not dedicated to analyzing intentionally "distasteful" food or lauding mouthwatering exotic dishes. Instead, we focus on the tense and awkward moment of discovery—the initial encounter of the unexpected that forces the anthropologist to reconsider accepted boundaries, both social and culinary. Some of these encounters are instantly delicious; other tastes must be acquired. All are productive in learning about cultural practices. These are experiences that all anthropologists have; knowing how to make such moments meaningful is an important skill in our discipline.

The literature on food is vast, and we could never hope to address it all in our brief introduction here (for more complete literature reviews, see Holtzman 2006; Mintz and DuBois 2002; Phillips 2006). The goal of this volume is to consider the questions of what food means beyond the immediate experience of eating it and how anthropologists learn from meals in ways that go beyond the dinner table. We hope this volume will serve as an introduction to newer anthropologists on how to approach the delicate matter of eating in the field—and how to turn food into food for thought for both oneself and the discipline.

SETTING THE TABLE

A brief summary of this volume is in order to "set the table," as it were, for the feast to follow. These chapters have been chosen to show a variety of perspectives, regions of the world (Figure 0.1), subspecialties in anthropology, length of time in the discipline (from advanced graduate students at the beginning of their careers to tenured professors), ages, backgrounds, and personal eating habits. Not all these authors consider themselves to be specialists in food; nevertheless, as anthropologists (cultural, archaeological, and physical) and as humans who eat, they all have interesting observations about how food, eating, and commensality affected their fieldwork in productive and sometimes unexpected ways.

At the beginning of each chapter, we have provided a brief biography of the author so that the reader can get a sense of each writer's perspective as both an academic researcher and an individual. Anthropologists are not objective recorders of culture (and never were, despite pretensions to such); they are people. As people, they have experiences, preferences, religious taboos, and food allergies, as well as simple dislikes. These are not obstacles to be overcome but rather part of what actually creates the data of anthropology.

We have titled the first section of this volume Main Courses, which for many of the cuisines of the world involve meat. Certainly in North Atlantic society meat is seen as the central part of the meal and its defining feature. This is true in many other parts of the world, where meat often has an importance disproportionate to its consumption. Fiddes (1991) discusses how meat is an object of both desire and revulsion; for most North Atlantic peoples, inappropriate animal products cause disgust. The true contents of sausages, as Otto von Bismarck once remarked, have long been a matter that most omnivores would care to know little about. Ground beef was once viewed with such suspicion in the United States that White Castle launched a publicity campaign in the 1920s to counter its image as something of low quality and easily contaminated, thus paving the way for fast-food hamburgers in general (Schlosser 2001:197–198). In contrast, vegetables may be disliked but are rarely a cause for true concern. Although the U.S. salmonella outbreaks of 2008 are worrisome from a health standpoint, few are concerned about eating tomatoes per se. There is something about meat that carries special meanings, and as such the essays included in this section focus on the consumption of meat in different cultures.

Lohmann begins this discussion by telling us about eating sago grubs and fertilized eggs with the Asabano of Papua New Guinea, and how he learned to enjoy only one of these delicacies. Meanwhile, he considers how the recent conversion to Christianity of his informants changed their eating patterns in ways that were not seen the same way by all, especially across gender lines. One of his friends assures him that this was not a loss of tradition but the very condition of possibility that allowed him to conduct his fieldwork without being cannibalized!

In her chapter Haines recounts how, as an archaeologist working in Belize, she managed to avoid the meat of the locally prized gibnut until an end-of-excavation party, when she realized that she had been missing out on a delicious treat all along. She comes to realize that her reaction to the "jungle rat" had more do with the linguistic associations of the term "rat" for North Atlantic English speakers, who assume that rats are not "good to eat," than it did with the nature of the creature in question. Her realization serves as an important lesson for anthropologists in the field to first consider why they react to something as "distasteful" before condemning it out of hand.

Goldstein's contribution also revolves around the issue of eating rodents, in this case, the Andean guinea pig. He is confronted with the challenge of not only learning to accept a rodent as a valued food but then telling his U.S. friends that he essentially eats their pets. His chapter recounts with amusement the horrified reactions of many North Americans to his eating guinea pig and the difficulties of trying to explain that in the Andes, these animals are domesticates raised entirely for meat. He also describes the challenges he faces when he tries to raise guinea pigs himself in order to compare the resulting material remains to those in the archaeological record.

Cattell describes for us how to eat termites after acquiring a reputation for liking them in Kenya. She gives a wonderful description of how the consumption of food and the meals offered to visitors change in the face of economic difficulties. Her long-term research gives a unique perspective on how to use unexpected methods—such as the "soda test"—to gauge peoples' overall well-being. Most food researchers see soda consumption as part of the increasing consumption of sugar and indicative of declining well-being, since these drinks provide only empty calories (Mintz 1985). But Cattell suggests that for those who are enmeshed in a cash economy, the need to forgo markers of hospitality, such as offering soda to guests, indicates serious economic difficulties. Even foods with no nutritional value still have social value and can be worth purchasing and gifting. One is reminded of Scheper-Hughes's realization while working in Brazil that baby formula was a way for fathers to socially acknowledge their children, not just to provide for them (1992:316–326).

The second section of this volume turns to Side Dishes and Condiments, those foods that are sometimes so central to cuisine that they often escape notice. Sammells's chapter on chuño, the freeze-dried potatoes that are a staple in the Bolivian Andes, muses on how anthropologists can acquire a taste for the unfamiliar, and why tourists are not encouraged to do the same. She finds that the unusual taste of chuño, combined with it being misunderstood as "just a potato," makes it far less interesting to foreign tourists seeking authentic Bolivian food than llama meat, which tastes like other red meats but transgresses North Atlantic food categories.

McBrinn's hilarious contribution describes her encounters with durian, "the King of Fruits," while on a short trip in Malaysia. In her discussion she recounts her numerous attempts to find a manner of eating durian that was pleasing to both her palate and her gastrointestinal tract. While she admits to not exactly acquiring the taste for it, she ends her chapter (and her trip) with a grudging respect for this unusual fruit.

Marte discusses the challenges of conducting fieldwork with a serious food allergy, a consideration rarely addressed in the literature on conducting anthropological fieldwork. Her frank discussion of her allergy, like Haines's contribution, serves as a platform for reflective discussions. Rather than allow her allergy to become an insurmountable obstacle, she uses it to find multiple solutions, including challenging some informants to cook differently, or in other cases leaving time to deal with adverse affects. Her chapter demonstrates that anthropologists sometimes must refuse foods and suggests ways that one can do that without detracting from fieldwork.

Our section on Table Manners is meant to highlight that *how* one eats is often just as important as *what* one eats. It is one thing to be willing to consume unusual foods, but knowing in what order to eat things, what utensils to use, and with whom one can eat is often essential. There are also intricacies involved in the roles of "guest" and "host" (to invoke Smith 1989 [1977]) and questions of whose morals take precedence when offering and partaking food offerings. Food is never just food, mere calories for the body. As a social act that creates a bond of commensality, and can just as easily breach those bonds, the consumption of food is always a multilayered, meaningful event.

In his chapter, Aimers describes how being served whale as food challenged not just his palate but his understandings about why Japan engages in whaling despite international pressures to end the practice. He starts by discussing his refusal to eat whale meat on moral grounds while he was a young man visiting and working in Japan, and the social tension that results from his choice. He contrasts his youthful position with his later, more mature perspective born from a greater understanding of cultural diversity as well as international whaling laws. Aimers's contribution highlights the fact that perhaps the moral high ground is not as clear-cut as many North Atlantic activists make it seem.

Chaiken writes about her food experiences while conducting her doctoral dissertation research on Palawan Island in the Philippines. Her chapter details how, over the course of the course of the two years she spent working there, she defined her own personal food taboos. Chaiken relates how she gracefully avoided eating chicken heads and dog meat and learned the valuable lesson of "to each their own taboos"—an axiom crucial for living and coping in today's multicultural world.

Contrary to North American dining traditions, pasta is not the main course in Italy, and Black discusses her discomfort at realizing this too late. Fortunately, while she fears she might be noticed for eating too much (often an unspoken social taboo for North American women), her Italian fiancé instead compliments her on her appetite. Documenting her time in Italy, she admires the Slow Food movement as a response to the homogenization of cuisine and the rise of fast food, even as she recognizes that many women do not wish to forgo careers in order to spend most of their time cooking for and feeding their families. This dichotomous position mirrors the dilemma felt by some working women in North Atlantic societies.

Zycherman addresses an issue that will resonate with many North Atlantic residents—how to remain a vegetarian while conducting ethnographic field-work among people who do not see that as a logical approach to food. Instead of abandoning her own culinary commitments, she instead discovers that what others might see as a disadvantage to her research becomes something of an advantage. Her dietary restriction becomes a catalyst that motivates her Argentinean informants to explain the importance of meat in their lives, precisely because she cannot partake herself.

Johnston's chapter ends this section by talking about her long-term research with the Blackfeet, a Native American group in northern Montana. She demonstrates that the presence of the anthropologist is never neutral and that moreover this position affects not only our relationships with people but also what is put on our dinner plates. Giving a history of how Blackfeet cuisine has changed as a result of their confinement on an U.S. reservation and involve-ment with the cattle industry, she shows how national discussions about the relationship between health and cuisine filters into Blackfeet understanding of their own eating and well-being.

In our section on beverages, Reminick discusses a favorite North Atlantic beverage—coffee—from the point of view of its place of origins (as well as possibly our own origins as humans), Ethiopia. There coffee cements friendships between humans as well as between humans and their ancestral *zar* spirits. He also touches on another favorite topic of anthropologists—sickness. It is a common experience to become ill while traveling, and illness is often the result of food-borne organisms. Reminick treats this ubiquitous, although frequently under-discussed, subject with commendable honesty and humor.

On the other side of the world, Palka also discovers that drink can be as much a means of building social cohesion and friendship as food. In his chapter, Palka address the language and codes of behavior associated with alcohol consumption among young Honduran men and notes how this compares familiarly in some regards and contrasts sharply in others to the beer drinking of young men in North American culture.

Finally, Chaiken provides the Last Course—whether that is dessert, cheese, or coffee we leave to the reader. She rightly suggests that this volume might fit into the larger American genre of shocking people through eating foods seen as liminally edible (and we will not deny that this is often a good opener for college class lectures!). But this is not the deeper purpose of our book. We might shock our readers, but our aim is to encourage them to reconsider their own definitions of "real" food—of what, literally, qualifies as dinner. We want to prepare students who are considering anthropological fieldwork for those very real, and sometimes very awkward, situations that arise—and to think of these awkward moments not as mere "problems" to be overcome (although often they seem that way in the short term) but as methodologically crucial moments when the friction between anthropologists' assumptions and informants' cuisine can produce new understandings. Anthropologists know that discomfort during fieldwork is often the sign that one is on to something—a new understanding that challenges one's own view of the world. It is those understandings that we hope to bring to the larger audience of anthropology and invite our readers to explore—even if we cannot invite them over for dinner to discuss it!

NOTES

1. Mezcal is a beverage produced from agave, an indigenous plant well-suited for the arid environment of the valley and a relative of the better-known tequila. It is generally stronger in both alcoholic content and taste than tequila and often has distinct smoky overtones from the slow roasting of the agave hearts prior to distillation.

2. Tanqueray is my favorite gin, although I have been know to drink Bombay Sapphire and even Beefeaters in a pinch.

3. The "other London" referred to here is London, Ontario, which was distinguished from London, England, by being referred to as "London in the bush."

4. Even today good tonic, such as Canada Dry Tonic Water, still contains real quinine, although only for taste and not in sufficient quantities to protect one from contracting malaria.

5. The term literally means "yellow tin can" and refers to Canada Dry Tonic Water, which comes in a distinctive yellow can.

6. The globalization of food is a worldwide phenomenon. Non–North Atlantic cultures are equally well-versed in the niceties of other cuisines and many of our comments may apply equally to other cultures. However, we have chosen to stress North American behaviors as the purpose of this book is to make anthropology students, and other readers, in North America aware that very real differences still exist among cultures when it comes to ideas about food.

REFERENCES

Appadurai, Arjun
   1988   How to Make a National Cuisine: Cookbooks in Contemporary India. *Comparative Studies in Society and History* 30(1):3–24.

Bourdieu, Pierre
   1984   *Distinction: A Social Critique of the Judgment of Taste.* Harvard University Press, Cambridge, MA.

Brockway, Lucile H.
   1978   Science and Colonial Expansion: The Role of the British Royal Botanic Gardens. *American Ethnologist* 6(3):449–465.

Coe, Sophie D., and Michael D. Coe
   1996   *The True History of Chocolate.* Thames and Hudson, London.

Dietler, Michael, and Brian Hayden (editors)
   2001   *Feasts: Archaeological and Ethnographic Perspectives on Food, Politics, and Power.* Smithsonian Institution Press, Washington, DC.

Fiddes, Nick
   1991   *Meat: A Natural Symbol.* Routledge, London.

Goody, Jack
   1982   *Cooking, Cuisine and Class: A Study in Comparative Sociology.* Cambridge University Press, Cambridge.

Hamilton, Jill
   2005   *Thomas Cook the Holiday-Maker.* Sutton Publishing, Thrupp, Stroud.

Holtzman, Jon D.
   2006   Food and Memory. *Annual Review of Anthropology* 35:361–378.

Ingle, Robert
   1991   *Thomas Cook of Leicester.* Headstart History, Bangor Gwynedd, Wales.

McLuhan, Marshall, with Quentin Fiore
   1967   *The Medium Is the Massage: An Inventory of Effects.* Bantam Books, New York.

Miller, Daniel
   2005   Coca-Cola: A Black Sweet Drink from Trinidad. In *The Cultural Politics of Food and Eating: A Reader*, ed. James L. Watson and Melissa L. Caldwell, 54–69. Blackwell, Malden, MA.

Mintz, Sidney W.
   1985   *Sweetness and Power: The Place of Sugar in Modern History.* Penguin Books, New York.

Mintz, Sidney W., and Christine M. DuBois
   2002   The Anthropology of Food and Eating. *Annual Review of Anthropology* 31:99–119.

Phillips, Lynne
   2006   Food and Globalization. *Annual Review of Anthropology* 35:37–57.

Sahlins, Marshall
   1972   *Stone Age Economics*. Aldine-Atherton, Chicago.

Scheper-Hughes, Nancy
   1992   *Death without Weeping: The Violence of Everyday Life in Brazil*. University
           of California Press, Berkeley.

Schlosser, Eric
   2001   *Fast Food Nation: The Dark Side of the All-American Meal*. Houghton Mif-
           flin Company, Boston.

Smith, Valene L., ed.
   1989   *Hosts and Guests: The Anthropology of Tourism*. 2nd ed. University of Penn-
   [1977] sylvania Press, Philadelphia.

Stoller, Paul, and Cheryl Olkes
   1989   The Taste of Ethnographic Things. In *The Taste of Ethnographic Things:
           The Sense in Anthropology,* by Paul Stoller, 15–36. University of Pennsyl-
           vania Press, Philadelphia.

Urry, John
   1990   *The Tourist Gaze: Leisure and Travel in Contemporary Societies*. Sage Pub-
           lications, London.

Veblen, Thorstein
   1899   *The Theory of the Leisure Class*. Penguin Books, New York.

Watson, James L. (editor)
   1997   *Golden Arches East: McDonald's in East Asia*. Stanford University Press,
           Stanford, CA.

The Main Course

CHAPTER TWO

Boiled Eggs with Chicks Inside, or What Commensality Means

Roger Ivar Lohmann

Biographical sketch. Roger Lohmann first visited the Asabano as a graduate student in 1991, during a self-funded trip to explore possible research sites. Idealistically hoping to live among people living an entirely indigenous life-style, he was disappointed to discover that everyone professed Christianity and had abandoned secret male initiations, the use of ancestral bones to aid hunting and gardening, and traditional food taboos. Fortified with an interest in discovering what kinds of evidence convince people to abandon and adopt religious beliefs, Lohmann decided to return to the Asabano for his Ph.D. research. With a Fulbright grant and approval from his anthropology commit-tee at the University of Wisconsin–Madison, he spent a year and a half during 1994–1995 in Papua New Guinea (Figure 2.1). After receiving his doctorate in 2000 and teaching at various institutions, he won a tenure-track position at Trent University in 2003. Together with his collaborator and wife, Professor Heather M.-L. Miller of the University of Toronto, he spent a month in 2005 with the Asabano, and in 2007, Lohmann returned with two students for two months.

2.1. Map of Papua New Guinea showing research location. (MAP BY ROGER LOHMANN)

APPETIZER

Most everyone in my New Guinea village loves sago grubs. Steamed in leaves, "[t]hey taste just like hot buttered bread!" a friend enthused. To me they look like tubes of fat the size of breakfast sausages, ribbed for your pleasure, only with sharp jaws on one end for gnawing their way through the decaying logs in which they live (Figure 2.2). Enthralled though I was with the idea of submersing myself in another culture, studiously living, feeling, and thinking as the Asabano did, I drew the line at eating grubs.

Unlike Helen Haines's (this volume) avoidance of jungle rat in Belize largely because of its name, I do not think the barrier for me was the admittedly unappetizing linguistic association with the word *grubs* (in American culture *grubs* are not food, although *grub* is slang for food . . . hmmm). I might have brought myself to eating them cooked, until I heard that people enjoyed them live as well. The fact that this seemed downright cruel to me was overshadowed with disgust on so many other levels. I discovered an implicit rule of my own culture: animals should not be eaten when they are still alive and moving (see Cattell, this volume, on the challenge of eating moving termites). Not only was this a bug, it was a huge, soft, juicy bug (for Cattell, small, living bugs were acceptable with effort, but large, cooked bugs were not). No, thank you. "We know; white people do not like these. They are black people's food," I was told in a way that simultaneously reassured me that I was accepted and underlined my difference. My friend Simolibo, perhaps to emphasize our common bond, commented that actually he did not like grubs raw, either. "It goes back to when I was little," he explained. "I was about to take a bite out of one when it bit *me*,

2.2. Sago grubs in 1994. (PHOTO BY ROGER LOHMANN)

and my lip bled!" Simolibo's story goes to show that food taboos are all built from experiences, and they are ultimately personal (see Chaiken, this volume).

Food taboos, implicit and explicit, call attention to differences among people through their use as barriers. However, they can just as easily invite—or dare—border crossings and mutual understanding. As Susan Johnston (this volume) notes, people may change their menus in an effort to reach out to culturally foreign guests. In my case, I prepared my body to accept foods that I expected to encounter in Papua New Guinea. A year or so before I began my longest sojourn in Papua New Guinea, I had become a vegetarian for reasons of environmentalism. As my time of departure drew near, I slowly began eating meat again, since I did not want to refuse local foods and in this way separate myself from the people I was to study. I also knew what kinds of food were available locally and doubted whether I would be able to physically survive on such a diet without meat. Had I remained a vegetarian in the field, I am sure that people would have been curious rather than offended, although I probably would have suffered from malnutrition on the protein-poor traditional Melanesian diet. Ariela Zycherman (this volume) relates that her own meat avoidance in meat-loving Argentina proved a boon for her research, as it inspired her informants to ponder the place of beef in their culture.

In this chapter I consider some of my adventures in eating as a North American doing ethnographic fieldwork among the Asabano at Duranmin, Sandaun Province, Papua New Guinea. There were some local foods that I ate with pleasure, like taro baked in hearth ashes and steamed bread made of sago flour and brush turkey eggs. Some foods I ate with apprehension, like bright red, greasy, and almost tasteless pandanus sauce. A few foods, like grubs and other insects, I would not eat. Boiled eggs with chicks inside fell somewhere in the middle and yet in a way outside this spectrum—both delicious and creepy—and ambiguous middles are among the most interesting places to explore. As Helen Haines and Clare Sammells conclude in their introduction to this volume, discomfort in the field is an anthropologically useful meter for registering cultural difference.

What were the meanings and social consequences of these acts of eating or not eating what my hosts offered? I first consider the matter in general and then dig in to my own situation. Sharing or refusing to share foods reflects diverse motives and marks social and cultural boundaries in distinctive ways and has different meanings as well. Ambivalent or problematic reactions to particular foods in cross-cultural encounters are often particularly revealing of this complexity.

FIRST COURSE: THE MEANINGS OF COMMENSALITY

In all societies, sharing food is a way of establishing closeness, while, conversely, the refusal to share is one of the clearest marks of distance and enmity. . . . Commensality, the act of eating together, is thus one of the most powerful operators of the social process. The reason is that the sharing of food is, and is always seen to be, in some way or other, the sharing of that which will cause, or at least maintain, a common substance among those who commune together. (Maurice Bloch 2005:45)

A number of complications surround these significant food facts outlined by eminent anthropologist Maurice Bloch. The first set of these relates to food itself. Even when we *want* to achieve closeness through commensality, eating the same things together can be a challenge. The proffered local cuisine does not always meet one's minimal criteria of delicious, palatable, or even "food," causing one to reject or be unenthusiastic about the menu. Therefore, rejecting food can appear as a false sign of social rejection. In the same manner, deciding to accept proffered food can be a false sign of social acceptance, closeness, or equivalence: one may simply be hungry.

The second batch of complications surrounding the truism that food sharing indicates social warmth concerns the type of relationship that one means to establish or reject. Foods may be shared or not based on a range of possible criteria for inclusion or exclusion, including social, political, sexual, ethnic, and economic criteria, to name but a few. And relationships come in more flavors than yes or no, member or outsider—they also come in maybe, sometimes, and just for today. They come in varying degrees of equality and inequality, dependence and independence, play and seriousness. Food acceptance can mean trust and an affirmation of common substance—or, it can mean something else or something more, as prosaic as needing nutrition, as political as accepting an inferior (or superior) status, and as convoluted as building false trust. Likewise, rejecting offered food can mean rejecting a relationship with the person who offers it—or, it can mean something else or something more. It might mean that one has been culturally conditioned in ways that make it difficult for one to stomach what is offered, even though one dearly desires to express comradeship and gratitude. Then again, one might simply be too full to eat what is offered.

These possible variations in the meaning of commensality establish a potential for misunderstandings in the moment when food is proffered. This is a danger present in any symbolic representation—the symbol's conventional meanings (we are eating together, which symbolizes our common substance) can be mistaken for solid evidence itself (our eating together *manifests* our common substance). Eating or not eating is easily—and reasonably—taken as an index of social warmth; but as a measuring device, it is not as accurate as a thermometer. Furthermore, on the other side of the exchange, the perspective and intent of the person who offers or chooses not to offer food can of course be very different from that of the recipient of the gesture. Giving one's own food can be a gesture of dominance, an expression of empathy, or an obligation of hospitality, quite as much as it might be an index of feeling of common substance, acceptance, and unity.

Having begun with a heaping plate of caveats (lumpers love them, splitters break up over them), I hasten to add a helping of recognition. The symbolic association between shared food and social warmth based on shared substance is ubiquitous cross-culturally, and opportunities for commensality, taken or missed, serve as a universal tool for sussing people out. This is nowhere more important than in cross-cultural encounters, where the meanings, the forms of sociality, and the foods are all up for grabs. And meetings of ethnographers and subjects are perhaps the most deeply personal and contemplated of all cross-cultural encounters. They always involve food and always inspire stories.

SECOND COURSE: REFLUX AND REFLEXIVITY

Stories of experiences with foods and food situations that are unfamiliar and interesting without being utterly revolting to one's audience are entertaining because, as Clare Sammells (this volume) puts it, their position at the interface between cultures makes them "good to relate." Certainly Maxine McBrinn's (this volume) first-contact-with-durian story is so charming and informative because of this quality.

All anthropologists have food stories with which to regale their students, colleagues, and friends, whether it be to gloat over the availability of excellent cappuccinos and biscotti at their field sites or to boast about daringly tried elements of local cuisine that would emphatically be classified as "not food" in their home society. They are often some of our best yarns, yet many are regarded as so personal or trivial that they neither receive formal analysis nor enter the ethnographic record, much like the wonderful tales of embarrassing fieldwork experiences Philip DeVita (1990) saved from oblivion in his volume, *The Humbled Anthropologist*.

Perhaps because some of these stories are on the surface more about ourselves than about the people we study, treating them as data seems narcissistic. Reflexivity (that is, being aware of our own perspectives and experiences in the field) is valuable, however, as an empathetic window on others as well as on ourselves (see Davies 2008; Meyerhoff and Ruby 1982). Furthermore, descriptions of anthropologists' life experiences are as much anthropological data as are any other ethnographic descriptions (Lohmann 2008). In any event, I begin my own yarn by describing my views before bringing in those of my hosts, the Asabano people, as they surfaced during my sojourns among them as an anthropologist. My tale is about what I was and was not willing to eat with my Asabano hosts, what I learned from our discussions about food, and what my categorizing their foods into edible and inedible (for me) signified in our ethnographic relationship. I should say at the outset that the Asabano were almost always willing to eat any of the various foreign foods I offered them, with the sometime exception of sweet rice pudding with cinnamon. But we were talking about *me*, so let's get back on topic.

Most Asabano foods were fine, if not downright delicious to me. Taro, sweet potatoes, sago wrapped in leaves, and tapioca baked in the ashes underneath hearth fires or steamed in hot stone leaf ovens are delicious (Figure 2.3). I found the steamed meats of pigs, marsupials, and birds of all kinds to be satisfying. I also really enjoyed wildfowl eggs cooked any number of ways. The Asabano make a wonderful sort of steamed bread out of wildfowl eggs and sago flour. They also boil the eggs all by themselves or fry them with recently introduced cooking oil and chilies. People collect them from broods that brush turkeys lay in mounds of vegetation, where the eggs incubate in the heat given off by the compost. When they hatch, the chicks look after themselves. Now that's effort-free parenting!

It is to these eggs that I want to pay particular attention. I am particularly fond of them, as I have already said, and friends kindly gave me more than my fair share. But early in my longest period of fieldwork, in 1994–1995, I made an unpleasant discovery. Because these eggs are wild, they are not necessarily undeveloped when people collect them. Some have blood in them, and others,

2.3. Eating boiled sweet potatoes from a common pot; *clockwise from left*: Roger Lohmann, Mandi, Diyos, Walen, Belok, dog, Sablaio, and child eating together in 2005. (PHOTO BY ROGER LOHMANN)

when cracked, reveal both a yolk and a chick, with feathers, bones, and beak encased in the shell. Some are almost ready to hatch. The thought of the poor chick inside being boiled to death disturbed me, but there was something else. Breaking open the shell to find a mixture of what my binary understanding of birds and eggs told me should be separate foods produced the sort of discomfort that Mary Douglas (1966) has described so well in *Purity and Danger*. However, while I guiltily refused to eat sago grubs, living or dead, when it came to boiled eggs with chicks inside, I was willing to cross the line and partake, telling myself that it was really just the same as eating eggs and meat together. I found this reasoning strangely comforting. Think of steak and eggs, after all—not merely an acceptable combination but one favored by cowboys and other Real Men. By eating these I could tell myself I was reaching a macho ideal—adventurous, independent, and also savoring home-style cooking.

A more recent visit to the Asabano in 2005 with my collaborator and wife, Heather M.-L. Miller, coincided with a bumper crop egg season. People brought many eggs to share and once even an already-hatched chick (Figure 2.4), discovered by a young mother named Davis whose family gave us use of a vacant house in the village. She brought the chick home to serve as a plaything for

2.4. The already-hatched brush turkey chick in 2005. (PHOTO BY ROGER LOHMANN)

the children until it would be injured or killed and become a delicious snack. This particular chick escaped that awful fate and became our houseguest with whom we *shared* our dinners rather than had for dinner. When our time to depart approached, we released the chick on the far side of the river that flows past the village, providing a second chance at freedom. Sablaio, an old man whose pig-keeping house we visited on our way to the release site, shook his head at our incomprehensible abandonment of meat. Our protests that the chick would grow up to produce more eggs in the future appeared to make no impression on Sablaio, who like other Asabano hunters is of the "a-bird-in-the-hand-is-worth-two-in-the-bush" philosophy.

Another favorite local food is red pandanus sauce, which I found disconcertingly bland considering its bright red color. It is labor intensive to prepare, as the fruit must first be steamed with hot stones in an earth oven, then repeatedly mixed with water, and hand-squeezed to remove the soft insides from the husks that surround each seed. The fruit is squeezed over a bed of mashed tubers, often sweet potatoes or taro, spread out on a piece of bark. Eating it is a charmingly communal experience, for everyone present (and there are always plenty of people present) sits on haunches around the spread with a spoon or sliver of wood in hand and eats from the outer edges in (Figure 2.5). This food

2.5. Eating "Papua New Guinea pizza"; cooking stones for leaf oven are in the background, 2007. (PHOTO BY ROGER LOHMANN)

I am willing to eat, but only a little as an expression of comradeship. I do not really like it. Locals call it "Papua New Guinea pizza," but this actually makes matters worse for me because pandanus sauce tastes nothing like tomato sauce. In fact, to me it tastes like nothing at all. It does exude a mild, greasy smell, which does not add to its appeal for me. As is the case for sago grubs, white people are famous in Papua New Guinea for typically not liking red pandanus. Indeed, not all Asabano like it either—so differing personal preferences of foods is another one of those pesky qualifiers to the social facts of commensality. Just because you do not like a local delicacy of your own people does not mean you will necessarily be regarded as an outsider.

By sharing a little pandanus pizza as a special ritual, I sought to magically overcome my cultural and social difference for a moment, to enjoy being one of the group, eating a quintessentially Asabano food. However, I have found that with each visit I make, I have less and less desire to eat this stuff. As the desire to follow local customs ("when in Rome") and to try new things for the sake of rigorous participant observation has diminished with greater familiarity, the motivation to do things that one would rather not do crumbles like the proverbial cookie.

During my times among the Asabano, I have wanted to eat local food as an index of my participation in Asabano culture, to honor and feel close to my hosts by sharing their experiences, to establish bragging rights, and to have a fuller participatory experience to enrich my ethnography. I also ate local foods because I was hungry. These desires were sometimes supported and sometimes thwarted by other factors. My culturally inherited familiarity with eggs in "bread," cooked tubers, and bird and mammal flesh made certain foods more palatable than others. At the same time, my cultural bias against eating larvae, developing eggs, and unfamiliar combinations of color, smell, and taste presented both a barrier and a challenge. All these factors contributed to the meaning of different foods in my own mind and influenced my ability to make use of them in commensality as an expression of real or desired social warmth and common substance.

THIRD COURSE: GUSTATORY DISTINCTIONS AND AMBIVALENCE

Maurice Bloch (2005:56–57) has observed that willingness to share certain sorts of food can be seen as a test of trust and intimacy. Indeed, in an intimate society such as a North American nuclear family, a foraging band, or a small horticultural tribe like the Asabano, basic necessities like food are shared relatively freely compared to less intimate societies. This accords with Marshall Sahlins's (1972) principle that sharing freely or generalized reciprocity is the rule for socially intimate groups. Similarly, sharing food, commensality, and partaking in a common cuisine symbolize and enact social intimacy.

Many examples of this pattern can be found in the ethnographic record. Elsewhere in Papua New Guinea, among the Vanatinai islanders, sharing food at feasts soothes sorcery suspicions following a death, and even more strikingly, a man and a woman declare their marriage by publicly eating together (Lepowsky 1993:245). By the same token, the closeness of friendship or the distance of dislike are expressed by the relative ease of food sharing in societies based on reciprocity, as the African San woman Nisa evocatively described to her biographer, Marjorie Shostak (1983 [1981]:88–89). Along with this, use of common access to food for feel-good intimacy can sometimes come suspicion that others are not sharing what they have (for an example from Sumatra, see Fessler 2005:53). This too is not merely a concern about equal access to nutrition; it also represents a sneaking suspicion that one's own society is not as intimate as it should be. If my neighbor is not sharing with me, I am not really a member of this society—I am an outsider.

At larger and less intimate social scales, such as those found in chiefdoms and states, reciprocity's stickiness as social glue is unsuited to the task of social cohesion. It is replaced by redistribution (making payments to a central authority that then redistributes wealth) and market economics, for which no personal relationships are needed for exchanges to keep a society interconnected and running. But common cuisines and even staples often provide a subtle bond every bit as sticky as the gluten in rice, which grain Emiko Ohnuki-Tierney (1993) argues is a powerful and long-lasting symbol of Japanese identity in opposition to foreigners. Foods can serve as markers of ethnic identity spanning societies of any degree of complexity (see Holtzman 2006:366; Whitehead 2000:91–92).

Shifting our gaze from distinctions between societies to variegations within societies, many internal social boundaries can also be marked with food prescriptions and proscriptions. As Anna Meigs (1984:17) points out in her Melanesian ethnography, food rules can be based on social relationships between individuals occupying different roles within societies. These "[r]elative rules define a relationship between a consumer, a food, and a source." In societies based on relative inequality, food's identity-building potential also makes it a powerful medium through which to pursue status. Leaders such as chiefs can differentiate themselves as superior to others while still indicating their belonging in the group by appearing to provide and share more or better food than others can manage. As Polly Wiessner (1996:6) puts it, "[a]s the basis for life, food attracts attention and is highly divisible, making the distributor or host the center of attention for food sharing. Commensal occasions create, affirm or reproduce a wide variety of social relationships."

For a member of a party to reject either eating simultaneously or eating the same food if offered is to indicate distinction—I am not like you. People can make much or little of this distinction, and it is in this degree and its consequences that culture varies around the universal facts. Thus the Asabano made me feel like one of the gang even though I did not always eat what they offered. Likewise, the warmth of our relationships was not at all harmed when some Asabano refused to eat my rice pudding, although on both sides we noticed the differences that these preferences displayed. My Asabano associates often called attention to the act of eating together, regardless of what was eaten, as an indicator of our closeness and equality. The fact that I sat and ate with local people was repeatedly held up as showing that in spite of my being a foreigner and a white man, I was unlike some whites they had met who refused to treat Papua New Guineans as fellow human beings by eating with them. These indices may not be intentional, desired, or reflective of what people actually think. On the one hand, one might desperately want to eat what one's companions are eating for the sake of companionship but be halted by finding the food unpalatable. On the other hand, one's attention may be squarely on the delicious food and not on the people with whom one is eating.

Once learned, gustatory distinctions are often motivated by *dis*gust for particular foods or the contexts in which they are consumed. Disgust is such a visceral sensation that it seems in the moment of experience to be completely biological and natural; yet it is clear that we learn to find certain consumables and contexts for consumption to be deliciously appealing or retchingly unappealing, and every measure in between. As Daniel Fessler and Kevin Haley (2006) note, disgust is most pronounced when it involves those body parts that are in most intimate contact with the environment. There is little more intimate contact with the environment possible than mouthing it; therefore, eating is a prime example of an activity with high potential for disgust—unfamiliar foods are particularly subject to disgust. One might observe, using the same principle, that those parts of one's cultural value system that come most intimately in contact with external or foreign *cultural* environments are also likely candidates for disgust. Facing a foreign delicacy, as I faced sago grubs and, to a lesser extent, eggs with chicks inside, brings these bodily and cultural vulnerabilities together, erecting particularly strong barriers to acquiring the needed taste proclivities with which to appreciate the food.

We know that cultural variation is distributed not only over space but also over time, so that even one's own past beliefs and practices change to the extent that they come to seem foreign. Traditional European practices of hanging meat before cooking it sound foreign and disgusting to me, although this was practiced by my own genetic and cultural ancestors. Likewise, medicinal cannibalism was practiced in Europe into the nineteenth century, as discussed by Beth Conklin (2001:8–13) in contextualizing her study of Wari' endocannibalism (eating the dead of one's own group) in South America.

There are also Asabano customs of eating that they have rejected in the last fifty years, following the first appearance of European trade goods in the 1950s, first contact (for most Asabano) with people of European descent when an Australian patrol arrived in the 1960s, and their mass conversion to Christianity in the 1970s (Lohmann 2001). The conversion in particular was powerfully linked with a change in dietary rules (Lohmann 2003). The traditional religion had centered on secret spiritual knowledge coupled with exclusive access for men to many foods, with successive initiations bringing access to more sacred and otherwise forbidden foods. These included a certain variety of red pandanus and culminated with the flesh of a marsupial, the terrestrial phalanger. One of the arguments of the Christian movement that swept away the old cult was that God had made everything for all people to enjoy freely. It was a "Satanic lie" that forbade women and children from enjoying the men's foods.

The few surviving older women who spoke to me about such matters in the 1990s confirmed that they had desired the forbidden foods but were not

2.6. Sablaio holding a steamed *kuyamodu* (terrestrial phalanger), formerly taboo to non-initiates, in 2007. (PHOTO BY ROGER LOHMANN)

allowed to have them. So in this case men at various levels of initiation expressed group exclusivity by favoring foods that had not come to be seen as disgusting by uninitiated outsiders but rather as desirable (Figure 2.6). This, considered with my own reaction of disgust for certain quintessentially Asabano foods, is consistent with a general principle that purposeful exclusion of certain people through tabooing foods does not cause an automatic disgust toward forbidden foods. As a foreign ethnographer, I desired to eat the local foods to show commonality with my hosts, but disgust sometimes prevented this for reasons other than desired social exclusion on either side. Disgust in such an encounter expresses ingrained and visceral cultural difference in assumptions about edibility, not necessarily perceived inclusion or exclusion in a social group. Reactions of disgust sometimes coincide with social boundaries, but ones of a different sort than those enforced by the traditional Asabano men's cult. Ultimately, emic boundary drawing between groups can make use of food proscriptions, but it is insufficient to explain the origins of disgust or food taboos (on etic explanations for the origins of food taboos, see Fessler and Navarette 2003).

I would like, finally, to consider another kind of food that, in contrast to the sacred foods of the men's cult that were once forbidden and are now free, was once free and is now forbidden. This food is human meat, the flesh of enemies killed in the feud warfare that used to rack the sparsely populated mountains inhabited by the Asabano and their neighbors. Among my favorite stories for sharing with students is my friend Belok's exasperated ejaculation that I should not idealize their traditional customs, since had I come before they had become Christians, I would have long since been killed and eaten. None of my informants admitted to me that they had eaten human themselves, but several people told of an old woman named Blogoi who had. By all accounts she was a great storyteller; alas, she died shortly before my first arrival in 1991. Judging by what people told me in the mid-1990s, human meat is not something all people wanted, even when it was allowed. It was something different—nutritious food, yes, but something more. Based on the reports of elders some people were, at least at times and to some degree, disgusted by the idea of eating human meat and would not partake when it was made available after a successful raid (Lohmann 2005:198–199). Yet there are plentiful Asabano folktales about killing and eating people. So it is difficult from my placement in the history of Asabano discourse to say exactly what sort of ambivalent hunger or social inclusion or exclusion cannibalism represented before contact. The fact that in cannibalism, what one is eating is, or at least was, physically part of a human social group is a further complicating factor. How, then, are we to account for *this* social distinction reflected in the question, to eat or not to eat?

There were no taboos for women and children, or any other segment of the population, on eating the meat of slain enemies. This would not have been your garden variety of forbidden yet desired fruit, expressing the sort of psychological ambivalence that the great psychologist Sigmund Freud made his stock in trade. It is true that human meat was formerly a person and, in the case of Asabano cannibalism, often someone who had been known to those who viewed their remains transformed into a dinner spread. Taboos or ambivalences regarding eating humans share features with attitudes about the prospect of eating companion animals, as pets can, in some cultures, become sorts of honorary persons. This shows up clearly in cross-cultural encounters in which a species of animal is regarded as pet in one and as food in another, as David Goldstein's (this volume) guinea pig example. Miriam Chaiken's (this volume) dog example shows that the line between pet and meat for the pot can also be contested and traversed within a society.

So, why didn't the pre-contact Asabano place age- or gender-based taboos on the meat of slain enemies? Perhaps the difference between humans and other animals in traditional Asabano thought holds the answer. In pre-contact doctrine, animals have no souls but are looked after by spirits—although humans can also appear in animal form (Lohmann 2005:199–201). In contrast, human beings are animated by a good "big soul" and an evil "little soul," the latter of which remains dangerous at the gravesite after death. Bones of ancestors, however, were retained to serve as media for contacting the good souls of the deceased in their forest homes. Taken together, these facts offer some indication that deceased human remains were the locus for the evil soul, a spirit who could strike down the living (Lohmann 2005:193–194). Clearly this notion was not worked out in detail, and these ideas had undergone change by the time I came on the scene. Nevertheless, I suspect this implication made some react with ambivalence or even disgust at cannibal meals. Human meat was a potential link to the vindictive portion of personality that survived death; animal meat had no such danger associated with it. The fascinating literature on cannibalism reveals the variety of cultural doctrines concerning who (if anyone) one is allowed to eat, under what circumstances, to what ends, and with what consequences (see, e.g., Conklin 2001; Lindenbaum 2004).

My three examples, then, leave us with three kinds of food discomfort or ambivalence. First is the visceral disgust at the idea of eating things that are emphatically not food in one's own culture. We become particularly aware of this reaction in cross-cultural encounters, and indeed people use these differences and their moments of gustatory transcendence to mark ethnic boundaries and *their* transcendence. My reflexive experience as an ethnographer among the Asabano is of this type. Second, there is the ambivalence about eating something that is forbidden to one as an outsider to a group within a larger society, as the male-only foods of the pre-contact Asabano exemplify. This sort of ambivalence is characterized not by disgust but by guilty and sometimes repressed desire. Third and finally, people encounter disgust or distaste for something that is understood to be dangerous, through either spiritual or physical causes, as the less-than-universal enjoyment of human meat among the pre-contact Asabano apparently exemplifies.

FOURTH COURSE: BLAND YET FILLING FOOD CONNECTIONS

On the flipside of ambivalence and disgust are fascination and desire, which, as the saying goes about love and hate, are separated by a thin line. Having moved beyond my own perspectives to Asabano ones, I now return to their reactions to the foreign foods that I brought with me. I mentioned that the Asabano were happy to eat almost all of the exotic foods I offered them. They were more than happy; they were thrilled to have canned meat or fish with rice almost every time they ate with me, often improved with other unheard of dainties such as cookies or rare favorites like coffee, tea, and Milo. These were the tangible attainables of global civilization, the "food of the white man," as they put it, that like Christianity, they wanted to join in claiming as fully their own. Here, again as with Christianity, the Asabano see ethnic boundaries as possible and desirable to transcend.

To counter the tendency for foreigners to see Melanesians like the Asabano as anxious to immediately accept anything representative of "global" or "modern" culture, I would like to note some of the ambivalent edges in the Asabano fascination with foreign foods. I asked a young man named Laurie in 2005 why he did not like my rice pudding, since he and other local people very much like rice, milk, and sugar, the main ingredients, in other contexts. "Rice shouldn't be sweet," was the clearest answer I received. I suspect the last ingredient, a good shake of cinnamon powder, which is unknown locally and is also spicy, is weird enough to local tastes to seal their rejection. This seems akin to my reaction of red pandanus; I *can* eat it, but something is just not right. It is a partial mismatch of cultural values, on the other extreme of the ambivalence scale from my full-out rejection of squiggling sago grubs.

The cinnamon points to another area of gustatory discomfort for Asabano, particularly elders: spicy food. The word for "food" in the Asaba language is *meole*, which literally means "taro-sweet potatoes." The subterranean taro corm and the sweet potato tuber, often simply baked or steamed and eaten with greens, are, like sago, famously plain (Figure 2.7). Traditional foods are bland, with the exception of medicinal plants such as ginger. In traditional Asabano taste aesthetics, one does not eat spicy food for the pleasure of the burning sensation. Nevertheless, when I offered spicy food to people, although they often commented on its "fight," it was rarely rejected. For my part, I came to love the simple and edifying starch and greens that made up a typical Asabano meal.

There is one more thing: a kind of food that the Asabano never tried but a few people saw in pictures. Desperate for the trappings of my own culture, in my year and a half in the field in 1994–1995 I gobbled up popular magazines and brought them back to the village from periodic visits to towns. As I was sitting one day with a couple of young women, one of them, named Seli, leafed

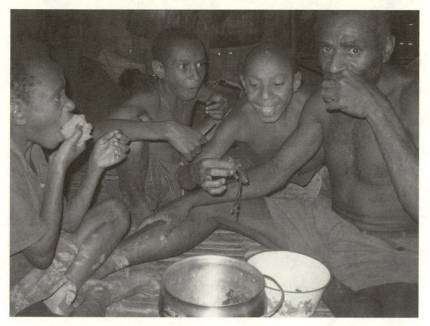

2.7. Nothing like a lump of gelatinous, tasteless sago pudding and a pot of boiled greens to fill one's belly; Belok (*far right*) and family digging in, 2007. (PHOTO BY ROGER LOHMANN)

through a magazine and expressed her amazement at photos of elaborate dishes. As a rule, Papua New Guinean food is not elaborate in either presentation or recipe. Why would anyone make such a detailed creation only to eat it, Seli appeared to ask, even as she clearly admired these culinary creations as visual art. This is one aspect of "white people's food" that is not sought after or emulated. Why this rejection? In some cases, rejection or idealization of a food is a statement of ethnocentrism or even domination, as Jim Aimers (this volume) describes in his examination of the debate over killing and eating whales, but there was something different happening in this instance. It would seem that here we have crossed to the other side of ambivalence, from disgust to disinterested acknowledgment. It is indeed an expression of a cultural boundary, where the difference does not violently contradict one's own ingrained aesthetic but rather presents something that is largely irrelevant and uninspiring to it.

Later that trip I was visiting a Telefolmin family from Duranmin in the nearby mining town of Tabubil. I contributed to the household food supply by bringing an exotic frozen custard pie from the supermarket. An older lady staying in the house served the pie that night; she plopped it right on top of the hot canned mackerel, greens, and rice that made up the rest of the meal. Clearly this complex food aggregate—a custard pie—was not considered unappetizing, and indeed it had been perfectly amalgamated into the local style of food presentation. Although I found the ensemble quite unappealing, I was not about to insult the cook by refusing to eat what she had created using ingredients I had myself supplied (see Marte, this volume, on how refusals of offered food can be interpreted as impoliteness, and Black, this volume, on how food surprises reveal that assumed familiarity with a culture can be illusory). I reminded myself that if I were to eat the components separately and in the order to which I had become enculturated in North America, the end result in my stomach would be the same. I dug in, excavating what I considered the main course out from under what I considered the dessert. What to me was a contradiction was to the cook a seamless integration of foreign and local foods. Social boundaries had been rendered null and void—or had they?

DESSERT

In this chapter I have told of my experiences of commensality with the Asabano and related this to a small portion of the great and wonderful anthropological literature on food. While I have concentrated on food's role as a saucy marker of identities and distinctions, this is but one of many recipes for understanding humankind through study of the anthropology of food and eating (Mintz and Du Bois 2002).

My purpose here has been to think about how eating or not eating proffered dishes reflects social inclusion or exclusion. While social consumption of drugs like coffee (Reminick, this volume) and alcohol (Palka, this volume) often act as social lubricants, psychoactive ingredients are not needed for the sharing of food and drink to serve this function in gatherings of all kinds. Some of my central points have been that commensality is not an all-or-nothing behavior—it occurs in degrees. Furthermore, while eating together and sharing particular cuisines often symbolize social inclusion through shared substance, they can also mean other things—and also occur in degrees. There are numerous kinds of boundaries within as well as between societies—based on ethnic, gender, religious, occupational, and other criteria—that can mark or express their existence through food taboos and obligations. This may be intentional or unintentional. Disgust often reveals cultural boundaries, while guilty desire can indicate social boundaries. Boundaries may be between equals or they may demarcate inequality—and those on opposite sides may have different perspectives on the matter. Ambivalence toward a particular food—like boiled eggs with chicks inside—indicates that these boundaries are not always or even typically firm and absolute; there are edgy zones in between. These liminal, in-between zones are some of the most interesting human arenas to

2.8. Rex unpacking eleven brush turkey eggs in 2005. They will be added to the dish of sago flour in the background to make egg and sago bread. (PHOTO BY ROGER LOHMANN)

investigate, through food and so much more (for example, in ritual; see Turner 2004 [1964]).

To conclude with a vignette, back among the Asabano in my adopted village, when we ate the same foods, particularly local foods, it did underline our commonality in my mind, and it seemed to me in theirs as well. The Asabano and other peoples dwelling at elevations that support brush turkeys often sell their eggs to people living in "cold places," higher in the mountains. I too had come from another sort of cold place sadly bereft of wildfowl eggs. I know it gave people pleasure and a sense that they had provided me with something I could not otherwise get when they gave me wildfowl eggs, with or without chicks inside.

On our last day in the village in 2005, before returning home, a young married man named Rex planned a little party for my wife Heather and me, featuring the sago and egg bread that I like so much (Figure 2.8). He had collected and set aside eleven eggs for this purpose. This was a major gift: one must make a difficult trek up forested mountains, locate the nests, gather the eggs, and then carry the fragile things, precariously wrapped in leaves, through mud, rivers, and over slippery logs for a several-hour journey back to the village. I think it was not just chance that eggs—albeit none with chicks inside—were

2.9. Laurie taking the baked egg and sago bread out of the leaf oven in 2005. (PHOTO BY ROGER LOHMANN)

the centerpiece of the party. Egg and sago bread is a distinctively Asabano dish, one that I happen to relish as much as they do. It is a point of commonality that expresses our relationship at its best, as both sides would like it to be: we are different peoples, but I hunger for them to teach me their customs. As an ethnographer, I was not there to become one of the Asabano but to stay for some short months to have a good long taste of their way of life. I was there as a "professional stranger," as Michael Agar (1980) cleverly designates the ethnographer's liminal position, and the egg bread was at once very Asaba and one of my favorite foods (Figure 2.9). When I returned in 2007, eggs were out of season, but I saw a string of eggshells hanging high in the rafters of one of the village houses—the shells of the eggs that had been made into bread for us two years before, kept as mementos of a moment devoted to celebrating our common humanity.

Acknowledgments. Thanks to everyone in Papua New Guinea for all the delicious and interesting foods you shared. This chapter grew out of a paper presented in 2005 as part of the session "Adventures in Eating: Anthropological Experiences of Dining from around the World," organized by Roger Ivar Lohmann and Helen R. Haines, at the American Anthropological Association,

Washington, DC. I offer my thanks to Helen Haines for providing the idea and impetus for the session and, as a result, for this chapter. She, Clare Sammells, and Maxine McBrinn provided valuable comments on an earlier draft, for which I am grateful.

REFERENCES

Agar, Michael H.
  1980   *The Professional Stranger: An Informal Introduction to Ethnography*. Academic Press, New York.

Bloch, Maurice
  2005   Commensality and Poisoning. In *Essays on Cultural Transmission*, 45–59. Berg, Oxford.

Conklin, Beth
  2001   *Consuming Grief: Compassionate Cannibalism in an Amazonian Society*. University of Texas Press, Austin.

Davies, Charlotte Aull
  2008   *Reflexive Ethnography: A Guide to Researching Selves and Others*, 2nd ed. Routledge, London.

DeVita, Philip R.
  1990   *The Humbled Anthropologist: Tales from the Pacific*. Wadsworth, Belmont, CA.

Douglas, Mary
  1966   *Purity and Danger: An Analysis of the Concepts of Pollution and Taboo*. Routledge and Kegan Paul, London.

Fessler, Daniel M.T.
  2005   Never Eat Alone: The Meaning of Food Sharing in a Sumatran Village. *People and Culture in Oceania* 20:51–67.

Fessler, Daniel M.T., and Kevin J. Haley
  2006   Guarding the Perimeter: The Outside-Inside Dichotomy in Disgust and Bodily Experience. *Cognition and Emotion* 20(1):3–19.

Fessler, Daniel M.T., and Carlos David Navarette
  2003   Meat Is Good to Taboo: Dietary Proscriptions as a Product of the Interaction of Psychological Mechanisms and Social Processes. *Journal of Cognition and Culture* 3(1):1–40.

Holtzman, Jon D.
  2006   Food and Memory. *Annual Review of Anthropology* 35:361–378.

Lepowsky, Maria
  1993   *Fruit of the Motherland: Gender in an Egalitarian Society*. Columbia University Press, New York.

Lindenbaum, Shirley
    2004   Thinking about Cannibalism. *Annual Review of Anthropology* 33:475–498.

Lohmann, Roger Ivar
    2001   Introduced Writing and Christianity: Differential Access to Religious Knowledge among the Asabano. *Ethnology* 40(2):93–111.
    2003   Turning the Belly: Insights on Religions Conversion from New Guinea Gut Feelings. In *The Anthropology of Religious Conversion*, ed. A. Buckser and S. D. Glazier, 109–121. Rowman and Littlefield, Lanham, MD.
    2005   The Afterlife of Asabano Corpses: Relationships with the Deceased in Papua New Guinea. *Ethnology* 44(2):189–206.
    2008   Introduction: Biographies of Anthropologists as Anthropological Data. *Reviews in Anthropology* 37(2–3):89–101.

Meigs, Anna S.
    1984   *Food, Sex, and Pollution: A New Guinea Religion.* Rutgers University Press, New Brunswick, NJ.

Meyerhoff, Barbara, and Jay Ruby
    1982   Introduction. In *A Crack in the Mirror: Reflexive Perspectives in Anthropology*, ed. J. Ruby. University of Pennsylvania Press, Philadelphia.

Mintz, Sidney W., and Christine M. DuBois
    2002   The Anthropology of Food and Eating. *Annual Review of Anthropology* 31:99–119.

Ohnuki-Tierney, Emiko
    1993   *Rice as Self: Japanese Identities through Time.* Princeton University Press, Princeton, NJ.

Sahlins, Marshall
    1972   *Stone Age Economics.* Aldine-Atherton, Chicago.

Shostak, Marjorie
    1983   *Nisa: The Life and Words of a !Kung Woman.* Vintage Books, New York.
    [1981]

Turner, Victor W.
    2004   Betwixt and Between: The Liminal Period in *Rites de Passage*. In *Sacred*
    [1964]   *Realms: Essays in Religion, Belief, and Society*, ed. R. Warms, J. Garber, and J. McGee, 177–184. Oxford University Press, New York.

Whitehead, Harriet
    2000   *Food Rules: Hunting, Sharing, and Tabooing Game in Papua New Guinea.* University of Michigan Press, Ann Arbor.

Wiessner, Polly
    1996   Introduction: Food, Status, Culture, and Nature. In *Food and the Status Quest: An Interdisciplinary Perspective*, ed. P. Wiessner and W. Schieffenhövel, 1–18. Berghahn, Providence, RI.

CHAPTER THREE

A Rat by Any Other Name

Conflicting Definitions of "Dinner" in Belize, Central America

Helen R. Haines

Biographical sketch. Helen Haines is an archaeologist specializing in the development of early state societies. She started working in Belize in 1990 (when the following adventure took place) with the Programme for Belize Archaeology Project surveying Maya ruins in the National Reserve. In 2000 she obtained her Ph.D. from the Institute of Archaeology, UCL, in London, England, specializing in Maya archaeology. Her postdoctoral research involved working in Oaxaca, Mexico, and she has also been an invited scholar on projects in Bolivia and China. She is currently directing the Ka'Kabish Archaeological Research Project (KARP) in north-central Belize and is based in the Belizean/ Guatemalan community of Indian Church, where she recently purchased a small house with a large kitchen. During the academic year she teaches at Trent University in Oshawa and resides with her tubby Tibetan Lhasa Apso dog in Toronto, Canada, where she is able to indulge her (their?) passion for different cultural foods.

One of my first fond memories of Belize involves food: fresh bananas handed to me by a stranger after I had been stuck for hours on the side of the road,

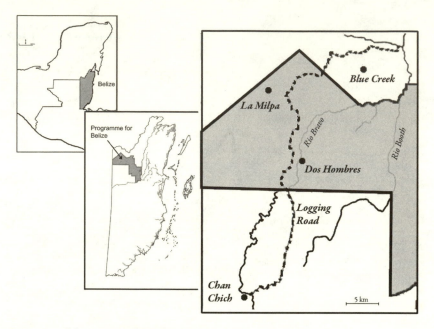

3.1. Map of the program for Belize National Park. (MAP BY H. R. HAINES)

miles from any village, in a Ford Bronco with a flat tire; no spare, jack, or tire iron; and only a temperamental CB radio for company. My companions had left me to watch the truck while they trekked off in search of help. It was my first trip to Belize, and stuck there sans map, water, food, and emergency equipment on a road that even twenty years later had no official name, I learned the first of many lessons about travelling—how sweet and important can be the gift of food. Despite all the anxiety and pains that day wrought (my pale Canadian skin was burned red for days), I still remember those bananas and how wonderful they tasted. I think what made that bunch so sweet was not their flavor but the fact that the people who offered them (colleagues I had never met before) had the forethought to pack them several hours earlier when they set out to rescue us. It wasn't so much the food that tasted sweet but the offer of hospitality, an act that forever endeared me to the country that would become my second home.

One might wonder how a twenty-one-year old Canadian, born and raised in one of Canada's largest cities and who had never travelled outside her own country, wound up in a broken truck on a deserted, unnamed back road of one of the smallest countries in Central America (Figure 3.1). At the time, I was an undergraduate archaeologist trying to find a culture or place that interested me enough to devote the rest of my professional career to it. Needless to say, the hospitality implied by the bananas won me over, and I've been a devoted Belizean archaeologist for almost two decades. The interesting thing about those bananas was they proved to be an omen of things to come, for much of my life in Belize has revolved around food. Indeed the majority of my non-excavation-related memories center around buying, preparing, serving, or eating various different foodstuffs, from homemade Mennonite sausages in the northwest to conch fritters on the southern coast. In the case of gibnut (*Agouti paca*), however, my memories are occupied predominately with my efforts to *avoid* eating this creature. These attempts all came to naught one night at a traditional end-of-season celebration when I was forced to confront my prejudice over what constitutes "suitable" food for dinner.

BIOLOGY AND HISTORY OF *AGOUTI PACA*

Agouti paca are small, furry piglike-looking creatures with a reddish-brown to dark-chocolate-colored coat; they are easily distinguished from their diurnal cousins, the agouti (*Dasyprocta punctata*), by the lines of irregular white spots that run lengthwise down their backs and across their haunches (Pérez 1992). Paca range in size from twenty-four to thirty-one inches (sixty to eighty centimeters), and an adult can weigh up to twenty-two pounds (ten kilograms), with little difference in size between the males and females (Beletsky 1999; Pérez 1992; The San Pedro Sun Visitors Guide [TSPSVG] 2005). They are nocturnal ground dwellers, emerging at night to feed. Although generally frugivores, their diet varies depending on seasonality, availability, and terrain; they are opportunistic foragers and in captivity have even been know to consume lizards, insects, and meat scraps (Pérez 1992). In areas where farming has impinged upon their ranges, they are considered pests as they readily adapt to feeding on, and subsequently damaging, agricultural crops (Smith 2005). During the rainy season they gain considerable weight in the form of fat that serves as a food reserve during the leaner dry-season months (Pérez 1992).

Paca exist in wide variety of habitats ranging from deciduous forest to mangrove swamps; regardless of the arboreal coverage, they prefer to be close to water and they can be found in most low- and middle-elevation wet forests throughout Mesoamerica (Beletsky 1999; Pérez 1992). The *Agouti paca* has five known subspecies whose ranges span Latin America from the Gulf Coast of Mexico along the Caribbean coast of Central America and down through the tropical regions of Ecuador, Peru, Bolivia, Paraguay, and Argentina as well as much of Brazil and the north coast of South America (Pérez 1992). The wide range of the paca means that it is known by a variety of different colloquial names, including paca, *tepezcuintle*, gibnut, and jungle rat (the last two being commonly used in Belize). The subspecies native to Belize and most of

Mesoamerica is *Agouti paca nelsoni* (Kirkpatrick and Cartwright 1975; Pérez 1992). The paca is a member of the Family *Agoutidae* in the Order *Rodentia*, thereby making it essentially a large rodent, one that looks (at least to me) like a large, long-legged, short-tailed squirrel.

Throughout its range, paca is a highly sought after and readily hunted animal (Smith 2005; Steinberg 1998). They are prized for their meat, which is described as "delicious and tender," and "highly appreciated throughout [their] range" (Pérez 1992:4; see also Beletsky 1999; TSPSVG 2005; Wilk 1999, 2006). In Manau, Brazil, gibnut comprises up to 8 percent of the meat consumed (Pérez 1992:4), while in northwest Panama, gibnut agouti and the nine-banded armadillo make up 80 percent of the hunted meat species (Linares 1976:338). In southern Belize, paca (or gibnut, as it's more familiarly called) and peccary are the two most frequently hunted animals of the indigenous Mopan (Steinberg 1998). Hunting gibnut has a long history in Belize; gibnut remains have been recovered from a variety of archaeological contexts. Historic accounts document their consumption as far back as the 1880s (Miller 1887), although it is logical to assume some continuity in the practice from the ancient Maya Formative period (ca. 600 BC–AD 250) through to the present period.

Despite its popularity, and unlike its *cuy* cousin (see Goldstein, this volume), only recently have attempts been made to raise gibnut in captivity for consumption. In 2005 a two-year grant was awarded to the Aguacaliente Wildlife Sanctuary to assist twelve Kek'chi Maya families in establishing gibnut farms (GEF Small Grants Programme 2006). The objective of this grant was twofold in that this provided people in the Toledo district (an economically disadvantaged area) with a means for income generation through the sale of gibnut meat while protecting the wildlife sanctuary from poaching activities (GEF Small Grants Programme 2006).[1] Both goals were supported by the local people, who readily acknowledge that "[p]eople hunt and they hunt for gibnut, they hunt for peccary, they hunt for several things and also it shows that the gibnut has a high value on the market." They understand the role this program plays in protecting the protecting the sanctuary and promoting wildlife protection programs (Floretino Pop, quoted in Noble 2006).

I was told that gibnut was occasionally sold in the "old" Belize market (originally located by the Swing Bridge), and I saw signs for it posted along the Southern Highway near Belmopan. In northern Belize, where I work, gibnut is still a "hunted" rather than a "ranched" food source. My experience has been that gibnut is either eaten by the hunter and his family or sold directly to other waiting consumers. Richard Wilk reported a similar situation in his study of the Kek'chi Maya of southern Belize before the GEF conservation and ranching initiatives occurred (1991:153–154).

It is perhaps unsurprising that attempts to domesticate gibnut should occur in Belize. Although long considered an acceptable meat source (see Wilk 2006:39), gibnut carries a special cultural cachet to Belizeans. In 1985, during Queen Elizabeth II's first visit to Belize, only four years after the nation achieved independence from Britain, a decision was made to include local delicacies in the state dinner. According to Richard Wilk, roast gibnut "was given the place of national honor as the main meat course" (Wilk 1999:251; 2006:167–168). The Queen, a consummate politico and well-versed in the social nuances involved in the offering and receiving of gifts of food at feasts, apparently both ate and commented favorably on the dish. British tabloids, however, concerned more with selling papers than cementing diplomatic alliances, ran severely derogatory headlines along the lines of "Queen Served Rat by Wogs" (Wilk 1999:251).[2] The incident fanned the flames of national fervor on both sides of the Atlantic. There were rancorous denunciations on the British side, while in Belize the gibnut became a rallying point for national identity. As a result of this incident, the gibnut remains firmly entranced in the Belizean national psyche as "The Royal Rat" (Wilk 1999:251; 2006:166).

MY FIRST EXPERIENCE WITH GIBNUT

My first experience with this animal was during my first trip to Belize in 1990. I was an undergraduate archaeology student working on a field project based in the Programme for Belize Biosphere, where we were mapping ancient Maya ruins in what was, and to a certain extent still is, a rather remote part of Belize (Guderjan 1991). Night falls very quickly in the rainforest, as I discovered. I was driving back to camp when darkness fell, leaving me to pick my way carefully along the narrow, rutted dirt road. I was worried all the while that I would hit a rut, lose control, and hit a tree in the dense forest that lined the road. This was also my first experience with driving on something other than well-lit, paved city streets (Figure 3.2). It was in the midst of this stressful situation that a couple of dark objects darted out of the dense jungle and dashed directly across the path of the old and somewhat temperamental Ford Bronco I was driving.

Already unnerved by the constant aerial display put on by the bats as they swooped in front of our car to catch the insects attracted by our headlights, I swerved quickly to avoid these clearly suicidal animals. As I was young and had never struck or killed any animal in my life, I was disconcerted when my efforts to avoid a collision were met with shrieks of protest from my companion—a young Maya woman—who attempted to grab the steering wheel from my hands while shouting, "Hit it! Hit it! It's gibnut—we'll have it for dinner!"

3.2. The road through the program for Belize Biosphere in 1990. (PHOTO BY H. R. HAINES)

I don't know what horrified me more at the time: the idea of deliberately hitting and killing an animal or the concept of eating roadkill. I am pleased to report that all of us—archaeologists and animals—survived the encounter. During the remainder of the drive back to camp I was treated to a lengthy lec-

3.3. Photo of an agouti in the Belize National Zoo. (PHOTO BY H. R. HAINES)

ture on the identity of our nocturnal traffic partners and introduced to this strange creature called a gibnut for the first time.

Subsequent discussions with the biologists who shared our research station, and field encounters with the gibnut's diurnal cousin the agouti, only served to reaffirm my belief that a gibnut was really just a large rat. Although I knew that in some places rodents such as squirrel and guinea pig were eaten (see Goldstein, this volume), I could not bring myself to do so. Nor could I understand how or why people would want to eat a rat when what I perceived to be more palatable options (i.e., beef, chicken, and pork) were available. Unlike Lohmann (this volume) I had not prepared myself, or in truth even considered, differences in food concepts when I set out from Toronto for the Belizean rainforest. I was as yet too unversed in cultural anthropological nuances to entertain the idea of consuming something outside the conceptual boundaries of the "food" with which I had been raised. Unlike Cattell (this volume), who prided herself on her reputation and ability for eating just about anything when working in Kenya, I was not yet daring enough to try anything out of my cultural comfort zone. Rather, like Chaiken (this volume) I opted to codify my rules on what constituted "food" and, more importantly, what I would, and would not, eat. Based on my observations of the gibnut, my cultural upbringing, and its name, I decided that that eating a rodent, no matter how tasty it was reputed to be, simply was not something I was going to do.

My sentiments toward this creature were solidified over the next nine years as I repeatedly heard people refer to this animal by its colloquial name—"jungle rat." Although viewing the gibnut in the Belize National Zoo enlightened me as to the distinct morphological differences between it and the lice-invested, disease-carrying rodents we envision inhabiting the sewers depicted in movies, it did little to change my mind abut eating the creature.[3] I simply could not wrap my head around the concept of eating something that was a "rat"—jungle or otherwise.

My feelings were only reinforced by reading Wilk's early account of how the British press had reacted to the Queen being "served rat" (Wilk 1999:251). Clearly if the entirety of the British press were aghast at the idea of "eating rat," then I was not incorrect in my thinking that this was not a foodstuff for "sensible" people. The fact that I was raised in a solidly British-Canadian household and therefore might be biased in favor of the opinion of the British presses did not impinge on my youthful consciousness at the time.

Looking back with the clarity age brings over the last two decades of working in Central America, it is clear that my aversion to gibnut was a sentiment largely induced by the language used to identify the animal. It was reinforced by my cultural upbringing and supported by the opinions expressed in the British papers of the early 1980s. The word "rat" had created an association with the sewer dweller of my urban imaginings, and the sentiments of the British papers had closed my mind to the concept of this animal as a legitimate foodstuff and underscored that it was certainly not something suitable to serve for dinner.

IT'S ALL ABOUT DINNER

As neatly illustrated by Wilk's account of the Queen's dinner and the subsequent British response, foodstuffs and their consumption may inform us on many levels about cultures not only in regard to available comestibles, resources, and diets but also in terms of national identity and social behavior. Consumption, or refusal to consume, also can inform us about ourselves and our own cultural backgrounds, behaviors, and preconceived concepts of what constitutes "dinner."

Dinner is a term common in everyday parlance. Yet, what do we mean when we speak of dinner? The Oxford Dictionary describes dinner as the "chief meal of the day, whether at midday or evening (a formal meal with several courses)" (Oxford University Press [OUP] 1976). The implication that the importance of this meal goes beyond its timing during the day is echoed by de Quincey in his discourse *The Casuistry of Roman Meals*. He notes that "time has little or no connection with [dinner]" as it "has travelled, like the hands of a clock, through *every* hour between ten, A.M. and ten, P.M." (de Quincey 1863:262). Instead, dinner should be considered "that meal, no matter when taken, which is the principle meal; the meal upon which the day's support is thrown" (de Quincey 1863:263).

But dinner can also be much more than a domestic meal. By the very nature of its formality it may easily transcend the confines of simply a moment when food is consumed and become "an artistic social construct" (Visser 1986:15). De Quincey refers to dinner as "the meal sacred to hospitality and genial pleasure" (de Quincy 1863:275), and it is perhaps this element of "hospitality" that serves to elevate dinner above the other meals of the day. It is logical therefore that the Oxford Dictionary should also define dinner as a "public banquet in honor of a person or event" (OUP 1976). In these cases food transcends the simplicity of being a meal and becomes a feast.

In anthropology the concept of a public banquet or feast has long been recognized as an important expression of social relationships. Examples of this can be found in Lohmann's understanding of what it means to "eat from the communal pot" in Papua New Guinea (this volume) and Sammells's discussion of the role of the *fiambre* in Bolivia (also this volume). Several compilation volumes have been published focusing on the different criteria for, intended results of, and social outcomes of feasts and associated activities (e.g., Bray 2003; Dietler and Hayden 2001; Mills 2004). While the term "feast" in its broadest sense may be defined as a "rubric to cover a wide range of cultural practices" (Dietler and Hayden 2001:3), most scholars agree that despite the manner of execution, the overwhelming purpose of a feast is to create or maintain important social relationships (Hayden 2001:30; Hendon 2003:205; van der Veen 2003:413).

This creation or maintenance of social relationships in feasting activities is manifested through the "communal consumption of food" (Dietler 2001:67) and may involve as few as two people or as many as several hundred, depending on the nature of relationship (Hayden 2001:38). Consequently feasting, or the offering of hospitality, may be viewed as a type of consumable gift. Like other types of gifts, commensal hospitality places an obligation on the recipient to reciprocate at some later point in time, either through a similar act of generosity or through a jointly acceptable alternative method such as labor, loyalty, or political support. Reciprocal obligation is only part of the bonding nature of a gift, for the recipient is also bound by the obligation to accept the gift, for "to refuse to accept is tantamount to declaring war; it is to reject the bond of alliance and commonality," whether the gift is food or material offerings (Mauss 1990 [1923]:13; see also Hayden 2001:35). The visual nature of the display noted by van der Veen (2003) only serves to bind the recipient more securely within the web of social networks through the presence of witnesses and the risk of losing prestige. This use of food and drink to create, maintain, and strengthen social relationships while also creating prestige for the host is a central theme in all the chapters in this volume. This volume highlights the important roles that food and commensal hospitality play in cultures around the world.

As with many types of gifts, the giving of food is highly nuanced and many subtle social distinctions may be encoded into the presentation of the meal. The status of the participants, both individually and relative to each other, may be reified by the food offered (Wilkins and Hill 2006:42; Wood 1995:48) or through the location and arrangement of diners during the feast (see Cattell's discussion of dinning alone and Lohmann's experience dinning communally, both this volume). Higher-status foods or choicer segments of certain foods may be ascribed to higher-status individuals or participants to whom one wishes to show respect or create a deeper bond of obligation. Sometimes, however, food may also carry the opposite connotation, a possibility that Chaiken (this volume) ponders in regard to the "gift" of chicken heads and feet.

Meat is frequently linked to ideas of status and obligation (Fiddes 1991; Grant 2002; McCormick 2002; Wilkins and Hill 2006:42–163). Meat not only carries connotations of status and prestige, it is also imbued with connotations of gender. Real men eat meat, not quiche; this is exemplified in Lohmann's attempts to psychologically and culturally rationalize eating "boiled eggs with chicks inside them" by paralleling them with the Western ideal of masculine "steak and eggs" breakfast (this volume). The association of meat and men has been viewed as inherently linked to subconscious associations of masculine expressions of strength in subjecting the environment and forcing nature to curb to will of man (Adams 1990:187; Twiggs 1983). Twiggs (1983:27) notes that in many cultures meat is imbued with a "symbolic potency" and that it is linked to masculinity and possesses "associations with strength, passion, aggression, and sexuality." In Smith's study of indigenous hunting practices in western Panama (2005), he noted that hunting trips were times of male bonding. They also provided the hunters with stories that could be shared with other men, and particularly successful hunters were accorded considerable respect and social status. Studies of ancient native populations at Chalcatzingo, Mexico, have suggested that differential consumption of meat existed in pre-Hispanic Mesoamerica, with men consuming substantially more meat than women (Schoeninger 1979:281). This gender inequality in access to meat is not unique to Mesoamerica but rather manifested in many cultures around the globe (Schoeninger 1979:281–282).

In the culture in which I was raised (British-Canadian), meat was central to any meal. As I was growing up the question "what's for dinner?" was likely to be answered with something akin to simply "roast beef," even though the meal included a variety of vegetables, possibly salad, Yorkshire pudding (a larger version of what is sometimes referred to as a "popover"), and gravy. This "meat-centric" mentality is oddly analogous to the experience Zycherman discovered when working in Argentina, half a world away (this volume). Many English people (like Argentineans, it would seem) don't consider a meal to be a meal unless there is meat, and certainly one would never have "dinner" without it. Willett's study among southeast Londoners noted the overwhelming sentiment among her subjects that "meat was what made a meal and a 'proper meal' always contained it" (Willett 1997:118). What makes this statement so compelling is that the subjects of her studies were all self-professed vegetarians yet admitted to consuming meat, some fairly regularly. Her study highlights the centrality of meat in the British diet and reflects both my cultural upbringing and the inherent cultural preconceptions I suffered from in my youth. The meats that formed their staple diet were also the ones that I had been raised to believe were acceptable, indeed expected, for dinner (beef, chicken, pork, and occasionally lamb).

THE END OF MY IGNORANCE

I spent nine years happily managing to avoid eating what I thought of as an unacceptable, and likely inedible, meat. The end of my blissful (and ethnocentric) ignorance, however, came swiftly in July 1998. The project I was working for at the time had for two years hosted a feast, similar to the *fiambre* Sammells discusses in this volume, to celebrate the end of each archaeological field season. Members from the local communities, our workers, and their families were invited to partake in the festivities. These feasts were used, albeit somewhat subconsciously, to finesse and reinforce the social relationships between the archaeologists (foreigners/employers/patrons) and the Belizean communities in which we lived and worked.

In the parlance of anthropological studies dealing with food and feasting, they fall into the category of what is called the "patron-role" feast. This is one of the key types of feasts identified by Dietler (2001) and is used to "symbolically reiterate and legitimize institutionalized relations of asymmetrical social power" (Dietler 2001:82). While these types of feasts normally exclude features of competitive feasting, aspects of gifting and reciprocity may still be present or incorporated. These may be deliberately factored into the display at the outset by the sharing of provisional responsibilities or through post-organizational offerings of unexpected gifts of food brought to the event.

Traditionally it had been our role as host, or "patron," to supply the venue as well as both the necessary foodstuffs and labor needed for the preparation of the meal. This year, however, in what may have been considered a gesture toward reciprocity for the feasts of the previous years, several members of the work crew decided to make a surprise offering of fresh meat for inclusion in the feast. As meat holds a high place in the ideology of human consumptive behavior, the ability to supply meat for a feast may translate into status and prestige for the provider.[4] Moreover, the prestige and high social value ascribed to meat makes it difficult to avoid consuming any meal in which it is contained, particularly in such cases where the providing of meat serves as both a gift and a sign of respect. Meat is heavily laded with social meaning, with highly prized game meat (particularly if freshly hunted) being viewed as superior to ranched or store-bought meat. In this case, the meat proffered was gibnut—more accurately, several gibnuts. These animals were hunted by several of our local workmen, and judging by the pride they took in describing their procurement, it is clear that they considered their ability to catch these animals an example of their masculine prowess (Collier and Rosaldo 1981; Fiddes 1991:146; Smith 2005).

Despite having successfully negotiated myself around the table of food offerings in such a manner as to avoid passing the gibnut, and therefore having a legitimate reason for failing to partake in the meat, it was not long before I was waylaid by the providers and my opinion was sought as to the tenderness and rich flavor of the gibnut. Upon learning that I had yet to try their offering, one of the men dashed off to claim a haunch for me. The other men remained to extol the delicacy of the meat and amount of effort spent in its acquisition, clearly in an attempt to impress me with their prowess and, by default, making me a hostage until their friend returned.

I was caught not just by the social situation but also in a clash of cultures. I was trapped under the double onus of being both a host, which in my culture implies an obligation for graciousness, and the recipient of a gift, with all its attendant social obligations of acceptance. If I refused to consume the food offered, I risked the very social relationship we were attempting to maintain. Faced with the option of the unpardonable double social faux pas of insulting the hospitality and masculinity of my givers, as well as being considered a bad host and losing prestige, I was left with little recourse but to consume the meat presented to me. Much to my surprise, the meat was tender and exceptionally flavorful.

As Shakespeare once said, "What's in a name? That which we call a rose, by any other name would smell as sweet" (Shakespeare 1925:1074). In regard to my experience in Belize I learned that which we call a rat by any other name can taste pretty good, actually! Although never having formulated a rational concept of how I anticipated rat meat to taste, it was apparent that I had subconsciously envisioned something greasy or slimy, reminiscent of gutters and sewers. Unlike Goldstein, who found that *cuy* tastes much like chicken (this volume), I found my rodent tasted more like rabbit, although less gamey. My preconceived notions and social abhorrence for rats in general had been transferred to this animal in specific, much to the deprivation my culinary repertoire.

In retrospect, I have come to the conclusion that language played a major factor in shaping my perception of gibnuts. As Levi-Strauss noted (1969, 1978 [1968]), food is more than just "good to eat," it is also "good to think" about. Clearly my concept of what constituted food, and could therefore be acceptably defined as dinner, was prejudiced by my cultural conception of what was considered an acceptable meat; nowhere in my cultural lexicon did rat construe dinner. I have often wondered if I had been introduced to the animal as "jungle chicken" whether I would have had the same immediate preconceived prejudices. I will never know the answer to that question, but pondering it has taught me to be more accepting of foods, regardless of what they are called in English.

NOTES

1. Although a license is not needed in Belize to hunt gibnut, hunting of any animals is forbidden in wildlife sanctuaries and reserves (Frost 1977).

2. "Wog" is a disparaging term found mainly in British English used to refer to a person of color, usually of African or South Asian decent. Fortunately, it has fallen out of general parlance.

3. For a good example of how rats are considered in the popular media see *Indiana Jones and the Last Crusade*, or as I like to think of it, "Archaeologist Meets Sewer Rats."

4. For a personal account of this phenomenon see Goldstein's discussion (this volume) of being offered the last *chaktado* in the house by his host.

REFERENCES

Adams, Carol
1990   *The Sexual Politics of Meat: A Feminist-Vegetarian Critical Theory*. The Continuum Publishing Company, New York.

Beletsky, Les
1999   *The Ecotravellers' Wildlife Guide: Belize and Northern Guatemala*. Academic Press, London.

Bray, Tamara L. (editor)
2003   *The Archaeology and Politics of Food and Feasting in Early States and Empires*. Kluwer Academic / Plenum Publishers, New York.

Collier, Jane F., and Michelle Z. Rosaldo
    1981   Politics and Gender in Simple Societies. In *Sexual Meanings: The Cultural Construction of Gender and Sexuality*, ed. S. Ortner and H. Whitehead, 275–329. Cambridge University Press, Cambridge.

De Quincey, Thomas
    1863   "The Casuistry of Roman Meals." In *Last Days of Immanuel Kant and Other Writings*, ed. T. de Quincey, 246–286. Adam and Charles Black, Edinburgh.

Dietler, Michael
    2001   Theorizing the Feast: Rituals of Consumption, Commensal Politics, and Power in African Contexts. In *Feasts: Archaeological and Ethnographic Perspectives on Food, Politics, and Power,* ed. M. Dietler and B. Hayden, 65–114. Smithsonian Institution Press, Washington, DC.

Dietler, Michael, and Brian Hayden (editors)
    2001   *Feasts: Archaeological and Ethnographic Perspectives on Food, Politics, and Power.* Smithsonian Institution Press, Washington, DC.

Fiddes, Nick
    1991   *Meat: A Natural Symbol.* Routledge, London.

GEF Small Grants Programme, The
    2006   Protecting the Biodiversity of the Aguacaliente Wildlife Sanctuary through Sustainable Income Generation (BZE/05/05). http://sgp.undp.org/web/projects/8910/protecting_the_biodiversity_of_the_aguacaliente_wildlife_sanctuary_through_sustainable_income_gener.html, accessed March 2009.

Grant, A.
    2002   Food, Status, and Social Hierarchy. In *Consuming Passions and Patterns of Consumption*, ed. Preston Miracle and Nicky Milner, 17–23. McDonald Institute for Archaeological Research, Cambridge.

Guderjan, Thomas H.
    1991   *Maya Settlement in Northwestern Belize: The 1988 and 1990 Seasons of the Rio Bravo Archaeological Project.* Maya Research Program and Labyrinthos, San Antonio, TX.

Hayden, Brian
    2001   Fabulous Feasts: A Prolegomenon to the Importance of Feasting. In *Feasts: Archaeological and Ethnographic Perspectives on Food, Politics, and Power*, ed. M. Dietler and B. Hayden, 23–64. Smithsonian Institution Press, Washington, DC.

Hendon, Julia A.
    2003   Feasting at Home: Community and House Solidarity among the Maya of Southeastern Mesoamerica. In *The Archaeology and Politics of Food and Eating in Early States and Empires*, ed. T. L. Bray, 203–233. Kluwer Academic / Plenum Publishers, New York.

Kirkpatrick, Ralph D., and Anne M. Cartwright
    1975   List of Mammals Known to Occur in Belize. *Biotropica* 7:136–140.

Levi-Strauss, Claude
    1969   *The Raw and the Cooked: Introduction to a Science of Mythology*, Vol. 1. Harper and Row Publishers, New York.
    1978   *The Origin of Table Manners: Mythologiques*, Vol. 3. Harper and Row Pub-
    [1968]   lishers, New York.

Linares, Olga F.
    1976   "Garden Hunting" in the American Tropics. *Human Ecology* 4:331–349.

Mauss, Marcel
    1990   *The Gift: The Form and Reason for Exchange in Archaic Societies.* Trans.
    [1923]   W. D. Halls. W. W. Norton, New York.

McCormick, Finbar
    2002   The Distribution of Meat in Hierarchical Society: The Irish Evidence. In *Consuming Passions and Patterns of Consumption*, ed. Preston Miracle and Nicky Milner, 25–32. McDonald Institute for Archaeological Research, Cambridge, UK.

Miller, William
    1887   Notes on a Part of the Western Frontier of British Honduras. *Proceedings of the Royal Geographical Society and Monthly Record of Geography* 9:420–423.

Mills, Barbara J. (editor)
    2004   *Identity, Feasting, and the Archaeology of the Greater Southwest.* University Press of Colorado, Boulder.

Noble, Alfonso
    2006   Tackling Poverty through Ingenuity in Toledo. http:// www.7newsbelize. com/sstory.php, accessed June 2009.

Oxford University Press (OUP)
    1976   *The Concise Oxford Dictionary*, 6th ed. Oxford University Press, Oxford.

Pérez, Elizabeth M.
    1992   Agouti Paca. *Mammalian Species*. No. 404:1–7.

The San Pedro Sun Visitor's Guide [TSPSVG]
    2005   The Paca. *The Island Newspaper*. Ambergris Caye, Belize. August 4, 2005, 7.

Schoeninger, Margaret J.
    1979   Diet and Status at Chalcatzingo: Some Empirical and Technical Aspects of Strontium Analysis. *American Journal of Physical Anthropology* 51:295–310.

Shakespeare, William
    1952   Romeo and Juliet, Act II, Scene ii. In *William Shakespeare Complete Works*, 1065–1099. P. F. Colliers and Son Corporation, New York.

Smith, Derek A.
   2005   Garden Game: Shifting Cultivation, Indigenous Hunting and Wildlife
            Ecology in Western Panama. *Human Ecology* 33:505–537.

Steinberg, Michael K.
   1998   Mopan Maya Forest Resources in Southern Belize. *Geographical Review*
            88:131–137.

Twiggs, Julia
   1983   Vegetarianism and the Meaning of Meat. In *The Sociology of Food and Eat-
            ing*, ed. A. Murcotta, 18–30. Gower, Farnborough.

Van der Veen, Marijke
   2003   When Is Food a Luxury? *World Archaeology* 34:405–427.

Visser, Margaret
   1986   *Much Depends on Dinner*. McClelland and Stewart, Toronto.

Wilk, Richard R.
   1991   *Household Ecology: Economic Change and Domestic Life among the Kekchi
            Maya in Belize*. University of Arizona Press, Tucson.
   1999   "Real Belizean Food": Building Local Identity in the Transnational Carib-
            bean. *American Anthropologist* 101(2):244–255.
   2006   *Home Cooking in the Global Village: Caribbean Food from Buccaneers to
            Ecotourists*. Berg, Oxford.

Wilkins, John M., and Shaun Hill
   2006   *Food in the Ancient World*. Blackwell, Malden, MA.

Willett, Anna
   1997   "Bacon Sandwiches Got the Better of Me": Meat Eating and Vegetarian-
            ism in South-East London. In *Food, Health, and Identity*, ed. Pat Caplan,
            111–130. Routledge, London.

Wood, Roy C.
   1995   *The Sociology of the Meal*. Edinburgh University Press, Edinburgh.

CHAPTER FOUR

The Delicacy of Raising and Eating Guinea Pig

David John Goldstein

Biographical Sketch. David John Goldstein is an anthropologist with a specialty in ethnobotany, the study of humans and plant interactions, and paleoethnobotany, the same area of study as it relates to peoples of past societies. For the most part he works with archaeologists and with modern farmers and botanists to develop resources for better interpreting archaeological data. He has worked on research projects in Great Britain, Italy, the United States, Belize, Peru, and Bolivia.

INTRODUCTION: THE CUY

There are three predictable questions that are asked of a foreigner by Peruvians upon arrival, departure, and any exchange with a taxi driver. First and foremost, "How do you like Peru?" Of course you say that you love it and can't wait to come back. What else can you say? Second, and perhaps most important, "Have you been to Cuzco and Machu Picchu?" I generally smile and say I didn't go this time but would be sure to go again someday. Critical to the topic of this book of collected essays is the third question, "How do you like the food?"

On the coast people simply ask, "Do you actually like ceviche?" The most well-known and signature dish of Peru is probably ceviche, raw fish with onions and chili pepper "cooked" in lime juice. But if you venture away from the coast, climbing up any of the country's river valleys, the highways to the highlands, where ocean fish are not often recommended as standard fare, this third and most critical food question often turns to the *cuy* (koo-ee). "Have you tried cuy?" and "Did you like it?"

Cuy is the popular term in Andean parlance for what we call guinea pig in English. The animal's scientific classification is *Cavia* sp. with a variety of species, *porcellus* (domesticate), *cobaya* (domesticate), *apera* (wild ancestor), and *tschudii* (wild ancestor) (Forstadt 2002). Although it is purported to be a rodent in its own branch of the Order Mammalia, classification terminology continues to be disputed between different wild and domesticated versions of the animal within the same genus; for some, its designation as a rodent is also in dispute (Forstadt 2002). Among those Limeños (denizens of Lima, the capital city of Peru) who are not consumers of cuy (an estimated six million people), however, it is often referred to as a rat or hamster, and a series of common jokes abound about the highland or *indio* tradition of eating tailless rats.

Within Peru the word cuy is widely used to refer to a guinea pig, the general assumption being that this word is Quechua, the largest indigenous language group in Peru. The Quechua and Aymara (the second largest Peruvian language group) terms for cuy are *jacca* or *aca* and *wanku* or *wankuchi*, respectively (Morales 1995:4). Popular lore has it that the term "cuy" refers to the cute little chirp that the animal makes. This cooing sound is also intoned or written popularly as "chivi-chivi" or "couy-couy." Curiously, the use of the term "cuy" lends considerable insight into the effects of long-term European colonization within the Americas. "Cuy" probably comes from one of the Arawakan or Tupi language groups that the Spanish first encountered as they moved toward the colonization of the Southern Hemisphere (Forstadt 2002). Whichever word was first encountered by the colonists, it was, in turn, transliterated from either Spanish or Portuguese and then translated back to lingua franca usage between indigenous peoples and the colonists during the sixteenth century. This tradition of colonizers appropriating and transmitting indigenous words throughout the colonized world is well-known and is similarly seen with foodstuffs such as maize (*Zea mays*), batata or camote (sweet potato, or *Ipomoea batatas*), papa (potato, or *Solanum tuberosum*), and yucca (*Manihot esculenta* var. *kranz*) (Morales 1995).

The cuy is traditionally a festival food, reserved for special occasions (Bolton 1979; Morales 1995). Guaman Poma de Ayala and Garcilaso de la Vega, both important chroniclers of the Spanish conquest of Peru, report that the cuy was a customary food for religious festivals, as well as an offering from at

4.1. Guaman Poma's representation of *cuy* offering, seventh century. (FROM G. POMA 2005 [1615])

least the Inca period onward (Figure 4.1; Guaman Poma de Ayala 2005 [1615]; Sandweiss and Wing 1997). We know from archaeological investigations that cuy were raised in households, consumed at festivals, and offered as sacrifices throughout the pre-Hispanic period as well (Sandweiss and Wing 1997). The extent to which they were consumed and their contexts for consumption, however, remain elusive archaeologically, as scavenging dogs and other taphonomic processes easily destroy their small bones (Valdez 2000; Valdez and Valdez 1997). Today, cuy is consumed mostly in traditional settlements where those villagers who raise them enhance their ability to hold village feasts and thus become political candidates (Morales 1995). In less rural settings, cuy consumption is regarded as something special and reserved for weekend outings with the family (Bolton 1979; Milliones 2002).

There are two main traditional preparations of cuy: fried (*chaktado* in Quechua) and roasted (known throughout Peru as *cuy al horno*) (Barrionuevo 1988:75–82). Roast cuy mainly consists of the animal, gutted and depilated, stuffed with *huacatay* (*Tagetes minuta*) and other seasonings, and baked in a wood-burning oven. Huacatay is used in Andean cooking as a major flavoring for sauces, stews, and roasts. The flavor is distinct and can be described as a florally fragrant parsley-like herb. It is the traditional preparation in the Cuzco region and the Urubamba Valley, also called the "Sacred Valley." Sometimes, true to its English "pig" reference, the mouth of the cuy is stuffed with a small chili pepper as decoration, akin to the occidental cooking style of serving a pig with an apple in its mouth (Barrionuevo 1988:80).

Chaktado, or fried cuy, has many variations. Chaktado actually refers to the manner of cooking by flattening the animal in a pan of frying oil and does not refer to the frying itself (Barrionuevo 1988). The animal's fur is first removed, and then it is gutted. The kidneys and liver are usually left in and are believed to have excellent nutritional value. The body is then sliced in half, ventrally, so that it lies flat in the pan (Figure 4.2). Often the filleted animal is then dredged in milk or an egg mixture and powdered on both sides with cracked corn or hominy flour (Ministerio de Agricultura 2004). As the meat is placed in the pan of frying oil, a large rock or heavy iron slab is used to keep the animal flat while frying. From here, the cuy is either served with its condiments or placed in a stew. Condiments for the fried cuy alone are roast potatoes, an acidic lime and onion salad (*zarsa*), and ground fresh chili pepper (Barrionuevo 1988).

FIRST ENCOUNTERS: ACCEPTANCE AND TOLERANCE

One of my closest friends and colleagues has the proud pleasure of being a Peruvian national. I say proud, as there are few people that I have encountered in my years of being an archaeologist who love their country and their traditions

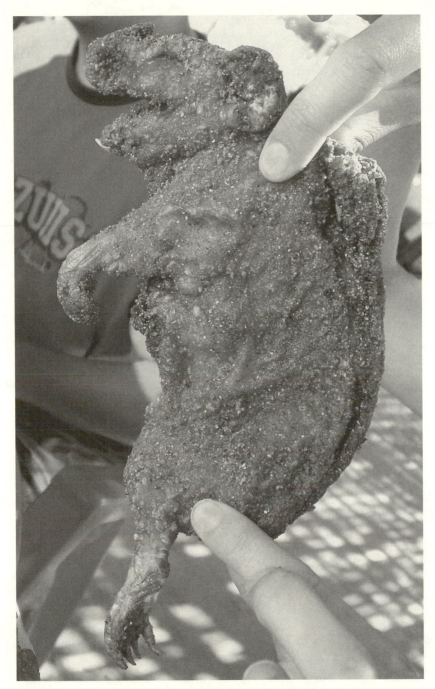

4.2. Fried cuy (cuy chaktado) in Moquegua, Peru. (PHOTO BY DAVID GOLDSTEIN)

with such profound, soulful introspection. Our first encounter prior to my admission to graduate school was during the attendance of a national archaeology meeting. We were in a group of colleagues and friends, and at one point in the night we found ourselves exchanging stories and sharing a drink. Almost immediately the subject turned to Peru. "Why don't you come work in Peru?" he asked. I said that I had been working in Central America for some years and felt committed to that work. He answered, "Yes, but there are relatively few archaeologists working in Peru, let alone paleoethnobotanists. Plus, where else can you eat a guinea pig?" I took the point of the guinea pig very seriously. He was right. While I had known several guinea pigs in my life, I had never eaten one.

He continued to tell his first cuy story of the night. Upon his arrival in the United States as a graduate student, he was enlisted by the local school district and his university's Office of International Students to give a lecture on Peru for a local group of third graders. He showed up on the appointed day, with his slide carousel and projector. The lights went out, and the majesty of Peru passed before this group of Midwestern schoolchildren: the Colca Valley, deepest canyon in the world; Huascarán, the highest mountain in Peru; Lake Titicaca, the largest and highest lake in the world; the Callejon de Huaylas, with its llamas and alpacas grazing at 12,000 feet above sea level. Naturally, the slide show turned to food, the third topic on every taxi driver's list and the nexus of Peruvian pride. This topic was illustrated with photos demonstrating the 3,000 varieties of potato, the bounty of tropical fruits, and eventually a picture of the traditional Peruvian kitchen (Figure 4.3). There, underneath the kitchen table, amidst all of the pots and pans, the dirt floor, and the sacks of grain, were the little beady eyes of the guinea pigs. "We call them 'cuy,' and we eat them," he said.

At this point there was a slight pause in his presentation, as he recalled the small cage situated at the back of the classroom that he had passed on his way in. From here the presentation rapidly sped up and came to a close. As the fluorescent lights flickered on, his eyes met with the tear-filled eyes of the teacher's, sitting next to the guinea pig cage in the back of the room (Figure 4.4). The conclusion of this story was that he, traumatized, vowed never to return to give such a presentation. He left, without asking for the students' reflections on the possibility of eating Fluffy at the back of the room. The greatest difficulty for him was in considering how on earth the teacher was to explain this culture clash with her students, who were more accustomed to fighting over who could take the classroom pet home for spring break. I found this story humorous and stimulating. As for working in Peru, I was sold.

Over the past ten years of working in Peru, I have become relatively skilled at getting through this contradiction between North American guinea pig

4.3. Traditional Highland Andean kitchen, Urubamba, Cuzco, Peru (note the cuyes under the table at the back). (PHOTO BY DAVID GOLDSTEIN)

semiotics (pet) and Peruvian guinea pig semiotics (food). When in the taxi, once the cuy-consumption topic is raised, often the Peruvian notes that it is fabled that North Americans are accustomed to keeping the guinea pig as a pet, not to be eaten. I respond with a resounding, "Yes, it is true; we are not accustomed to eating our pets."[1] Often this leads to the discussion of other culinary traditions that North Americans often consider "pet eating," for instance, the Chinese and Vietnamese with dogs and cats, the rabbit as a delicacy in Europe, and of course the people in Chincha in central Peru famous for eating house cats, a topic for another chapter in a book like this one.

In the popular Peruvian press, however, this contradiction is used as a way to describe the culture clash between the Western world and the more remote, traditional areas of Peru. On the first page of a national newspaper's Sunday magazine section on tourism (Rocha Revilla 2005:40) is an illustration of a typical blond European or North American holding a cuy and sitting next to a Peruvian guide. In this case the Peruvian's identity marker is the use of the hat and the colors of the hatband, which likely relate to the region and even the district from which he comes. As this is in the Peruvian press, based in Lima, most readers would recognize this person as "traditional," in stark contrast to

4.4. Author's nephews and their classroom guinea pig in Lexington, Massachusetts. (PHOTO BY CAROLYN GOLDSTEIN)

the braided blond hair, tall stature, and "white" skin of the foreign tourist. The caption reads: "To one it is a pet, to the other, a food resource. The cultural contrast permits each to learn about the other." While this is true, in my colleague's predicament, these "learning" activities and cultural exchanges can sometimes be unpredictably traumatic. Food traditions clearly offer this kind of exchange and additionally offer an anthropological view into national pride, cultural traditions, and other forms of accepted practice. Clearly, in Peru, cuy consumption encompasses these themes. For me it was easy to become a participant observer to this cultural practice of guinea pig eating, and I eagerly anticipated my first experience.

Relatively new to Peru, I spent my second, brief field project in 2000 in Ayacucho, a city in the south-central highlands of Peru. The city is famous for two things: its incredible colonial churches, which remain well-preserved and revered in the city, and as the seat of the Sendero Luminoso, a ruthless Maoist rebel group that ravaged the countryside during the 1980s and 1990s (Perú 2004) and was equally matched in savagery by the government's military reprisal against them. This recent situation made Ayacucho a "no-go" destination for foreign and national tourists for almost twenty years. As I arrived in February 2000 for a short stay to work with a joint Peruvian and U.S. archaeological team, I felt quite privileged to be allowed to visit and take it all in. Many of my Peruvian friends and colleagues had never been to Ayacucho, the city or the department (state), because of the security situation. My previous experience in Peru had been on the north coast of Peru, the land of ceviche, and faraway from cuy country. Meals on this project in Ayacucho were taken in a local restaurant accustomed to serving meals to "gringo" archaeologists. We arrived on a Saturday night, and Sunday afternoon was our first big meal. Additionally, Sunday afternoon is the weekly big family meal for Peruvians. The place was packed, and my U.S. host, the group photographer, and I were the only foreigners in the restaurant. Cuy was on the menu, so I ordered it. My U.S. and Peruvian comrades, seasoned cuy-eating experts all but one, were hyping the experience: "Go ahead, try it; there is a first for everything." The waitstaff, on the other hand, wanted to know if I was hungry enough for a whole one. I sort of chickened-out and ordered a half.

My first half cuy arrived chaktado that day, and, I admit, my first instinct was to take a photo. There it was, one-half of a guinea pig. Exactly one-half: head cut in half, one single kidney, and with great luck, the half with the liver as well. It was impressive to be served my first cuy. I didn't take a photo, as I thought that it would be too "gringo" or touristy to do so. I found out later, after many years, that even Peruvians do this, often when traveling as tourists within their own country, and I eventually lost my anthropologist's inhibitions for taking pictures of flattened fried guinea pigs (Figure 4.2). But my first impression really was of tenth-grade biology class with Mr. Gorrill, when we were each given a fetal pig. All of the anatomy of the cuy, just as with my fetal pig who we affectionately named "Flash," was in plain view and easily distinguished: the eyes, sinus cavities, brains, and so forth. So I spent more time studying, rather than eating, my first cuy. My principles of documentation and investigation, however, were a huge mistake. The cuy got cold.

I began eating what I thought was the least offensive part, the hind leg; indeed, it tasted and looked like a Cornish game hen and went down easy. The guinea pig has an incredibly high protein to fat ratio. As a result, the meat is low in fat and cholesterol, a selling point for the export market (Horkheimer 2004). I then moved to the foreleg—less meaty but still within the poultry range of flavor, so relatively inoffensive. This left me with a head, a liver, and a rib cage. With these as the options, I returned to the legs and sucked and pulled every last piece of meat from these areas. Again, I didn't realize that I was wasting time. After I realized that you could actually crunch up the bones with your teeth, I began to lose fear of the next part. So I moved to the rib cage. It was too late. The cuy had cooled just enough that the tough, leathery skin had contracted, making an almost impervious shield-like covering over the slender and almost meatless ribs. I looked around to other tables on that Sunday and noticed that most people avoided this problem by going at the skin first.

I moved to the liver, convincing myself that the liver was a healthy thing to eat. Here I was following my New York delicatessen instinct that told me, just like with chicken, livers are a delicacy. The liver went down easy and was rather tasty. This left the job of the head. I went for the cheeks, remembering that with fish, another small protein-filled treat, the cheeks are a delicacy in Japan. And the cheeks were less work than the tough outer skin. I stopped with eyes and brains, deciding that someone else could take that on if they wanted to eat off my plate. There were no offers from around the table.

I survived, and in the end, it tasted like chicken. I had learned my lesson about studying my food too much. I was now convinced that I was prepared for any combat situation as an anthropologist. I felt prepared to be airlifted into a highland Andean festival to negotiate a mining contract or gain access to an archaeological site while dining on guinea pig. I could now eat cuy with the best of them.

POST-INITIATION: RAISING THE GENERAL STATE OF THE CUY

About three years later, having learned much more about Peru and having completed my dissertation fieldwork there, I realized that there were still many things yet to know about Andean living. I began working with an archaeological project in Moquegua, a small city in southern Peru. The project team had twenty years' experience working in the region and, as a result, had developed a collection of animal, plant, ceramic, and mineral reference materials that were used to identify and classify the archaeological remains recovered from the region. One day I began talking about the cuy with the zooarchaeological specialist on the project, Dr. Susan DeFrance of the University of Florida and an expert on the subject. The town of Moquegua and its adjacent settlements are renowned for the quality of the cuy that they produce. One nearby town, Los Angeles, is the location of several weekend *cuyerias*, or guinea pig eateries. I was surprised to find out from her that every weekend (Friday through Saturday) and on holidays, these places serve 300 to 400 guinea pigs. My conversation with Susan then led to a discussion of cuy quality. What is the best cuy, male or female? How are they selected for flavor? By age? Physique? If you raise them, which ones do you cull and when? Last, and most important, what might this industry look like archaeologically? For me, as an anthropologist, the best way to answer some of these questions was to try my hand at raising them myself.

Another colleague, Robin Coleman (a student from Northwestern University), and I decided to purchase and raise our own guinea pigs. The initial requirements were readily available. The house that the project had rented came with its own empty cage. Now all we had to do was fill it. We decided that we would start with a mating pair and go from there. With a short gestation period, eight weeks, and an expected first *cria*, or brood, of at least four (standard size is generally two to seven), we were sure that they would reproduce like rabbits.

Moquegua's daily market is vibrant with commerce. The town sits at the nexus between the highlands and the coast at an elevation of almost 5,000 feet (1,500 meters). Most importantly, the recently paved highway that links Bolivia to the coast goes straight through town, which makes coastal and highland products available. On one side of the market is a small animal market, which sells everything from goats to cuyes.

We decided that we wanted to buy a "quality" pair, and among the four or five women selling cuyes, we quickly learned that the important traits, as far as taste quality is concerned, are the ears and toes. The more toes that a cuy has, the tastier it is; the more wrinkled the ears, the more *sabroso* (flavorful). In Moquegua six- and seven-toed cuyes are common (Figure 4.5). Information supplied by the local Moquegua Cuy Husbandry Association, Asociación Moqueguana de Crianza de Cuy, indicates that pelage color is also a critical comment on flavor and on the overall durability of the animal for sustained production (Valcárcel Salas, Villegas Suarez, and Revilla Layme 1998). Pelage comes in curly, straight, or long hair, and color varies among brown, mottled, orange, white, and black. In the end, we selected two seven-toed, wrinkled-ear cuyes: Lucas and Madeline. They were young, about three months old, and not about to mate anytime soon. So we came upon our first problem: our excavation season would end well before our cuyes could go to their next generation. As one of our primary questions of our cuy-raising experiment was to see how long they could survive without being eaten, as well as to get a sample of bones

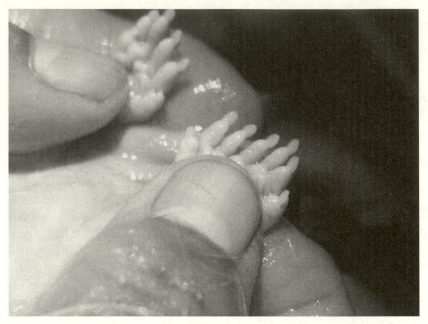

4.5. Vendor displays seven-toed cuy in Moquegan market. (PHOTO BY DAVID GOLDSTEIN)

from aged cuyes, we decided that we would leave our original mating pair with a friend in Moquegua until we returned the following year.

Much like the North American guinea pigs that are household pets, Peruvian cuyes require an incredible amount of care, and to raise them for food they require a strictly controlled diet (Palomino Mendoza 2002). Animal scientists at the National Agricultural University at La Molina (UNALM), near Lima, Peru, have developed strict breeding and food regimens for successful cuy raising. Recent investigations into traditional cuy raising indicate that, overall, the cuy population has increased nationally to almost 22 million, nearly one per person in Peru (Palma 2005); the overall quality of the gene pool, on the other hand, has dramatically declined (Morales 1995). Cuy produced today are much smaller, less hearty, and potentially less meaty than in previous years and certainly than in antiquity. This situation has led to the development and implementation of cuy-raising programs throughout the country using the UNALM and the Ministry of Agriculture as national coordinators for the program. Both the ministry and the university offer "super-cuyes" for sale. These are animals that have been bred from the heartiest stock found in the country. These animals can grow up to five pounds in weight; this is substantially greater than the less-than-two-pound variety typically offered at local restaurants (Morales 1995). At the same time, the national authorities have organized local cuy-growers' associations throughout the country to aid in refortifying the cuy gene pool and to develop these animals as a meat product for export.

In the end, our cuyes died in the care of our friend. Apparently, we had not chosen a pair that could thrive at the level of industrial production that we had hoped. Our friend, however, caught the cuy production bug from our pair and over two years has developed a population of 800 cuyes. She and her husband have an apparently thriving business selling cuyes to the local cuyerias, making a $100.00 per month in profit, which supplements their incomes from their jobs doing roadwork for the local municipality (the average household income is a little over $150.00 per month). There are issues, however, with this level of success. First is the care. The cuyes have to be fed four times each day and at the same time each day (Valcárcel Salas, Villegas Suarez, and Revilla Layme 1998). One of the meals is a fortified grain supplement that has been engineered by Animal Scientists at UNALM; the other three consist of fresh alfalfa. While alfalfa is readily available in and around Moquegua, several pounds are necessary at each feeding and have to be bought twice a day in order to maintain production. Hence, my friends comment frequently that most of their time each day is spent transporting alfalfa around Moquegua. Additionally, within any population of more than 300 cuyes, plagues and mites—among other ailments—are common, and constant cleaning, and often individual washing of the cuyes, is necessary to maintain the population in healthy and good breeding condition. This does not include the monetary investment of medicines and cleaning supplies for this many animals. Overall, this couple sustains about fifteen breeding pairs and can sell two to three dozen cuyes per month, which seems to be the maximum sustainable household level of production (Sarria 2005).

Recent reports in the national press have presented cuy raising as everything from a sustainable get-rich-quick scheme to a rising industrial market on the verge of exploding onto the international export scene (Palma 2005; Palomino Mendoza 2002; Sarria 2005). At the local level, the meetings of the Moquegua Cuy Husbandry Association seem to corroborate the pending interest in the development of the export market. Rumors have developed that a company called Cuysa is selling frozen cuyes to the growing market in China and the United States (Palma 2005; Palomino Mendoza 2002). Simultaneously, rumors exist that restaurateurs from the regional metropolis of Arequipa (population 1 million and growing) are arriving weekly to purchase Moqueguan cuyes to supply the weekend restaurant market in the neighboring province. No one from the Moquegua cuy-raising association, however, has entered into either of these "markets" in the past two years. In fact, the association's membership has shrunk, with some would-be entrepreneurs deciding not to deal with the hassle of raising cuyes. Returning to the photo using the cuy as an opportunity for cross-cultural comparison, it is difficult to believe that the so-called developing North American market will ever be significant enough to spur cuy production to levels above that used for national (i.e., Peruvian) consumption (Manjeli et al. 1998).

Two and a half years after our initial experiment of cuy husbandry began it yielded results. Two animals, both with six toes, fell victim to old age and became new accessions to the Museo Contisuyo's zooarchaeological reference collection, part of the archaeological project in Moquegua. The female was nearly three years old and died of a head wound while pregnant. She was almost ready to give birth to a single seven-toed female. The other was a male that died of internal wounds caused by "rough play" with other males. Interestingly enough, both of these animals fit into rather common patterns. Females are usually at the end of their breeding potential after two years, giving birth to four pups when younger and only one pup after two years (Palomino Mendoza 2002). Males are generally "sacrificed" after four months for the food market. Our unfortunate male was kept around as a breeding pair, but few males live longer than a year (Palomino Mendoza 2002). Ultimately, our experiment generated good comparative specimens for investigating cuy husbandry in antiquity.

CONCLUSION: HOPES AND DREAMS OF *CAVIA PORCELLUS*

The cuy holds an honored place in the folklore of the Andes as a mythical trickster. In one story the cuy outfoxes the other great trickster, the fox, who wants to eat the cuy. The cuy gently coaxes the fox into doing the menial tasks that are supposed to be the dedicated work of the cuy, for example, digging holes, removing rocks, and moving boulders. The cuy argues that he is just too clumsy and delicate to do the work, and the fox kindly lends a hand. The cuy realizes that once the fox finishes with his work, he is likely to be eaten. So the assignment of tasks eventually allows the cuy time to escape. The story ends with the fox losing interest, leaving the cuy in peace (Martinez Parra 1999:170–172).

In retrospect, I think that this myth serves as a metaphor for my own experience with the cuy. After a while, one loses interest in the novelty of eating or raising the cuy. It is too much work for the little meat that you get, and raising them is too much work to sustain a limited amount of additional income. Why work so hard for something that, frankly, tastes like chicken but comes in a much more cumbersome package? When offered, I now know how, without making a fuss or a mess, to eat one. Many Peruvians clearly feel great pride that a food eaten by the Incas is still available on many plates in the country. At the same time, many Peruvians find the idea of eating cuy rather distasteful and disavow the consumption of what I have heard many nationals call a "hamster."

4.6. Cuy as sporting club mascot, Moquegua, Peru. (PHOTO BY DAVID GOLDSTEIN)

There are a great number of Peruvians who have never tried their own national dish and so they seek it out and, with great interest and pride, consume their first, second, and third cuy. It does not appear, however, that from this novelty a renewed nationalist or pride-based cult will develop around cuy consumption. Nor, as it was recently reported in the national press, is it likely that national chains of cuy restaurants will start up anytime soon.

Yet, the cuy is a symbol of national pride. To some extent it is difficult to understand how a rodent, or a rodent-like animal, could become a national or local symbol. Then again, not all national symbols have universal charisma; Benjamin Franklin wanted the United States to appoint the turkey as its symbol, and the Canadians use a beaver to this day. One local sports club in Moquegua uses the cuy as its mascot and symbol (Figure 4.6). It is not likely that the "Fighting Cuy" will supersede team names like the Warriors, Falcons, or Giants. Popular culture, however, has endorsed the cuy as a center of Peruvian national pride. Many Peruvians remember a famous, long-running comic strip in which the protagonist was a cuy aspiring to greatness, and this legacy remains (Figure 4.7). Overall, the cuy as a symbol as well as a food maintains a dear place in the hearts of many Peruvians, even if it probably will never reach the fast-food status of McDonald's hamburgers. That is probably a good thing.

Cuy production, on the other hand, may increase slightly. This level of production will only be as sustainable if and when new markets become available. It may be that the Chinese will become aficionados of the cuy, but the European and North American markets still seem uncertain. A colleague at Northwestern University was able to acquire a frozen cuy, which was proudly labeled as a product of Ecuador and had a nice picture of a long-tailed cuy on the front—more like another well-known rodent. She remarked, however, that she had to cajole a restaurateur into selling her the cuy, as many South American restaurants do not advertise cuy because they fear attracting the attention of

4.7. Cuy graffiti depicted with political aspirations behind the Faculty of Social Sciences, National Major University of San Marcos, Lima, Peru. (PHOTO BY DAVID GOLDSTEIN)

animal-rights groups in the United States and Canada. On a recent visit back to Lima, however, my wife and I encountered a canned, precooked cuy in a shop in Chinatown; sadly, it was only one-half of the animal. The label on the can declared that it could be heated and served with ease and had instructions in one of the main Chinese languages, Russian, English, German, Japanese, and Portuguese. It became such a novelty item among our Peruvian friends that we went back a month later to buy more, but we were distressed to see that they had sold out. When asked if they were going to get more, the storekeeper looked at me a little oddly.

The level of production currently advocated in Peru by both national authorities and animal-science experts is a level between cottage production and industry. Traditional cuy husbandry in small towns, within kitchens or courtyards in rural or semi-urban areas, is likely to continue as it relates to traditional feasting, political responsibility, and cuisines. The level advocated by the Moquegua Cuy Husbandry Association has been relatively stable since the 1970s in Peru, and it is not likely to change as the market served is largely local and mostly a function of weekend consumption (Manjeli et al. 1998). An indication of the unlikelihood that cuy will become a more mainstream national and international commodity is that both a national restaurant guide and a national tourism guide neglect to offer any information about cuyerias or eating cuy, while ceviche and potatoes are both highlighted (Findley 2002; Hinostroza 2002). In every instance, like the fox, we are likely to always encounter the cuy in the Andean context, but it is never likely to be the focus of great attention as an international export.

Personally, I still eat cuy and have chosen several times to go out for cuy with Peruvian friends and colleagues. Often, in the Peruvian house of my colleague's family—the same colleague who had the classroom experience described above—cuy is served. This situation leads to discussions of where the best cuy comes from, the best way to prepare it, the best way to accompany it, and so on. On one occasion, as the visitor, I was offered the honor of eating the last half cuy in the house, much to my friend's mother's chagrin. She had just returned to Lima, her home of forty years, from a trip to her small hometown in northern Peru and brought with her a fresh batch of home-style (chaktado) cuy. I think that she had been saving the last portion for herself to eat one afternoon when no one else was around. As she offered it to me, I had to say yes, but the cuy had been fried several days previously, and the skin was tough. It took about an hour to get through the half rodent. I finished it, a process that included a great conversation, knowing that it was, for her, a sense of pride to serve me her last cuy.

So now when the taxi driver asks his third question about the food, and after discussing ceviche, we reach the cuy topic, I say, "Yes, I have tried it, several times. I think that it tastes like chicken, don't you?" Generally, they agree, some profoundly disagree, stating that although cuy may taste a little like chicken, cuy es más rico ("guinea pig is much tastier").

Next, I am most afraid of being asked to try the house cat.

NOTE

1. For the complete North American perspective I direct the reader to the Web site http://www.guinealynx.com/plea.html.

REFERENCES

Barrionuevo, Alfonsina
    1988   Qori Manka: Culinaria en Olla de Oro. CONCYTEC, Lima.

Bolton, Ralph
    1979   Guinea Pigs, Protein, and Ritual. Ethnology 18(3):229–252.

Findley, Tom (editor)
    2002   Silver Llama Dining Guide. Enterprise Perú Consultant SAC, Lima.

Forstadt, Michael S.
  2002   History of the Guinea Pig (Cavia porcellus) in South America: A Sum-
            mary of the Current State of Knowledge. http://cavyhistory.tripod.com/,
            accessed May 24, 2010.

Guaman Poma de Ayala, Felipe
  2005   *Nueva Cronica y Buen Gobierno*. Fondo de Cultura Economica, Lima.
  [1615]

Hinostroza, Rodolfo
  2002   The Great Cuisine of Perú. In *The Inca Guide to Perú*, 50–56. Promoción
            Editorial Inca S.A., Lima.

Horkheimer, Hans
  2004   *Alimentación y Obtención de Alimentos en el Perú Prehispánico*. Instituto
            Nacional de Cultura, Lima.

Manjeli, Y., J. Tchoumboue, R. M. Njwe, and A. Teguia
  1998   Guinea-Pig Productivity under Traditional Management. *Tropical Animal
            Health and Production* 30:115–122.

Martinez Parra, Reynaldo
  1999   *La Fabula Quechua: Estudio y Recopilación de la Mitología Andina*. Edito-
            rial "San Marcos," Lima.

Milliones, Luis
  2002   The Traditional Feast. In *The Inca Guide to Perú*, ed. Walter H. Wust and
            German Coronado, 59–63. Promoción Editorial Inca S.A., Lima.

Ministerio de Agricultura
  2004   *Recetero de Cuyes*. Consejos de Criadores de Cuyes Regionales, Ministerio
            de Agricultura, Lima.

Morales, Edmundo
  1995   *The Guinea Pig: Healing, Food, and Ritual in the Andes*. University of Ari-
            zona Press, Tucson.

Palma, Rudy (editor)
  2005   Crianza de Cuy es Una Oportunidad de Negocio. Serie de Pymes: Especial
            2, *Perú21* October 24, 2005:4.

Palomino Mendoza, Ricardo (editor)
  2002   *Crianza y Comercialización de Cuyes*. Colección Granja y Negocios, Edi-
            ciones Ripalme, Lima.

Perú
  2004   Hatun Willakuy: Versión Abreviada del Informe Final de la Comisión de
            la Verdad y Reconciliación. Comisión de Entrega de la Comisión de la
            Verdad y Reconciliación, Lima.

Rocha Revilla, Álvaro
  2005   Camino Descubierto. *Somos* (Editorial "El Comercio," Lima) 21(46):40–
            46.

Sandweiss, Daniel H., and Elizabeth S. Wing
   1997   Ritual Rodents: The Guinea Pigs of Chincha, Peru. *Journal of Field Archaeology* 24(1):47–58.

Sarria, José
   2005   *40 Maneras Prácticas de Hacer Negocio.* Ediciones Ajá, Lima.

Valcársel Salas, Julio, Ever Villegas Suarez, and Juan Revilla Layme
   1998   *Crianza de Cuyes:* Cavia cobaya *(Granjas Familiares).* Caritas Moquegua, Programa Suiza, IV Fase. Flores Impresores Editores, Moquegua.

Valdez, Lidio M.
   2000   Aproximaciones al Estudio del Cuy en el Antiguo Perú. *Boletín del Museo Arqueología y Antropología* 3(3):16–19.

Valdez, Lidio M., and J. Ernesto Valdez
   1997   Reconsidering the Archaeological Rarity of Guinea Pig Bones in the Central Andes. *Current Anthropology* 38(5):896–898.

CHAPTER FIVE

Termites Tell the Tale

Globalization of an Indigenous Food System
among Abaluyia of Western Kenya

Maria G. Cattell

Biographical sketch. Maria Cattell has done research among Zulus in South Africa and older white ethnics in Philadelphia, but Kenya remains her first love. She lived among Abaluyia in rural western Kenya for two years and has made a number of four- to six-week return visits to renew friendships and carry out short-term research projects on issues of current interest, such as place and identity (Cattell 2005). When she returned for the first time in 1987, Maria was amazed when people hugged her. Kenyans are publicly undemonstrative, and these were big hugs—in public! Finally someone told her, "Now we know you really love us because you have come back." And so Maria has gone back, many times, and has shared many more meals (and hugs) with her Kenyan friends.

ADVENTURES WITH TERMITES

One day my co-researcher, John Barasa "JB" Owiti, and I were walking through the Nangina Hospital's grounds in rural western Kenya. As we approached the outpatient clinic, JB rushed to the side to a large hole in the ground. He squatted, then reached toward the hole, and put his hands to his mouth again and again. I squatted beside him. JB was catching little white-bodied insects as they flew from the hole—and he was indeed eating them! "Termites?" I asked. "Yes," said he, throwing a few more into his mouth. I watched for some time, longing to try them because I was born with an adventurous palate and love trying new foods—but termites? Do they bite? Taste awful? An image popped into my head: the man in the seat ahead of me on the country bus who bought a bag of live termites from one of the women who appear at every bus stop to sell snacks like bananas, popcorn, and roasted groundnuts (peanuts). As the man popped handfuls of the termites into his mouth, some escaped and crawled over his head and the back of his neck. He paid no attention to them. But I wondered, how can he eat those things? And how can he let them crawl all over him?

But in spite of that memory, suddenly my hand reached out, almost on its own, grabbed one termite, flung it into my mouth—and I ate it. Just that one, but I ate it. When we stood up, I heard a voice behind me: "Maria, did you eat?" I turned around. "Yes, I ate!" I told the inquirer, my friend Fosca, a nurse's aide. She was with a small crowd that had gathered on the veranda of the outpatient clinic to watch the *musungu* (European or American) at the termite hole. I am sure word quickly spread far and wide by "bush telegraph" about my exploit: "The *musungu* eats termites!"

For the most part I had no problem with Kenyan foods. The staple *ugali* (in Swahili; *obusuma* in Luyia), a stiff porridge made by boiling white maize-meal and water, was easy. Ugali is similar in flavor to grits, which my family ate often although we lived among meat-and-potatoes Pennsylvania Dutch farmers (my father was a Southerner). When people served "black ugali" made with millet or sorghum or stickier ugali made with cassava, it was no problem. Goat meat—again, no problem; we had eaten goats on our Pennsylvania farm. The ubiquitous *sukuma wiki* (collards or kale), chopped, boiled, and seasoned with onion and tomato—no problem; my father grew these greens in his garden. New foods, like *emjombola* (a fruit) and "slippery vegetable" (*omutere*), also offered no challenges because of my eagerness to try new foods. So after eating that one live termite, I was sure I could eat anything my Kenyan friends offered me, including termites. So I ate termites, lightly fried and salted, as often as I could. I ate them with pleasure, enjoying their flavor and preserving my self-image as someone who can eat anything.

But then I met my comeuppance. Occasionally I visited Gladys, the eighteen-year-old "matron" who supervised the boarding students after the day scholars went home from Nangina Girls' Primary School. One day, as we drank the super-sweet tea she always served, Gladys opened a paper bag and took out a largish insect, about an inch long, which she popped into her mouth and crunched like a potato chip. "Dried termites," she said, offering me one. I took one and held it in my hand for a long time, staring at it. The longer I looked at that termite, the more it looked like a cockroach. My stomach was telling me, "If you put that thing down here, it's coming right back up." Whoops! What about the person who can eat anything? But finally, reluctantly—but also with relief—I held the termite out to Gladys as I said: "Sorry, Gladys, I just can't eat that. I'd like to, but my stomach is refusing." Luckily, Gladys was not offended—although since this was a private occasion and Gladys was a very junior person, and in fact was from another Luyia area, it would not have mattered if she had been. But we remained friends, and I drank many more cups of overly sweet tea with her. To this day I doubt I could eat one of those termites! Well, maybe . . . I'd like to think I could. But I doubt it.

TERMITES ARE GOOD TO THINK

Even if the occasional termite is not good for me to eat, termites are "good to think" about food in the social life and cultural imagination of Luyia people. Food sustains life. But food is never just food. It is rich with meaning and power. It is woven into history, into the fabric of daily work and social relations, hospitality and special occasions. It is used for gifts and as a medium of exchange. It figures in stories grandmothers tell grandchildren about *amanani*, the antisocial ogres who overeat, consuming even the plates and also humans. It is embedded in ordinary speech as metaphors, as when someone remarks that so-and-so is "only cooking" for her husband (meaning that she is refusing sex) or a widow says, "I refuse the brothers-in-law because they would just eat me" (meaning that she refuses to marry her deceased husband's brother, as is the custom, because he would consume her resources and give nothing in return). Plenty of food makes a person's body fat, and a fat body signifies good health, wealth, power, and authority. So if you lose weight, people worry and ask if you are ill. Thus, "you are fat" is a compliment. I wish I could discuss this, and more, in this chapter, but doing so would probably take half the book, so I will stick to the theme of the transformation of the Luyia food system from localized to globalized and how that process has resonated in social relations.

Initially my research was inspired partly by modernization theories, which grapple with issues such as the impact of modernization on family structures and social roles. Although these theories have inspired a great deal of research, modernization remains hard to define because of the complexity and ever-changing nature of the processes involved. But surely *something* is going on as indigenous societies move from relatively closed subsistence economies following local customs and lifeways into societies connected to the wider world and the global economic system. We can name that something "modernization" or "social change" or "globalization" (the preferred term now).

There have been many factors influencing the enormous changes Abaluyia have experienced since about the 1880s, when the first Europeans arrived in their land. The environment—droughts, floods, locusts, epidemics, epizootics, soil degradation—plays a part. Demography figures in the story, especially in regard to the people/land ratio (land abundance or scarcity). The impacts of colonialism and postcolonialism have reached into every aspect of life, including governance, education, healing practices, religion, and incorporation into the global capitalist political economy. Incorporation into the global economy involves such things as the introduction of money and commodification of goods, labor, and land, which have led to extensive labor migration and the development of cash crops and agricultural exports to other nations. Among other things, the modernization (or globalization) of the food system has changed people's relationships to food and their relations with each other as expressed through food. Because food is fundamental to life and an ongoing daily concern for everyone, it is an excellent lens for examining these changes.

RESEARCH SITE AND METHODS

My adventures with termites occurred in the mid-1980s when I was doing my dissertation research on aging, gender, family life, and the lives of older persons under circumstances of far-reaching socioeconomic, political, and cultural change (Cattell 1989). For two years I lived among Samia (Abasamia, Basamia) people in rural western Kenya, in Busia District (county), in the land they call Samia or Busamia. I also made brief visits to Banyala, culturally similar neighbors to the south, in the land called Bunyala. Since then, return visits have enabled me to keep my knowledge up-to-date, develop longitudinal data on contemporary life and individuals and families I have known for over a quarter century, and investigate special issues and events as they have arisen.

Samia and Banyala are two of seventeen subgroups of Abaluyia (or Luyia, also spelled Luhya), who together numbered about 4 million persons in the 1999 Kenya census. Abaluyia means "Luyia people," which is indicated by the "Aba" prefix. (Luyia can refer to the people or be used as an adjective; the "Bu" prefix indicates place.) Luyia homelands are in Kenya's Western Province, bordered on the west by Uganda. Bunyala and Samia (or Busamia) lie along the northeastern shores of Lake Victoria. Most Luyia women and men are peasant farmers and use hand-tools (such as hoes and machetes) on small acreages to grow food and cash crops. Poverty is widespread and persistent. To increase incomes many people make and sell artisanal items (such as baskets and clay pots), engage in petty trading (especially of food), and are active in a variety of self-help groups. Some are employed in the modern sector as teachers, medical workers, or government administrators. Some practice a trade such as tailoring or carpentry. Others are shopkeepers or traders in local markets. Near Lake Victoria men and women work in the fishing industry. Theft (another form of self-help) is also common. Many become migrant laborers, going to Kenyan cities like Mombasa and Nairobi or cities in nearby Uganda and elsewhere in Africa and beyond to look for hard-to-find employment.

In my research I have used field-designed formal instruments (including, in 1985, an Old People of Samia survey of 200 women and 216 men aged fifty years and older), but my knowledge has come mostly from participant observation: being with people in various settings, watching what they do and how they interact with each other, trying some of their activities myself, talking with them (often with JB or someone else as interpreter, since my ability to speak the Samia language was not as good as I would have liked), and, of course, eating with them.

Kinship is a primary determinant of position among Luyia (and other Kenyans and Africans generally), and—like many anthropologists—I was "adopted" by two Samia families, JB's and the family of Tadeyo and Regina Makokha, whose daughter Teresa worked for me in 1984. The Mahagas of Bunyala also made me one of theirs. These relationships are not mere formality; I am expected to behave appropriately with other family members and participate in family reciprocity. For example, I have contributed to educational fees for family members and have been asked for money for a really important event such as a funeral, which I hear about quickly now via cell phone and e-mail. I have learned much through these relationships. I have also observed and interacted with numerous other people in homes, on roads and footpaths, and in public places such as markets, churches, and schools. I have shared many meals and daily activities, joys, and problems including serious illness, marriages, births and deaths, theft, house fires, and the struggle to educate children. My contacts have included females and males of all ages with a range of social and economic characteristics.

Relative age is another important determinant of an individual's social status. Being older brings respect and, often, authority. In many encounters, like the one with Gladys and her crunchy termites, I was the elder (I was then in my mid-forties). Other characteristics frequently put me on the top of the social ladder, even with persons older than myself, because I was an educated person with a college degree and an American and, therefore, wealthy according to local standards (I always had money for food, bus fare, and so on). Another source of respect was being a white person, a *musungu* (*mzungu* in Swahili, the lingua franca of East Africa). Probably this was in part a colonial hangover but most of the thirty-five or forty other whites in the county (Busia District) were nuns or priests, and I was commonly thought to be a nun. People called me "sistah" (sister) even when I said, "No, I am not a sistah, and I even have a husband and four adult children, including three sons" (another source of respect). As JB said to me in a recent visit, "You know, with you people [whites], we always have to respect you." Respect keeps distance between people.

Years ago JB asked if he could call me mama. I replied, "Yes, but I'll be your American mama, which means we can talk about many things, even sex, which you cannot discuss with your really mama." (I had my research needs in mind.) So JB called me mama or mom, but we developed a relaxed, comfortable joking relationship, like that between grandparent and grandchild (Cattell 1994). With some people it has been difficult or impossible to get beyond the respect relationship, although older people often are willing to talk about many things regardless of status difference. Elders have fewer behavioral constraints, and as people age they become more self-confident and ready to speak out (this is especially true of women, who as girls are taught to be meek and submissive).

Sometimes I have used my high status (or perhaps, as I am not easily put into a category, it is more of an anomalous status) to escape from rules of behavior. For example, the custom is to leave visitors alone in a house to eat, not to isolate them but as a sign of respect. Families usually do not eat together. Men and older sons eat in the house while women, older girls, and young children eat in the kitchen. But Samia say that if you have "eaten from the same pot" (even if not in the same space), you have strengthened your relationship with everyone who ate from that pot. So being left alone is a courtesy, and you have eaten with the family symbolically. But when I finish my meal, I often go out and walk around the homestead. That way I catch people living their daily lives—bathing a child, peeling cassava, eating the chicken I had left in the serving bowl, washing dishes—and daily lives are what I want to learn about.

GLOBALIZATION OF AN INDIGENOUS FOOD SYSTEM

As a culinary item, termites are a vestige of the nearly self-sufficient indigenous food system of Abaluyia and other peoples of the East African interior. In the indigenous system, termites were one among many wild foods, including other insects (such as locusts, beetles, moths, and bees), birds, fish, mammals, and plants. Domesticated livestock and cultivated crops provided other foods. The main cereal crops, finger millet and sorghum, are native to East Africa. Cowpeas and probably sesame are also of African origin. But other foods had non-African origins and reached East Africa in the distant past. Goats, sheep, and zebu cattle were domesticated in India and Southwest Asia about 10,000 years ago. Bananas (including plantains) came from Southeast Asia. New World foods—beans, groundnuts (peanuts), maize (corn), peppers, squash, and sweet potatoes—first reached Africa (often via Portuguese traders) in the sixteenth century as part of the "Columbian exchange" (Plotnicov and Scaglion 2002 [1999]; Viola and Margolis 1991). The globalization of East African diets began long before the British arrived.

In the nineteenth century, people had a local orientation and met nearly all their needs from local resources and their own labor. In addition to producing food, they built houses, tools, and other utilitarian items from local materials. Education, carried out by parents and grandparents, taught the technical and social skills needed for daily living with no schools or books, no reading, writing or arithmetic. There was no money. Chickens, livestock, grains, and iron hoes (*embako*) and other items made by Samia blacksmiths served as media of exchange. Regional exchange systems with regular markets and long-distance traders moved food, livestock, and locally made goods throughout the Lake Victoria region (Alpers 1974; Ndege 1990). Famous rainmakers also traveled far beyond their homes to provide their services. But for the most part, the orientation was local.

Historians portray nineteenth-century Samia as turbulent and dangerous, with cattle raiders, ivory hunters, slavers, and people of different ethnicities moving over the land in numerous local migrations (Seitz 1979; Were 1967).[1] Consequently, people lived in fortified villages (*olukoba*, pl. *engoba*) surrounded by mud walls, a yard wide and about fifteen feet high (1 by 4.5 meters), and dry ditches (fosses) of a similar depth. These villages were symbolic of the relatively closed world in which people lived. An olukoba village contained ten to twenty households and 200 or more inhabitants (Soper 1986). Inside the walls, people lived in extended family groups: a husband, two or more wives, their children, and elderly parents (and probably other kin too). These families were the basic social and production units of Luyia societies. During the day people went outside the walls to graze their cattle, sheep, and goats; cultivate their crops; and hunt and gather wild foods. By sundown people and livestock returned to the village and the gates were shut (Wandibba 1985). Men and older boys gathered in the male space of cowsheds around a fire called *esiosio* to eat their evening meal and chat, while women, older girls, and young children ate in the preeminent female space, the kitchen (*amaika*)—gendered eating spaces that reflected the gendered nature of work and other activities.

Daily, people ate *obusuma*, the stiff porridge made from flour cooked with water or milk that is still the daily staple. (Luyia today say, "If you haven't eaten obusuma, you haven't eaten.") Obusuma was eaten with side dishes such as meat, chicken, peanut sauce, and leafy greens. People cultivated bananas, beans and other legumes, grains (millet, sorghum, maize), and sweet potatoes.

From livestock they got blood, milk, butter, and meat. They ate fish, insects, honey, wild-collected fruits and vegetables, and wild birds and animals. Drinks included water, milk (often soured), and *amalwa*, beer prepared from finger millet in a large pot and drunk through long reeds by men (a privilege of gender) and older women (a privilege of age).

The first European explorers appeared in the 1880s. Twenty-five years later, British control over western Kenya was firmly established (Maxon 2002). The British colonial government brought radical changes to the indigenous economy, including the introduction of money, wage labor, and cash crops, which the colonial government pushed aggressively. Among these cash crops was white maize, which displaced what were regarded as local varieties of colored maize (maize that had originated in Mesoamerica). White maize eventually became the staple food throughout Kenya and much of eastern and southern Africa. Other new foods (such as kale, onions, white potatoes, tomatoes) and ways of preparing foods came with the influx of administrators, missionaries, traders, and laborers from England, the United States, and India. Indians brought chapattis and samosas, which became nearly ubiquitous in Kenya. Imported salt from mineral sources saved women the work of producing salt from the water-filtered ashes of various plants, but it had to be purchased—like so many things in the new cash economy. Tea was established as a commercial crop in Kenya by about 1925. By the mid-1930s, *chai* (tea) was the main drink served to visitors in Christian and "progressive pagan" households among Bukusu and Maragoli (Luyia subgroups). It was served in proper British style, in imported china cups (not in the homegrown gourds that served as local "cups") with plenty of milk and sugar, the sugar also being new (Wagner 1956:74). Serving a proper cup of chai required money.

European and U.S. missionaries brought Christianity. Their daily lives modeled a very different lifestyle. They also promoted "the gospel of domesticity" as part of the process of "civilizing" Africans. For example, in the 1920s, Quaker missionaries at the Girls' Boarding School in Maragoli (in Luyialand) taught African girls domestic skills including U.S.-style cooking, cleaning, and sewing (Thomas 2000). They promoted the notion of woman as housewife, ignoring Luyia women's productive roles, which were as, or more, important as men's, since women contributed the bulk of agricultural labor in addition to doing domestic work and childcare (Cattell 2002).

As Abaluyia became increasingly integrated into the global political economy, they added new foods to their diet and ate fewer wild foods, a process of dietary change still going on—and not always for the better. For example, today people eat more cassava and maize than the more productive and nutritious local grains, millet and sorghum. Cohen and Odhiambo (1989), writing about Luo people in Siaya District (in western Kenya, not far from Samia), show how "maize means hunger" because Kenyan governments (colonial and independent) have pushed maize as both local staple and export crop. This has led to maize largely replacing local grains in people's diets.

As food became a commodity (something bought and sold) and new foods became available, more and more food was purchased rather than grown at home. And eating wild foods has come to be regarded with scorn as something poor people must do. People have taken to many nonlocal foods such as bakery products like bread and cookies, fat for cooking, and margarine for bread, sodas, and fruit drinks. Some innovations I have noticed since the mid-1980s include Knorr's dry soup mixes, peanut butter, rice pilau seasoned with Mchuzi mix (packaged spices), and spaghetti. But when times are hard, food becomes expensive, even unaffordable. In a 2004 tour of the small market town of Funyula, I noticed many small packets of things—like a sliver of soap, a bit of salt, a little sugar—so a person could buy just enough for a day instead of larger, more economical sizes (Cattell 2008). Thieves steal ripening crops from fields as well as anything they can get by breaking into houses—and so more and more homes are surrounded by fences and high walls. There is less sharing of food within extended families. That old enemy *enjala* (hunger) used to show up seasonally or in drought years. Today enjala has become a more constant companion for many people. While much of the world is experiencing the "nutrition transition," the shift from under-nutrition to over-nutrition and obesity (Popkin 2007), in western Kenya over-nutrition is not a problem. Rather, endemic under-nutrition and child malnutrition are ongoing problems. Most people are struggling just to survive.

FROM ABUNDANCE TO SCARCITY

Overwhelmingly, the images of pre-colonial and early colonial western Kenya are images of abundance, whether they come from the writings of Europeans who first went there or the memories of older Kenyans. Although people everywhere have a tendency to romanticize the past, to remember the best and forget difficulties, there is much evidence supporting the view of past abundance. For example, Joseph Thomson (1885), a British geographer who in 1883 walked on a mapping expedition through Luyialand (including Samia and Bunyala), was impressed with "the surprising number of villages, and the generally contented and well-to-do air of the inhabitants" (481). "Food at Kwa-Sundu [a trading center about twenty-five or thirty miles from Samia, now called Mumias] was surprisingly cheap and apparently inexhaustible . . . we were in a veritable land of Goshen" (487–488). Thomson remarked on the number of cattle, the vast expanses of cultivated fields, and the abundance of food, which local people were happy to exchange for beads.

In the 1980s many Luyia elders remembered food being abundant in the past. "Food was plenty," they said, or "food was cheap" or "food was free." In 1985, in response to the survey question, "Was life better in the old days?," 77 percent of 122 elders in my Old People of Samia survey said yes, life was better in the old days. They gave two main reasons: greater material prosperity (more food, more land, less need for money) and better relationships. A woman born around 1934 said: "Long ago food was easy. We harvested much and food was cheap. Or you could be given sorghum or maize free; nowadays that is not easy, not even with relatives" (Agneta interview, September 1984). At a group interview in a private home, an old Samia man (age not recorded) recalled: "Long ago life was good. There was organization in the home and people stayed together, worked together, ate together. Brothers and cousins [half-brothers] might stay in the same home. All the wives cooked for a meal, and all the men ate together, and all the women, and all the children [in separate groups]. There used to be much milk, and after a meal we drank milk. And there was much meat, especially *emitanda* [dried meat]" (Then and Now interview, June 4, 1984). Others spoke longingly of emitanda and of having so much milk that obusuma was cooked with it. Today, obusuma is always cooked with water.

Over beer and food in a Nairobi hotel, Paul Okumu Oyiikamo described the feasts of his grandfather Omonyo, who was a very old man when he died in 1954 (Okumu interview, January 1985). Omonyo, a blacksmith with twelve wives, lived a life of abundance and generous hospitality. "Three times a year he had his wives brew much beer and killed a bull or even two. Then he invited his relatives and neighbors to his home, and they would pass two days eating and drinking and doing no work." On ordinary working days, Omonyo had six wives cook food just for the men working at his forge: "Food was ever there. First one wife would bring obusuma and beef, then another brought sweet potatoes, another brought *amayengere* [maize and beans]. So people were enjoying to eat."

Weddings and funerals were also occasions for feasts. Traditional Luyia wedding ceremonies included several feasts and a procession from the bride's home to her new husband's home. The bride's body was oiled and covered with sesame seeds, symbolizing health, wealth, and fertility. In the 1980s many old people described their own weddings as having been like that, in the early to mid-twentieth century. But by the 1980s, marriages often began with no ceremony: the woman simply moved into the man's house one night, and if she was still there in the morning, that was it.[2] In 1985 I attended a church wedding followed by a feast (for which I made the wedding cake), but the old-style ceremonies and multiple feasts were a thing of the past. I never saw or heard tell of a modern bride covered by the sesame seeds of abundance.

When I first went to Kenya, funerals were major social occasions. They took place over three or four days (three for a woman, four for a man), with all the mourners being fed by the family of the deceased—a heavy burden for the family. But now, thanks in part to the efforts of saved (born-again) Christians (Cattell 1992) and stimulated by the increased numbers of deaths because of AIDS, funerals take only one afternoon, and people may not be fed even one meal. That reduces the burden on the family but also diminishes the sociability that used to be an important aspect of funerals.

Other food customs have also changed in the direction of reduced sharing. Older men described the elaborate protocol for sharing meat when a man slaughtered one of his cows. But today few people have cows, and meat sharing is virtually unknown. Older people also said that beer groups were common when they were younger. At the end of the day, men sat on their four-legged stools (symbols of male authority, even today) with their senior wives sitting at their feet. They sipped beer through long reeds and discussed everything. Now such beer drinking is almost gone—in part because of the cost of brewing beer, but also because the Kenyan government requires a person to get a permit for such a party. Beer drinking in Africa as a significant social activity has been much written about by anthropologists, but in Samia, at least, it seems to be a fading custom. In all my years in Kenya I have seen only two such parties. (And yes, I sipped the beer—which is thick, milky-colored, and a bit sour—through a reed.)

In 1984 and 1985 I often walked by the fields of Leo Balongo, then about eighty years old. Sometimes Balongo would be there, sitting on the ground to weed his cassava (he sat because he was nearly blind and needed to get close to see what to pull). One day Balongo told me: "Modern life is terrible in that relationship is slow. People used to visit each other and converse, especially in the cowsheds at the time of eating. Now people have a gap, they don't visit each other" (Balongo interview, October 1984). All but a few of the 216 old men in my survey said that when they were young, they took their evening meals at the men's *esiosio* fire (at the cowsheds, as Balongo said) and learned from the discussions and advice of the older men present. Nearby neighbors and relatives would gather at one fire or another, so the practice helped build community. That custom was gone probably by the 1950s, and today a man eats in his own house with his older sons while his wife, daughters, and young sons eat in the kitchen (a separate building because of the hazard of cooking with open fires under a grass-thatched roof). Or families even eat all together behind the closed door of their house, because they have so little they cannot feed visitors who might drop in, or even share food with others (especially elderly parents) in the extended family homestead (Cattell 2008).

Günter Wagner (1956), in his research among Bukusu and Maragoli (other Luyia groups) in the 1930s, observed much informal hospitality with neighbors and relatives moving about and freely dropping in on other households to share food and conversation. He took this to be "an indication of a quantitatively fairly high level of food supply, which allows people to display a certain generosity" (73). In the 1980s I observed such behaviors in Samia. But in western Kenya today, poverty and scarcity have become the norm.[3] Food sharing is much diminished, not just within a family but at public events such as funerals and community gatherings. And as food sharing has diminished, what Balongo said—"relationship is slow"—seems ever more true.

GLOBALIZATION AND ENJALA (HUNGER)

"In the old days food was free," the old people told me, meaning if you cultivated your crops, you would eat. "But today it is a world of money." The old people were right. Globalization changed people's relationships to the land, to food, and to each other, in the sense that today they are mediated by money. Today is indeed a world of money. And without money there is hunger.

With a declining national economy and high unemployment, many Kenyans are unable to earn enough money to meet even minimal needs. Although the majority of Kenyans live in rural areas, many experience hunger even when there is no drought (or, in Bunyala, floods) because of the competition for limited cropland between cash and food crops. Also, people may sell their food crops to get money for daily necessities—and later buy the same foods back at high prices or go hungry. Inflation has played a part in making things more expensive, but also people now buy many things they once made themselves or simply did not have, such as salt, sugar, cooking fat, kerosene, matches, soap, TVs, cell phones, clothing, and furniture. Today most people buy even meat and milk, when they can afford them, since many do not have cows. And they pay for services that used to be done by family labor, such as grinding maize into flour. In the 1980s most homes had grinding stones (and I learned the womanly skill of grinding from Marita, an old woman who earned money by selling *obusara*, a thin porridge similar to cream of wheat, served in dried gourds). Today, women pay a small fee to have their grain ground mechanically—and very fast. By the end of the twentieth century, grinding stones—like so much else of indigenous origin—were things of the past.

As farmers, Abaluyia are accustomed to seasons of lean and plenty. A pre-harvest *enjala* (hunger) is normal. In 1992 I was in Kenya in August, the month of maize harvest. There was plenty of maize obusuma in homes but also much "strong tea" (*echai strongi*), tea with neither milk nor sugar. Most people prefer "milk tea," tea that is half milk and sweet with sugar. The strong tea made me suspect that people were really struggling. The abundant maize harvest compensated for that temporarily, but many people no doubt experienced hunger once the maize was eaten (or sold). The next year was a drought year. When I visited in July, it was obvious people were struggling. They were eating obusuma of cassava, sometimes with sorghum, sometimes just cassava. Cassava (introduced around 1915) is a famine food, because its roots keep in the ground for up to five years. Magoba Anyango (then in her late sixties) told me: "We have enjala nowadays because there is very little cassava. If you don't want enjala to invade your house, then you plant cassava. So you can be adding there just a little sorghum and that will chase away enjala" (Magoba interview, May 1985). Cassava keeps hunger at bay but is not very nutritious.

In July 1993, Nangina Hospital administrator Nicholas Habala told me, "We're already seeing malnutrition"—well ahead of the maize harvest, which might be "zero yield" because of drought. Everywhere, people were talking of money, rising prices, and how they could not afford this and that. One man went without lunch every day so his wife, who was breastfeeding, and children could eat. I also noticed the absence of sodas. In earlier years when I visited homes, I would usually be offered sodas, two at a time. I would arrive and a kid would be sent off, on foot or bike, to buy sodas (you do not buy the sodas or catch the chicken till the visitor reaches the homestead, as you cannot be sure when or if the visitor will show up). I recalled that in 1992 only one person served me a soda. The same thing happened in 1993. Sodas remained nearly absent from the hospitality scene until 2004. In that year I was served sodas (and once, Dasani mineral water, something new on the scene) on a number of occasions but only by people who were better off than average. Perhaps my "soda-meter" indicator of prosperity (or diminished adversity) was pointing the right way in 2004, as the Kenyan economy has experienced growth since then. I hope that means less enjala for my Luyia friends.

GLOBALIZATION AND SOCIAL CHANGE

The processes of modernization/globalization have had many social impacts. For example, in pre-colonial Luyialand elders (male and female) were the advisers and decision makers. But intergenerational and gender relationships were transformed as young men gained access to money through education, employment, and political power in the colonial government and then in Kenya's independent government. Wealth and power shifted from older to younger generations and particularly to males (it is likely that British gender ideology and practices strengthened indigenous patriarchal leanings). At the same time, with most men engaged in labor migration, women found themselves as household heads and having to make decisions and do the work that would have been the husbands' responsibility.[4] These days some women are also labor migrants or join their husbands away from home. And in recent decades women (especially older women) have been taking more leadership roles in their families and communities (Cattell 1992, 2002).

In family and community life, the giving of food has been fundamental to relationships. When food is plentiful it can help expand or strengthen relationships. When food is scarce, it has a diminished role in relationships. In prosperous times, food is given as gifts in many situations. A visitor may take a gift of food to the host and receive a gift of food when departing. During my two years in Kenya I was given various foods, including several kilograms of beans—enough to last me for months!—and a number of chickens (which rode home on my hip and then I doubled the gift by giving them to someone else). Grandmothers like to give visiting grandchildren eggs, and adults remember fondly the food they received from grandmothers as being "very sweet." Family members carry food from home when they visit family members working away from home. But nowadays migrant workers may not go home even for Christmas because they have no money for gifts, not even a kilo of sugar, and home folks may not visit the migrants because they have no food to give.

Food giving is an intensely emotional means of creating, maintaining, and strengthening relationships. It is preeminently a female activity. Indeed, a woman becomes a mother not just by giving birth but by feeding her children, day after day, year after year. And a mother's curse is much feared. She will shake her breasts at you and say: "With these breasts I fed you! How can you deny me now?" Many people, when asked about caring for their frail old parents, say simply: "They fed me when I was young. Now they should be able to just sit and eat." This is the obligation of the gift and the emotional basis of female power (Counihan 1999). But in these difficult modern times, people lament their inability to care properly for their old parents—although they do what they can. In some cases the old parents themselves are caring for grandchildren orphaned by AIDS, which strikes hardest among middle-generation adults who provide most of a family's labor and income. Parental deaths from AIDS have created many orphans among Abaluyia (and neighboring Luo too)—and have left many grandparents struggling to feed their grandchildren (Nyambedha, Wandibba, and Aagaard-Hansen 2003). Such grandparents cannot just sit and eat.

Women grow food, decide what foods to eat every day, and prepare and apportion the food. The kitchen is female space, the domain of women and usually not entered by men, not even by a woman's husband. One evening JB and I made a "pop-in" (unannounced) visit to his cousin Michael. I was invited to visit Michael's wife, Beatrice, in her kitchen. It was a big kitchen, dark but for the light from the cooking fire. Kitchen things and seven of Beatrice's nine kids were scattered about the room. Beatrice sat in one corner, stirring a big pot of obusuma. She mounded the obusuma on two plates, one big mound (about two quarts) and one huge (more than three quarts). The big obusuma went into the house for Michael, JB, and me, along with a huge *embuta* (Nile perch)—enough food for five or six people. The huge obusuma and a small embuta remained behind for Beatrice and her children to eat. I am sure they also got to eat what JB, Michael, and I did not eat, which was most of what was served to us. But the nutritional hierarchy was clear: the man of the home and visitors came first.

In cooking and distributing food as Beatrice did, women are daily structuring or reaffirming (or denying) relationships, each individual's status, and the nutritional hierarchy within their families. But when money and food are in short supply, their decisions about who gets what are made more difficult. It may be that only the nuclear family eats together, and there is no food to share with the extended family (such as old parents) in the homestead. So the widespread, persistent poverty that has developed with globalization has made food giving difficult and has impoverished relationships—within the family and beyond, at public occasions such as weddings and funerals, and in the diminution of gifts of food.

EPILOGUE: BECOMING MUSAMIA, OR WE ARE WHAT WE EAT

In 1985, toward the end of my two-year stay among Samia people, I was visiting JB's family as I had done many times before. When it came time to eat, everyone except JB left the house. JB, as the "owner" of the visitor, was to eat with me. On this day we got chicken, which is often served to visitors, especially in-laws (for whom it is mandatory). The chicken was prepared the usual way, cut into chunks, boiled, and served with the broth. It was accompanied by rice. We were being served by JB's younger sister Pauleen, who added a bowl of fat-bodied termites to the table—live termites, crawling around their dish and onto the tablecloth! By then I had eaten termites several times but always sautéed and sprinkled with salt (they taste rather like mushrooms). The only live termite I had eaten was that one caught on the wing as it flew from its underground nest two years earlier. I had no problem looking at the termites crawling around the bowl, nor did my stomach issue any warnings, but they did not look all that appetizing. I certainly did not want to pop some in my mouth and have escapees crawling around my neck and down my shirt, like the man on the bus! But even more, I did not want to insult JB's sister (by kinship, my daughter), who had gone to some trouble to please me because she had heard I liked termites. What to do?

My solution was to mix things up. I poured chicken broth over my rice, added a couple spoons of termites, and stirred everything up. The hot broth and rice slowed the termites down—and it tasted delicious. After a few bites, I did not really mind the crawling critters. Then JB, who had been quietly watching me, said: "That looks like an interesting recipe. May I try it too?" I felt I had truly learned to eat local food if I could create a new recipe for termites! And that, because we are what we eat in more ways than one, I had become—as JB put it—"almost Musamia" (a Samia person).

Acknowledgments. I am most grateful for the invaluable help over the past quarter century of my Luyia co-researchers, especially my son John Barasa "JB" Owiti of Siwongo village in Samia and my daughter Frankline Teresa Mahaga of Port Victoria (in Bunyala) and Nairobi. Special thanks to Frankie and JB and their extended families for their love and hospitality over the years, and also to the family of Tadeyo and Regina Makokha of Samia. I especially recognize here JB's real mama, Nabwire, who died in October 2007. She hosted me for many a meal. Sadly, I salute JB himself, who died unexpectedly at the age of forty-eight in August 2008. For a quarter century, JB fed my anthropological inquiries and his wife, Mary, fed my body. *Pole sana*, Mary, and JB—*mareba*! Thanks also to Medical Mission Sisters at Nangina Holy Family Hospital (especially Sr. Marianna Hulshof, now retired); the many pupils and staff at Nangina Girls' Primary School (now St. Catherine's) who have welcomed me over the years; and Samia officials, particularly my old friend, Fred Wandera Oseno, once a teacher at Nangina and now retired as Chief of Funyula Division. Above all, mutio muno to the many people in the Luyia areas known as Samia, Bunyala, and Bungoma (and the Kisumu and Nairobi families of some) who have allowed me to share their lives in various ways. The research was partially funded by the National Science Foundation (grant BNS-8306802), the Wenner-Gren Foundation for Anthropological Research (grant 4506), a Frederica de Laguna Fund grant from Bryn Mawr College, and the generosity of my late husband, Bob Moss, who loved to teach at Nangina Girls' Primary School. I was a research associate at the University of Nairobi's Institute of African Studies in 1984 and 1985.

NOTES

1. Although there were no written languages in East Africa (except for Swahili at the coast) and hence no written records before the British came, research has unearthed much information on life in western Kenya during pre-colonial times. Reconstructions of African history depend on a variety of sources including colonial documents, missionaries' and travelers' accounts and other written materials (e.g., Jackson 1930; Thomson 1885), archeological and linguistic evidence, oral traditions (proverbs, stories, songs, etc.), and field research conducted by anthropologists, historians, and others and usually involving interviews with older persons in a community. To reconstruct

political and economic history, Gideon Were, a Luyia historian, interviewed Luyia clan elders, probably all men (Were 1967); and U.S. historian Jacob Seitz interviewed Samia individuals (mostly men) of various ages and social statuses (Seitz 1979). A research team from the University of Nairobi's Institute of African Studies interviewed women and men during field research in Busia District in the mid-1980s. Their report (Soper 1986) provides much information about daily life among pre-colonial Abaluyia. In the mid-1980s I too asked Samia women and men about life "in the old days" in what I called "then and now" interviews (Cattell 1989).

2. The woman's family will still expect bridewealth (cattle and/or money), which is likely to be paid over many years (if at all). Some have civil or church weddings—although sometimes after years of living together as spouses.

3. For a history of the growth of widespread poverty in colonial and postcolonial sub-Saharan Africa, see Iliffe (1987).

4. In my Old People of Samia survey, 187 of the 216 male interviewees had been labor migrants (only 7 of the 200 women had done this).

REFERENCES

Alpers, Edward A.
1974 The Nineteenth Century: Prelude to Colonialism. In *Zamani: A Survey of East African History*, ed. B. A. Ogot, 229–248. EAPH/Longman Kenya, Nairobi.

Cattell, Maria G.
1989 Old Age in Rural Kenya: Gender, the Life Course and Social Change. Ph.D. dissertation. Department of Anthropology, Bryn Mawr College, Bryn Mawr, PA.
1992 Praise the Lord and Say No to Men: Older Samia Women Empowering Themselves. *Journal of Cross-Cultural Gerontology* 7(4):307–330.
1994 "Nowadays It Isn't Easy to Advise the Young": Grandmothers and Granddaughters among Abaluyia of Kenya. *Journal of Cross-Cultural Gerontology* 9(2):157–178.
2002 Holding Up the Sky: Gender, Age and Work among Abaluyia of Kenya. In *Ageing in Africa: Sociolinguistic and Anthropological Approaches*, ed. Sinfree Makoni and Koen Stroeken, 157–177. Ashgate, Aldershot, England.
2005 African Reinventions: Home, Place and Kinship among Abaluyia of Kenya. In *Home and Identity in Late Life: International Perspectives*, ed. Graham D. Rowles and Habib Chaudhury, 219–235. Springer, New York.
2008 Aging and Social Change among Abaluyia in Western Kenya: Anthropological and Historical Perspectives. *Journal of Cross-Cultural Gerontology* 23(2):181–197 (DOI 10.1007/s10823–008–9062-x).

Cohen, David William, and E. S. Atieno Odhiambo
1989 *Siaya: The Historical Anthropology of an African Landscape*. James Currey, London.

Counihan, Carole M.
1999   Food, Power, and Female Identity in Contemporary Florence. In *The Anthropology of Food and Body: Gender, Meaning, and Power*, ed. Carole M. Counihan, 43–60. New York, Routledge.

Iliffe, John
1987   *The African Poor: A History*. Cambridge University Press, New York.

Jackson, Frederick
1930   *Early Days in East Africa*. Edward Arnold, London.

Maxon, Robert M.
2002   Colonial Conquest and Administration. In *Historical Studies and Social Change in Western Kenya: Essays in Memory of Professor Gideon S. Were*, ed. William R. Ochieng', 93–109. East African Educational Publishers, Nairobi.

Ndege, P. O.
1990   Trade since the Early Times. In *Themes in Kenyan History*, ed. William R. Ochieng', 117–132. Heinemann Kenya, Nairobi.

Nyambedha, Erick O., Simiyu Wandibba, and Jens Aagaard-Hansen
2003   "Retirement Lost": The New Role of the Elderly as Caretakers for Orphans in Western Kenya. *Journal of Cross-Cultural Gerontology* 18(1):33–52.

Plotnicov, Leonard, and Richard Scaglion
2002   *The Globalization of Food*. Waveland Press, Prospect Heights, IL.
[1999]

Popkin, Barry M.
2007   The World Is Fat. *Scientific American* 297(3):88–95.

Seitz, Jacob
1979   A History of the Samia Location in Western Kenya: 1890–1930. Ph.D. dissertation. Department of History, West Virginia University, Morgantown.

Soper, Robert W. (editor)
1986   *Kenya Socio-Cultural Profiles: Busia District*. Republic of Kenya, Ministry of Planning and National Development, Nairobi.

Thomas, Samuel S.
2000   Transforming the Gospel of Domesticity: Luhya Girls and the Friends Africa Mission, 1917–1926. *African Studies Review* 42(3):1–27.

Thomson, Joseph
1885   *Through Masai Land*. Edward Arnold, London.

Viola, Herman J., and Carolyn Margolis (editors)
1991   *Seeds of Change: A Quincentennial Commemoration*. Smithsonian Institution, Washington, DC.

Wagner, Günter
  1956   *The Bantu of North Kavirondo*, Vol. 2: *Economic Life*. Oxford University
          Press, Oxford.

Wandibba, Simiyu
  1985   Some Aspects of Pre-colonial Architecture. In *History and Culture in
          Western Kenya: The People of Bungoma District through Time*, ed. Simiyu
          Wandibba, 34–41. Gideon S. Were Press, Nairobi.

Were, Gideon S.
  1967   *A History of the Abaluyia of Western Kenya: c. 1500–1930*. East African
          Publishing House, Nairobi.

Side Dishes and Accompaniments

Ode to a Chuño

Learning to Love Freeze-Dried Potatoes in Highland Bolivia

Clare A. Sammells

Biographical sketch. Clare Sammells first went to Bolivia during the summer of 1993 as an undergraduate to research the consumption of llama meat in the city of La Paz. After graduating with a degree in folklore and mythology from Harvard College and living for two years in Costa Rica, she began graduate school at the University of Chicago in 1997. She returned to rural highland Bolivia to conduct an anthropological study of tourism at Tiwanaku, that nation's most important archaeological site. She traveled to Bolivia again in 1998, 1999, 2000, 2007, and 2010 and lived there for two years from 2002 to 2004. She completed her Ph.D. in 2009 and is now an assistant professor at Bucknell University. She loves Bolivian food and misses her *comadre*'s amazing cooking when in the United States.

I like *chuño*.

This statement sometimes surprises highland Bolivians but surprises Americans[1] who know the region even more. The former find it pleasant that I like Bolivian food. But some North Americans believe that this is clear evidence that I will eat "anything"—something I certainly aspire to but cannot claim to have fully achieved.[2] Meanwhile, those who have never been to the Andes usually have no reaction at all. Chuño? It's just a potato, right?

Chuño is a freeze-dried potato, but tastes nothing like a fresh potato.[3] When cooked, it looks like a whole truffle: small, round and wrinkly, dark gray or black in color, and a little larger than a ping-pong ball although often flatter in shape. Generally it is eaten with the fingers (sometimes with a spoon) and breaks apart in sections radiating from the center. Its texture is firm, not mushy like a fresh potato. It is dense, a little mealy, and slightly bitter. It is very filling. It can be eaten with various sauces, such as *llajwa*, which is a sauce made of ground tomato, *locoto* (an Andean chili pepper), and *kirkiña* (a green herb). Breaking the chuño apart with one's fingers, one uses it to scoop the spicy sauce. Or chuño can be broken into smaller pieces and mixed with crushed peanuts or scrambled eggs and served as a side dish. Raw chuño can be ground into a flour to be used as a base for soups such as *chairo*. Chuño can form an essential part of a dish or be placed in a communal bowl for diners to complement their individual plates. It is a versatile staple, and in my time living in Tiwanaku (a rural highland village), it was included in one-third of all the meals I ate.[4]

In addition to being tasty, chuño is also a product of a pre-Colombian technology that allows potatoes to be stored for decades and transported easily. The Inca empire had an elaborate system of storehouses used to provision travelers and soldiers; among the items stocked there were chuño and other freeze-dried foods, such as *charq'e*, a form of dried llama meat (and, later, sheep or beef) for which our own jerky is named. These storehouses were so well-provisioned and operated so efficiently that in one area they continued to function and in some places provision the Spanish for twenty years after the conquest (D'Altroy 2002). Indigenous miners sent to work in the colonial-era mines of Potosí were fed with chuño produced elsewhere in the highlands, transported by llama caravans, and either sold in enormous markets or brought to workers directly by their communities. Many of the caravan llamas were then slaughtered and consumed in the burgeoning city (Mangan 2005).

Despite its usefulness, the Andean technology of creating chuño did not cross the Atlantic with the crop. Studies of the potato's introduction into Europe tend not to comment on the failure to transfer this knowledge (see Messer 1997; Salaman 1949; Walvin 1997; Zuckerman 1998). Awareness of this technology has fallen out of North Atlantic stories about their love affair with the tuber. These accounts also usually fail to return to the Andes to consider recent misguided efforts to introduce North Atlantic varieties of potatoes into the Andes. European and U.S. varieties of potatoes are considered by most highland Bolivians to be watery and tasteless, and wealthy Bolivians who had traveled to the United States told me in no uncertain terms that the potatoes they encountered in their travels were inferior.

HOW TO PLANT A CHUÑO

In Tiwanaku some locals tell variants of a tale about the Spanish conquistadores who came to the highlands in the early colonial period. Impressed with chuño, they forced the local people to plant it on the assumption that it was a unique crop. When the locals balked at this ridiculous request, the Spanish accused them of laziness. Of course, it was the Spanish who were disappointed to discover that their fields of chuño did not sprout.

This story highlights the fact that from the point of view of those who eat Andean cuisine without participating in its production, chuño seems so completely different from potatoes that it would be easy to assume they were from different plants altogether. This is not true in a biological sense, but it is true in a culinary sense. Socially and culinarily, chuño is not a potato at all.

In Bolivian cuisine, *papas* are specifically fresh potatoes; chuño is not included in that category by highland Bolivians. Nor are the two interchangeable in all dishes. Without chuño, some dishes cannot be properly made. For example, *chairo* is a soup that must be made with ground chuño. While other ingredients are expected in the soup (grains of wheat, carrots, and other items) these can be substituted or omitted without changing the identity of the soup. Likewise, the soup *jakonta* must include whole chuño—otherwise it is something else. One cannot make chairo without chuño, just as one cannot make French fries without potatoes.

Papas, chuño, and other tubers can be substituted for each other in some dishes, similar to the way that side dishes can be substituted in U.S. cuisine. Unlike U.S. dishes, which tend to include only one staple carbohydrate, Bolivian dishes regularly contain two or more staples—such as rice and papas, or papas and chuño—especially in dishes that involve meat (such as beef, mutton, or guinea pig). Chuño is a common option, but it can be replaced with multiple varieties of fresh potatoes, *oca* (a sweeter, oblong orange-colored tuber), or *isaño* (resembling a large oca but with a tart taste, which is also sometimes turned in to a frozen ice-cream-like treat called *thayacha*). Non-tuber staples include rice, pasta, and less commonly maize, *quispiña* (steamed biscuits made from *quinua* flour), sweet potato, and plantain.[5]

MAKING CHUÑO

Bolivia has hundreds of varieties of potatoes with vastly different characteristics. Only certain varieties are appropriate to be freeze-dried. Chuño is created from bitter potato ("*papa amarga*"; for a description of potato varieties, see La Barre 1947; and for detailed descriptions of chuño processing, see Condori Cruz 1992; Mamani 1981). Potatoes are generally harvested in May. Those potatoes chosen for making chuño are picked on the basis of variety and size; medium-sized potatoes are preferred (slightly bigger than a golf ball) as very large potatoes may not freeze evenly. Also potatoes with many *gusanos*—large worms that tunnel into the potatoes and are removed by hand after cooking—are avoided.[6]

The potatoes selected for making chuño are placed outside in the month of June, which is the coldest month of the year. The potatoes freeze during the frosty nights and then thaw in the bright sunshine when temperatures rise above freezing. This alternation of freezing and thawing is essential to making chuño and may explain why this technology did not travel to Europe, where winter temperatures often remain below freezing even in the daytime.[7]

Once the potatoes have alternately frozen and thawed for three consecutive days, the water must be squeezed out of them. My first experience with this was unplanned. I was walking in the rural countryside with my *compadre*.[8] We had gone to his village in part to see the raised fields, called *suka kollus*, that were once a mainstay of the region's pre-Columbian agriculture and had been restored in the 1980s (Kolata 1993, 1996). Nothing was growing at the time, because it was winter (June). But on the way back, we happened on two of his relatives who were in the process of making chuño.

The chuño they were making had already been left to freeze and thaw for three days and nights, and they were stepping on the tubers to remove the liquid. They invited me to join them. I am not sure they expected me to actually do so, but I happily sat down and took off my shoes and socks. They showed me how to gather the potatoes into small piles with my bare feet and then "dance" (*bailar*) on top of them. Here the Spanish verb meaning "to dance" describes the movement, although there is no music or imposition of rhythm. Each person steps on the potatoes while removing the potato skins with their feet (although the process is incomplete and is continued by hand after the tubers have dried and then finished when they are soaked in water before cooking). One alternates between stepping on the chuño and gathering them back together in a pile, using only the feet.

I found that the potatoes were firm but spongy. A cool, dark-purple liquid squirted through my toes and onto the hard ground as I tried to keep the slippery tubers in a compact pile so they did not scatter everywhere when stepped on. The ground was hard-packed with only very short grass on it, as is typical in the dry, cold Andean winter, and this grass stuck to our feet as we worked. They insisted I had the hang of it, but I suspect—as was the case with the majority of agricultural labor I helped with in Bolivia—that I was far slower than a woman my age should have been at such a task. Nevertheless, we had a great time, and they insisted on photos to commemorate the event. That moment was remembered fondly when I saw them even years later.

Once the liquid is removed and the chuño is dried, it is light, easy to move, and can be stored for years. I have visited houses of farmers who had rooms with bags of chuño from floor to ceiling, some of which were more than a decade old. This ability to store food is important in a region were periodic droughts can destroy a year's crop; chuño provides the food needed to survive.

In its dried form, chuño feels like Styrofoam packing peanuts. To cook it, it must be soaked overnight in water. The chuño is then boiled and served either in soup, as a side dish, or in a *fiambre* (explained in the following section).

Two other varieties of freeze-dried potatoes deserve mention. One is *chuño fresca*, which is only consumed in June, when chuño is made. Lighter in color, this is prepared by stopping the preparation process before the tubers are stepped on. Having undergone the freezing and thawing process for three days, they are immediately boiled and served, and thus they are only eaten a few times a year. The other is *tunta*, where the tubers are placed in a body of water or stream for a month after the freezing and thawing process. The tuber is then dried out and can be stored like chuño. Tunta is white in color, has a different taste, and is generally more highly prized. Much as a chuño is not a potato, a tunta is not culinarily a chuño. There are dishes that require tunta to be properly made and are assumed to include it even though the name of the dish does not mention the tuber (such as *sajta de pollo*).

THE BEGINNING OF A LOVE AFFAIR WITH A NOT-EXACTLY POTATO

When I moved to the rural village of Tiwanaku in 2002 (having already lived there for three months in 2000), I lived in a house with my *compadres*. I soon learned—through experience and the grapevine—that my *comadre* was an excellent cook. I miss her soups when in the United States. She told me that sometimes others would ask her what she had to cook for me—and when she replied that I ate what everyone else did, they were surprised. Apparently, some assumed that foreigners would require, or perhaps insist on, specific kinds of foods or preparations. But given my comadre's and her daughters' culinary skills—which I tried, unsuccessfully, to learn—it is hardly shocking that I found little to be picky about.[9]

At first I did have to get used to chuño being a much larger part of the diet than it had been for me during my previous time in urban Bolivia. On these visits, which ranged from one to three months in 1993, 1994, 1998, and 1999, I lived in the capital city of La Paz with middle-class Bolivian families or other foreigners and often ate in *pensiones*. While my research in marketplaces often led me to eat market food, which included chuño, I encountered it infrequently in other parts of the city. Chuño was eaten and enjoyed throughout the highlands by Bolivians of all social and economic classes, but it was eaten far more frequently by rural highland peasants and the indigenous urban poor. Members of the urban middle and upper classes tended to eat chuño less often, although they still enjoyed it and considered it an important part of their cuisine. Among Bolivians living in the United States, for example, chuño was important for recreating a taste of home while abroad (Katherine McGurn Centellas, personal communication). My own interviews with upper-class residents of La Paz in 1994 revealed that many of them found potatoes in the United States disappointing and bland compared to their more flavorful counterparts in Bolivia; the lack of chuño was part of their observations.

There was a turning point in my relationship with chuño. My compadres had hired a tractor that fateful day in mid-November 2002 in order to plant a large piece of land. The tractor picked us up at their house near the village—my compadres, their children and other relatives, the resident anthropologist, and heavy bags of seed potatoes—for transport to their field in a nearby rural community. There were few seats on the tractor so many of us rode hanging on—I clung to the outside of the driver's door, hands slippery with forty-five-plus sunscreen to protect myself from the tropical sun at more than 13,000 feet (4,000 meters) in elevation, and holding my three-year-old goddaughter in her seat as we bounced along the uneven dirt track. A few of the men came behind on bicycles, taking some of the smaller children with them.

Reaching the field, I discovered that planting with a tractor is faster than with ox-pulled plows, but also far more intense. The religious ceremonies associated with potato planting were hurriedly performed. Four women quickly ran to plant seed potatoes in the furrows created by the tractor before it turned around at the end of the field and came back to bury what they had just planted and open new furrows for planting. *Choq' siwa!* became a constant refrain—"Potatoes, she says!" as the women demanded that the men bring them more potatoes to plant (Figure 6.1).

Women plant potatoes (although in rare instances, if no women are available, men will do so). I was clearly the slowest planter in the group, which was acceptable for planting behind an ox-plow, but not for keeping up with the pace of a tractor. So I was sent to help the men cut larger potatoes in half before planting so the seed would go farther. We did this in between rushing out to give the women more potatoes for planting, pouring the seed out from textiles wrapped around our shoulders for easier carrying. The planting was finished in a mere forty-five minutes—quite a feat for a half-hectare field.

My compadres had assumed that we would have our *fiambre* at the field and then walk the two hours back to their house. They had brought the fiambre, already cooked and wrapped in a large textile bundle. But it turned out that the tractor was going most of the way back to the village. Since there was leftover seed that would be heavy to carry, we decided to take advantage of the tractor to return. The tractor left us and the potatoes at the junction with the

6.1. Preparing to plant potatoes on the Bolivian altiplano, November 2002. (PHOTO BY CLARE SAMMELLS)

highway, still a mile from the house. We waited for a passing public minivan to take us the remainder of the way.

Finally, back at their house, we were ready for lunch, a fiambre. Fiambres (also called *meriendas*) are meals where a common pile of food is placed on a blanket on the ground. They can include any combination of mixed tubers (potatoes of various varieties, chuño, tunta, oca, isaño, sweet potato), *fideo* (cooked pasta), rice, *mote* (maize kernels), *choclo* (maize on the cob), *quispiña* (a salty steamed *quinua* biscuit), and *postre* (boiled plantains sliced into thick circles with their skins, which are removed by the eater). During fiambres, each person is expected to eat the section closest to them in a wedge pattern, like a slice of pizza. Only fingers are used. Late in the meal the remaining food may be redistributed by one of the older women if it is clear that a particular individual is not eating as much. Allowances are made for young children who are still learning proper etiquette; small children sometimes raid preferred foods, such as sweet postre, from outside their areas. Foreigners can discretely avoid those tubers they dislike (Figure 6.2).

Fiambres can be planned events, such as when a family gathers friends, extended relatives, and "fictive kin" (such as compadres, godparents, or god-

6.2. A woman and her two children dine with other family members at a *fiambre* with *chuño, papa, mote,* and a spicy sauce in the center, November 2003. (PHOTO BY CLARE SAMMELLS)

children) to help with planting, harvesting, or building a house. But they can also be more spontaneous—for example, when a group of vendors who sell in a marketplace gather at midday and collect together what each woman brought for lunch, or when unexpected relatives visit around lunchtime and soup is made to go farther by adding a blanket of tubers, sometimes brought by the visitors themselves.

During a fiambre, one woman generally gives out portions of non-staple foods to the diners to eat with the staples. These are foods with higher status and protein and fat content, including locally made "country cheese" (*queso de campo*), fried eggs, portions of cooked meat (commonly beef or mutton, but occasionally guinea pig, chicken, or more rarely high-status pork), and fried or boiled lake fish, such as carachi or ispi. Also included in this category are *tortillas* (not to be confused with Mexican *tortillas*), which consist of a dough of wheat flour, eggs, and onions fried into thick patties. These non-staple foods are categorized into one word in Aymara, *irxata*, which covers the non-staples eaten in a fiambre that give flavor to the staples.

During impromptu meals, the staples each person has brought are mixed together on a single textile on the ground. One woman may be given all the non-staples to divide between those present, or each woman may distribute what she brought herself. In fiambres that take place in the home where the cooking occurred, soup may also be served, ladled from a large pot into individual bowls. People eat from the fiambre while soup is served to each in turn. Soup is served roughly in order of status, with men, visitors, godparents, and older people served first, and women and then children last. This order is extremely flexible, however, depending on the circumstances. For example, a particularly hungry and fussy young child might be served sooner if there is the threat of a tantrum. Likewise, if one of the older men is washing his hands when the soup is being served, the women will serve others first, fitting him in when he arrives. Often there are not enough bowls for everyone, so those served first eat relatively quickly and hand the bowls back so that others can be served. No liquids other than soup are consumed until the end of the fiambre, when soda or *refresco* (a non-carbonated drink) is sometimes served, again roughly in order of status. As with bowls, there are fewer cups than people—sometimes only one—so each person quickly pours a small amount on the ground as a libation for Pachamama (the Earth Goddess), drinks, and returns the cup to be filled for the next person.

On this particular day, after our exhausting planting session, there was no soup, no plantains, no cheese. And there was no leeway for pickiness, since the blanket we gathered around was piled high with chuño with only a few fresh potatoes scattered among them. A dish of sauce was placed in the center to give the tubers flavor; it was made with chopped hard-boiled egg and *aji*, an Andean chili pepper that is commonly used to spice foods. The sauce was delicious and reminiscent of deviled eggs. My compadre had quickly bicycled into town and returned with a tin of Lydita-brand sardines in tomato sauce, which his daughter mixed with chopped onions to make a second sauce. I was very, very hungry, and I ate more chuño that day than I ever had before. My love of chuño was sealed. I now often prefer it to fresh potatoes.

CHUÑO-LESS TOURISTS

When my partner (now husband) first visited Bolivia in 2000, I wanted to share chuño with him as part of the Bolivian experience that he was signing up for. But, remarkably, he spent a week in Bolivia without ever trying chuño, despite my best attempts to put one on his plate. When he visited Tiwanaku for a day, my comadre made a local specialty for him that did not involve chuño—*pesq'e*, a quinua porridge served with milk or cheese, which he has been fond of ever since. Once traveling on the tourist circuit, we ate in places accustomed to serving foreigners in Copacabana and the Isla del Sol on Lake Titicaca. Chuño simply was not on the menu or even, as became apparent once I started asking specifically for it, in the kitchen.

Chuño was almost never offered to tourists because it was assumed they would not like it. One tourist restaurant owner in La Paz whom I spoke with in 2000 had even removed chuño from the menu because of the negative reactions of clients. This situation was not immutable, however. In my own field site, two of the restaurants began in 2004 to offer buffets to tour groups that included chuño. Neither put chuño on the individual plates ordered by tourists; it was served as a culinary curiosity rather than as a standard side dish. By 2004 some tourist-oriented restaurants in Copacabana had begun to offer chuño as well (Elayne Zorn, personal communication, 2005).

Despite the importance of chuño in the local diet, the tour books that influenced so many travelers in Bolivia often warned their readers away from experiencing it. Of course, descriptions of food in these guides are extremely brief and focus on guiding the visitor toward understanding the unfamiliar, finding the palatable, and experiencing the *típico* (a term that we can gloss in the Bolivian context as "authentic"). These books give tourists a food vocabulary that allows them to negotiate menus and advertisements, ensuring that readers know what they are getting into when confronted by unfamiliar foods.

Many of these books offered ambivalent descriptions of chuño, such as "[f]ew foreigners find them [chuño or tunta] particularly appealing, mainly because they have the appearance and consistency of polystyrene when dry and are tough and tasteless when cooked" (Swaney 1996:108; see also Swaney 1988, 2001; Swaney and Strauss 1992), or described the tubers as "gnarled looking and tasting, though some people love them" (Gorry et al. 2002; Lyon et al. 2000).[10] One even made the unusual comment that chuño "is rumored to be used by Bolivian women to suppress their husbands' sexual desires"

(Murphy 2000), a rumor I never heard elsewhere (although Coe [1994] provides evidence that this effect was attributed to the tuber isaño in the colonial period). A more generous description tells us that "these dehydrated potatoes have an unusual texture and a distinctive, nutty flavor that takes some getting used to. They're often boiled and served instead of (or as well as) fresh potatoes" (Read 2002). Descriptions are often repeated, verbatim, in reprintings of guides. Most guidebooks mentioned chuño as integral to dishes such as chairo, while others mentioned it only in passing (Cramer 1996). But none presented chuño as an integral and essential part of Bolivian cuisine that *must* be tried by the visitor.[11]

So why is it that chuño was so central to the highland Bolivian diet and yet so neglected by those trying to explain Bolivian cuisine to the foreign tourist market? Most Bolivians and North Americans seem to agree that the unfamiliar taste of chuño was the primary reason why it did not appear in Bolivian tourist cuisine—simply put, tourists did not usually like it.

I do not find this to be a complete explanation, however. Restaurants make money from what is ordered, not from what tourists discover that they like to eat. Touristic cuisine is constantly being re-presented to new diners who are at least partly willing to try unfamiliar local specialties, even if they are unconvinced they might enjoy them. Additionally, serving food to tourists is not entirely about money: most people take pride in their own region's food and want visitors to try, appreciate, and respect their cuisine.

Tourists, in short, do not single-handedly determine what they eat while traveling. They are limited, in large part, to the offerings of the establishments they visit. These establishments may be chosen by tour guides, recommended by tour books, or chosen by tourists on the basis of location, availability of menus in their language, appearance, or any number of other factors. Additionally, because of the networks of their travels, tourists often do not have the opportunity to eat in locals' homes or cook for themselves.

Touristic cuisines are predetermined by negotiations that occur on multiple levels of interlaced perceptions, such as what locals think are their tastiest dishes and those most appropriate to serve in a restaurant context; the seasonality, availability, and price of ingredients; what restaurant owners think tourists want to eat; what restaurant cooks think their employers want them to cook as well as what they think tourists want to eat; and what tourists think are the best choices available to them based on a variety of criteria (taste, freshness, exoticness, price, perceived sanitation, and the advice of tour books and guides). Tourists are sometimes served foods that they may not readily like (e.g., *poi* in Hawaii) because these foods are locally meaningful and presented as part of a local experience that tourists should participate in. But for tourists to try a particular dish, it must first and foremost be on the table.

Instead of focusing purely on taste, we must consider seriously the structures in place that reinforce chuño's neglect in tourist cuisine. In the touristic context—and every other eating context—there are different ways in which foods can be palatable. To make this point, I will compare chuño to llama meat, another Andean food I have researched (Sammells 1998, 1999; Sammells and Markowitz 1995), on three levels: the sensory experience of what is considered "good to eat," the cognitive aspects of what is "good to think" about these foods for both tourists and those who feed them, and finally what tourists find "good to relate" about their dining experiences once they return home.

Despite emphasis on the touristic search for the "authentic," the fact that some foods are locally produced or consumed is not sufficient to make them "good to think" or "good to relate" for visitors. Both chuño and llama meat were local to Bolivia. Both foods are indigenous to the pre-Columbian Andean highlands, currently produced locally, and served in few places outside the Andes. Llama was consumed less than other "non-native" (but still locally produced) meats, such as beef and mutton. Chuño, on the other hand, was ubiquitous. Nevertheless (and perhaps because of this discrepancy), llama garnered touristic attention in ways that chuño did not.

Since 1997, llama meat became an important authentic highland Bolivian dish served to tourists (Sammells 1999), even though many Bolivians (especially urban Bolivians) ate llama on rare occasions, if at all. This situation might seem counterintuitive. Llama meat was more highly marked as a food of the poor (especially the rural indigenous poor) than chuño. Despite the prejudices against its consumption, it underwent an incredible transformation into a meat lauded by expensive tourist-oriented restaurants.

Why has llama meat become widely popular in tourist cuisine since 1997, even though chuño—which was more widely consumed throughout Bolivian society than llama meat—has not? Llama captured the imagination in multiple ways. As a live animal it was depicted and photographed everywhere, appearing on tourist postcards as well as the Bolivian coat of arms. As meat it made a tasty dish lauded for its low fat and high protein. It was "good to eat" in that it was similar to red meats that North Atlantic visitors were familiar with. It was also "good to think" because of the position of llamas in both Bolivian cultures and touristic imaginaries. And llama meat was "good to relate" once tourists returned home to share tales of their culinary adventures in places where llamas were exotic animals and potatoes were boringly quotidian.

GOOD TO EAT

We should start with Mintz's (1996:93) warnings about ignoring the experiential aspects of food. We cannot ignore that tourists are seeking something that is "good to eat" within a cuisine that has both familiar and unfamiliar elements. The amount of space in tour books and other tourist literatures dedicated to describing, explaining, and promoting food and the large proportion of tourist budgets spent on dining indicate how important eating is to travelers' overall experiences.

In this respect, llama meat was "good to eat." While it is a common joke in the United States that all unknown meats "taste like chicken," llama actually tastes like beef or mutton—so much so, in fact, that stories abounded of llama being added clandestinely to street food, sausages, and hamburgers (Sammells 1998). As a steak, llama meat is slightly paler in color but similar in taste to other red meats. For a North Atlantic tourist, and even for many Bolivians, the difference would be difficult to detect. For tourists who like beef, llama tastes familiar.

In contrast, chuño could never be substituted secretly for potatoes. It is a completely different sensory experience from a potato in both taste and texture. In highland Bolivian cuisine, where tubers are eaten at least twice a day, these differences among fresh potatoes, chuño, tunta, oca, isaño, *papaliza, remolacha*, and other tubers are prized and relished. But what made chuño prized among Bolivians—the fact that it does not taste like a potato—was what made it difficult for some foreigners to appreciate. Tourists who were in Bolivia for a relatively short time might not become accustomed to the taste or texture of chuño.

GOOD TO THINK

Foods are not just "good (or not) to eat" but also "good to think," as famously stated by structural anthropologist Claude Levi-Strauss. The understanding that foods have social meanings beyond the purely nutritional, and that these meanings interact with social structures in other parts of society, has been elegantly demonstrated by Levi-Strauss (1963, 1969, 1978 [1968]) and Mary Douglas (1966, 1972, 1983 [1977]). Tambiah's work on food and incest taboos (1969) showed how animals can have related meanings in the realms of sex and edibility. All these authors discuss how foods are eaten or avoided for reasons that are not entirely based on how they taste. Food is part of a coherent system of meanings, interwoven with the other ways that people make sense of their lives and relationships.

Llama is "good to think" for tourists in part because it is a meat and therefore forms the centerpiece of meals where it is included. The now-outdated airline-food joke "chicken or beef?" highlights the emphasis we put on meat as the identifying feature of a meal, the key item on which decisions of edibility and preference depend. To give an example that may be familiar to some readers, in

U.S. holiday meals such as Thanksgiving, the turkey is an essential part of the meal. Even vegetarians are pressured to replace it with something turkey-like, such as tofurky. Other Thanksgiving dishes can be modified or substituted to suit individual taste or preserve ethnic traditions; one can serve either corn or wheat bread, baked or sweet potatoes, pumpkin pie or English trifle. Even in quotidian meals, staple foods—the everyday carbohydrates that make up our daily bread, such as wheat, maize, rice, manioc, millet, and potatoes—tend to play second fiddle to the more glamorous meats that flavor them.

This explains why meats are the focus of more food taboos than vegetables or grains (Douglas 1966; Fiddes 1991).[12] When Americans think about strange food experiences, they often focus on meats. They tend to be easily disturbed by meat products and the processes (especially industrialized ones) that create them (Sinclair 1906). I am not immune from this cultural bias. I, like many of my fellow Americans, was unaccustomed to consuming organ meats and preferred muscle; offering delicacies such as sheep's head to me was a source of mirth for Bolivians who found it amusing to watch me squirm (although I did eat it the first time). This focus on meat as potentially more upsetting to travelers often sidelines the importance of staples. In this sense, chuño is less "good to think" for tourists, who are more likely to choose their meals on the basis of the meat rather than the side dishes served with it.

Of course, llama was "good to think" for tourists precisely because it was unfamiliar to them. Llama had pseudo-pet status in the North Atlantic (similar to horses), and some North Americans reacted to the idea of eating it with pseudo-cannibalistic horror. My thoughts on this are informed by the reactions I received from U.S. residents when describing my undergraduate thesis research on the consumption of llama meat in La Paz (Sammells 1998). This topic quickly broke the ice at any party. Many would ask if llama meat tasted like horse meat—not because they had eaten either animal but because the two animals had similar social positions in the United States as four-legged luxury pets. (As I have not tried horse meat, I am forced to make more mundane comparisons.) Interviews I conducted with U.S. llama herders indicated they had mixed feelings about the possibility of consuming the animals. One who did occasionally slaughter camelids asked not to be identified for fear of negative reactions from peers. This concern was not misplaced; the editors of a U.S.-based llama magazine sent me a nasty letter rejecting a short article I wrote for them on the topic of eating llamas in Bolivia, even though I had first queried and they had indicated their interest. Clearly the topic was a sensitive one for the editors.

Llama meat may be transgressive for tourists, but urban Bolivians avoided eating it for completely different reasons. Middle- and upper-class residents of La Paz (whom I interviewed in 1993–1994) assumed that llama was something eaten by poor, rural, and indigenous peoples. They avoided llama meat and even places that served it—although few establishments did.[13] Llama meat was nevertheless sold in large quantities in the street markets of La Paz, where it quietly found its way into ground-meat products. Urban La Paz residents often denounced cheap, no-brand processed meats sold in street markets—sausages, hamburgers, and the like—as being made of llama or even stray dog. Stories abounded about cheap locales that would surreptitiously serve llama instead of beef to unsuspecting customers. Many that I spoke with believed that despite their best attempts to avoid it, they might have consumed llama unknowingly. Others were convinced that they had eaten llama disguised as beef, only later realizing the truth. These stories invariably placed suspicion on meals eaten while traveling in rural areas or on street food.

Despite these prejudices on the part of some urban Bolivians, llama meat had become integral to Bolivian touristic cuisine by 1997. Peña Huari in La Paz began offering llama meat to tourists and the local upper class in 1997—one of the first restaurants to successfully do so.[14] Located on Sagarnaga Street in the center of the tourist district, an area that sported colorful artisan stalls, tour operators, and backpacker hotels, the restaurant offered a nightly two-hour *peña* show of folkloric dances and music from all regions of Bolivia. The restaurant's walls and tables were decorated with masks, ceramics, and other contemporary Bolivian art, all of which the menu declared to be for sale. Llama meat was first on the list of house specialties on what was, by Bolivian standards, a very pricey menu. The owner, who was from the city of Oruro (where llama meat was more accepted restaurant fare than in La Paz), estimated in 1999 that 65 percent of his foreign clients ordered llama rather than beef, lamb, chicken, or Lake Titicaca trout.[15]

In the rural touristic village of Tiwanaku, home to that nation's most important archaeological site, llama meat had entered the menus of several tourist restaurants by 2002. Ironically, while urban La Paz residents often associated llama meat with rural cuisine, in this particular part of the altiplano there were few llamas—thus the meat was imported from La Paz to be served to tourists. Locals in my field site almost never ate llama meat themselves, although they valued it. For these Aymara people, eating llama meat was associated with strength. One man correlated the success of a neighboring village's soccer team with the fact that they had large llama herds and thus ate the meat frequently.

Despite the taboo against their meat among some, llamas have long been an undisputed symbol of Andean authenticity. Llamas appeared on the Bolivian national emblem and on many of the national currencies. This was neither contradictory nor coincidental. Trouillot (1991) has provided us with the useful concept of the "savage slot": while the content of the meanings attached to "othered" concepts and objects—and foods—may change, their position of alterity does not.[16] It was precisely because the llama was so marked—that is, as a rural and indigenous animal, to the point where it was even questionably edible to some Bolivians—that it also became a national symbol and useful as a representation of a national cuisine to present to outsiders.

Despite llamas' symbolic importance, consumption of llama meat had declined precipitously since the colonial era, corresponding to similar declines in the consumption of other native foods. Today rural Aymara purchase imported and processed foods, such as cooking oil, rice, bread, and cookies, and often view the cuisine of the past with nostalgia. Many in Tiwanaku agreed that their ancestors' better health and longer life spans were the result of eating llama and other traditional foods, including chuño. *Quinua, cañahua, p'itu,*[17] and other native grains are now eaten far less often than bread, pasta, and heavily sugared *mates* (herbal infusions). Rural Bolivians told me that their current dietary patterns were less healthy. They and their children consumed far more sugar, pasta, and bread than their grandparents, which had a negative impact on their health, strength, and life expectancy. The increasing incorporation of Western-style foods into rural Bolivian cuisine and an accompanying decrease in nutrition have been noted in rural Bolivia and elsewhere in the Andes (Orlove 1987; Weismantel 1988). Llama and guinea pig are now far less common in the highland cuisine than mutton and beef (although individual diets depend on the region, and there are areas where llamas are still the dominant meat source).

Llama meat is generally higher in protein and lower in fat than beef or mutton, however, and the animal is less damaging to the highland environment. This motivated several groups to make efforts to promote its consumption both within Bolivia and as a foreign export in the hopes that this would result in increased incomes for llama herders, better nutrition for the rural and urban Bolivian poor, and less damage to the environment (McCorkle 1990; Sammells and Markowitz 1995; Valdivia 1992). At the same time, there is a small but growing movement by Bolivians to promote llama as both a healthier meat and a source of national pride.

In short, llama meat is local and "authentic." It is neglected, yet available; promoted as both traditional and healthy for the future, but under-consumed in the present. MacCannell (1976) observed that tourists often take particular interest in things perceived to be part of the disappearing, premodern world. While Andean peoples are not premodern in any sense, tourist literature tends to present them as both descendents and members of ancient Andean cultures, always on the brink of suffering the consequences of incorporation into a global capitalist economy. (In reality, Andeans have been participating in that system for centuries.) The llama, as the animal most closely associated with this pre-Columbian past and the indigenous present, therefore takes on special meaning in these touristic narratives.

There are many accounts of locally denigrated foods becoming part of national cuisines or touristic fare (e.g., Wilk 1999, 2006). Llama meat's transformation from undesirable meat to authentic Bolivian cuisine is not at all surprising. Its clear association with the poor and indigenous was exactly what made it interesting to tourists—it served as a truly authentic representation of the "indigenous culture" that many came to highland Bolivia to see. In the touristic imagination, "Bolivianess" is intimately connected to indigenousness, with representations of Bolivians ranging from the "real" indigenous people who line the market streets of the city (who, despite being touristic attractions, receive little benefit from this industry) to those who play and dance to folkloric music at peñas.

In contrast to llama meat, potatoes and chuño are staples for all highland Bolivians (albeit in different proportions). Because chuño is eaten by all social classes, it was never clearly associated with only the poor or indigenous. Thus, it never became emblematic of "Bolivianess" (meaning, indigenous Bolivian) in the touristic imaginary in quite the same way. Chuño was part of an only loosely hierarchical arrangement of staples (in order from lowest ranked to highest ranked, chuño, *tunta*, potato, rice). However, this hierarchy was not stable; certain dishes and contexts required specific staples and granted them higher values. Chuño was not marked enough to keep on tourist plates and therefore was easily replaced with higher-status staples more familiar to tourists and more appropriate to their economic status in the Bolivian context. This suggests a self-reinforcing effect. Those who wrote tour books and marketing brochures did not write about chuño (or said little that was positive or interesting about it), perhaps in part because it was not offered. Thus, tourists who visited Bolivia did not think to seek it out.

GOOD TO RELATE

I argue that there is another reason why chuño has not been fully incorporated into Bolivian touristic cuisine. Chuño was also not "good to relate" in the sense that the tuber did not serve as an emblematic marker of travels in Bolivia specifically. In North Atlantic countries, the potato is a quotidian part of diets and national histories. It is common knowledge that the potato's nutritional and agricultural qualities led it to be adopted as a staple peasant food and later incorporated into several national cuisines (Salaman 1949). Whether we consider the spread of McDonald's French fries or the devastation of the Irish Potato Famine, the potato has been omnipresent in North Atlantic history for more than two centuries. Tourists were often told about the incredible variety of potatoes in the highlands but were less well-informed about the extraordinary qualities of chuño.

Potatoes are integral to the diet of the "modern" world and thus are generally ignored in the touristic imaginary. The potato is not disappearing—on the contrary, it is an important part of North Atlantic diets. The potato is Andean, but mentioning this fact in touristic marketing does little to distinguish "local" cuisine from what North Atlantic tourists believe they have already experienced. The chuño was not "good to think" or "good to relate" because tourists categorized it as a kind of potato—which, as I have argued, it is not.

Llama meat, in contrast, was "good to relate" for a number of reasons. When tourists talk about their experiences after returning home, their audiences probably know what a llama is but have rarely eaten one—if the idea has occurred to them at all. Eating llama has a certain shock value that adds to the value of the tourist's tale. For North Americans, eating llama was transgressive, much like the tales of eating guinea pig discussed by Goldstein (this volume). That made such tales all the more captivating.

Eating while traveling—whether as a tourist or an anthropologist—is not only about eating what is familiar. Travelers generally want to experience foods with unfamiliar tastes that will be interesting to talk about later. The popularity of cooking magazines and TV shows like *Iron Chef* demonstrates that we love to read about, hear about, and watch others eat unusual things, even when we are not in a position to replicate the dishes we see or even imagine what they taste like. In fact, this is one of the premises that underlies this book. Nothing I write here will allow you to taste chuño or any of the other foods described by my coauthors. Nevertheless, here we are—we as authors trying to create a taste in your mouth that we often cannot even recreate in our own kitchens at home, and you as readers trying to imagine these dishes and wondering if you can trust our assertions that you might like them.

TOURISTIC CUISINES

This comparison of llama meat and chuño brings me to my final point, one that I think can be expanded to an examination of touristic cuisines more generally. Bolivian touristic cuisine—meaning, the cuisine served to tourists in Bolivia—is not a watered-down, bland version of local food. Nor is it an attempt to cater to North Atlantic desires for McDonald's (which is itself not a uniform monolith; see Watson 1997) or other familiar dishes. Touristic cuisines have their own logics, ingredients, spices, styles of presentation, and dining contexts that derive from the cultural situations in which these dishes are cooked and served—specifically, the structured interactions between locals and visitors within a touristic context. The status that foods have within both Bolivian and North Atlantic societies entered into the cuisine that one prepared for the other, and ingredients and dishes were transformed by a distinct culinary logic that emerged from a touristic encounter fraught with inequalities and anxieties as well as steeped in cosmopolitan sophistication and entrepreneurial acumen.

Bolivian touristic cuisine is certainly different from the highland Bolivian cuisine typically consumed by locals. This is true of touristic cuisine in most places—the claim may be made that it is authentic, *típico*, or local, but what is served in tourist restaurants is usually not the same as what people cook in their own homes. Some travelers might see this as an obstacle to be overcome in the search for the "real" or the "authentic." Some anthropologists might even consider their knowledge of local home cooking to be part of what separates them from tourists (Crick 1995). I prefer to see this division as part of regional culinary diversity; in other words, touristic cuisine is one part of the diverse culinary knowledges and practices that make up local cuisines rather than one that is external to them.

There is a long debate on how to best define the word "tourist" (for examples, see Boorstin 1961; Chambers 2000; MacCannell 1976; Nash 1996; Smith 1989 [1977]; Urry 1990). Any universal definition of this term is inherently unsatisfying precisely because this word takes on meaning through specific local interactions. These encounters are not limited to "host and guests" but include infrastructures that facilitate exchanges of currencies, images, goods, literatures, and services. An important part of these interactions is culinary.

In the context of Bolivian touristic cuisine, restaurants catered to a clientele that was not only foreign but also seen as upper-class. The word *turista*—which did not apply to all leisure travelers within that nation—carried the connotations of a short-term, foreign visitor (usually European, U.S., or Canadian but also those seen as racially "white" from other nations, including Latin America). This term also had class connotations, as turistas had substantial economic resources compared to most Bolivians (Sammells 2009:84–97). In this context, where turistas were not defined solely by the activity of travel but also by their race, nationality, and economic position, llama and chuño acquired very different meanings.

Thus, llama meat served with rice, a common dish in Bolivian touristic cuisine, combines ingredients with different class associations for Bolivians into a tourist cuisine with its own culinary logic. Llama is presented proudly as the truly Andean, quietly accompanied by rice and perhaps potatoes, both higher-status staples. Chuño and tunta generally go unmentioned and unserved in this context.

So, if you go to Bolivia, try the chuño. But wherever you go, recognize that it is not just your head and heart entering into a relationship with the people you visit, but also your stomach.

Acknowledgments. My deep thanks to Helen Haines and my fellow contributors to this volume, who gave many helpful suggestions, feedback, and food for thought. Conversations with members of the Gringo Tambo, including Maria Bruno, Stephen Scott, and Katherine McGurn Centellas, and comments specifically on this paper from Alison Kohn have been indispensable. I also thank Michel-Rolph Trouillot, Alan Kolata, Manuela Carneiro da Cunha, and John Kelly for their support and comments. I thank my compadres Paulina and Anaclo for making sure I was so well fed in Bolivia and for all the wonderful conversations we had in their kitchen. This research was supported by the Fulbright-Hays Doctoral Dissertation Research Abroad Program, the Tinker Foundation, the Orin Williams Fund, and the University of Chicago Center for Latin American Studies.

NOTES

1. By "American" I mean people from the United States of America. It is a misnomer, since "American" should rightly apply to people from the entire hemisphere. But this term is far more elegant in English, which lacks an alternative word such as *estadounidense* to describe those from the United States more specifically. My apologies to those who might be offended.

2. For example, I strongly dislike olives. This is a matter of some amusement among my friends.

3. I should note that *chuño* was the word applied to the raw product by Aymara speakers. If cooked and served whole (such as a side to a meal, or in a *fiambre*), it was referred to as *phuti* (also written *p'uti*). Phuti also referred to cooked *tunta*. In this essay, I will use the term "chuño" to refer to both the raw and the cooked product for the simplicity of those readers who do not speak Aymara and also to distinguish it from tunta.

4. I kept a detailed food diary for twelve months while conducting dissertation research. The one-third figure includes midday and dinner meals in Tiwanaku but excludes *tecito*, which usually consisted of only a hot drink and bread and was served twice a day, at breakfast and in the early evening.

5. In rural areas, the exact proportions of consumption of each staple depended on the climate and agriculture of the region. Regions that grow maize or *quinua* will obviously consume more of those grains. This paper shows my own bias in having done research in La Paz and Tiwanaku, but I recognize that cuisine can change radically even over short distances. For example, communities on Lake Titicaca eat far more lake fish and have a microclimate conducive to growing maize, whereas Tiwanaku, a mere ten miles (seventeen kilometers) from the lake, grows little maize, and residents tend to eat fish only on Sundays when it is sold at the weekly market.

6. One particular type of potato, *pitikilla*, was actually more delicious when it had worms. The worms were not eaten—they were removed while eating—but as a result of the worms, the potato's flavor resembled that of chestnuts. It was generally agreed that while the worms are troublesome to remove, the flavor was superior.

7. Informants in Tiwanaku often found it strange that although Chicago was colder in the winter than the altiplano and Chicagoans ate potatoes, no one made chuño. My description of bitter cold even during the day, high snowbanks, and short daylight hours seemed odd to them indeed (as did my description of the long daylight hours of summer). When I brought them a photograph of a Hyde Park, Chicago, street in winter, they were as interested in the parked cars lining the street—a clear sign of widespread wealth—as in the thick layer of snow covering them.

8. A *compadre* is a "fictive kin" relationship where two unrelated individuals are linked through one being the godparent—for the baptism, wedding, high-school graduation, or other kind of sponsorship—of the other's child. I had a number of *compadres* in Tiwanaku.

9. Again, this is not to claim that I ate everything with equal relish. I did try everything, but it quickly became clear to those who knew me well that there were certain dishes I was less fond of. My *comadre* did not insist I eat these things, because that meant there was more for everyone else. Fried liver (fresh from a slaughtered sheep) was a particular treat that I ate conspicuously less of than everyone else, but the children were happy to divide up whatever I did not want.

10. The 2002 edition of Lonely Planet's *South America on a Shoestring* displayed on its cover a photo of two of the artisans of Tiwanaku, Bolivia, playing soccer. When I contacted the publisher, they sent a complementary copy of the book for each of them.

11. Compare written guides' treatment of chuño to that paid to *salteñas*, a meat-filled pastry, which almost always received high praise and a detailed description.

12. I do not wish to suggest that all food taboos involve meats. In Bolivia, there were food taboos involving non-meat foods in particular contexts, such as in the diets of postpartum women.

13. No La Paz establishments offered llama meat openly during that time, although in the city of Oruro dishes made of llama meat, such as *charquekan*, were sold as specialties and very popular.

14. In addition to Peña Huari, another La Paz restaurant aimed at tourists also began serving llama meat around this time, although it had closed by 1998.

15. Trout from Lake Titicaca was another mainstay of Bolivian touristic cuisine that was rarely eaten by Bolivians, who tended to consume smaller native species of fish. The trout are not native to the region and were often farmed.

16. In fact, from the perspective of North Atlantic nations, Bolivia itself could be seen as squarely within the "savage slot"—as an underdeveloped, poor, "Third World" nation—or, as postcards and tourist brochures declared, as the "Folklore Capital of South America" that drew foreigners to see its vibrant indigenous culture and unspoiled natural landscapes.

17. *P'itu* is a preparation that can be made from *quinua*, *cañahua*, wheat, or fava beans. It involves toasting the grains and then grinding them into a powder. The powder is then served in a bowl with a mug of a sugared hot drink (usually an herbal tea). The drink is poured into the powder and then mixed to form a porridge. This was usually served for breakfast but has been largely replaced with bread. When made more watery, p'itu can also be served as a *refresco*, or beverage. P'itu falls somewhere between a food and a drink.

REFERENCES

Boorstin, Daniel J.
    1961   *The Image: A Guide to Pseudo-Events in America*. Vintage Books, New York.

Chambers, Erve
    2000   *Native Tours: The Anthropology of Travel and Tourism*. Waveland Press, Prospect Heights, IL.

Coe, Sophie D.
    1994   *America's First Cuisines*. University of Texas Press, Austin.

Condori Cruz, Dionisio
    1992   Tecnología del chuño. *Boletín del IDEA* (Puno, Peru) 2:70–97.

Cramer, Mark
    1996   *Culture Shock! Bolivia: A Guide to Customs and Etiquette*. Graphic Arts Center Publishing Company, Portland, OR.

Crick, Malcolm
    1995   The Anthropologist as Tourist: An Identity in Question. In *International Tourism: Identity and Change*, ed. Marie-Françoise Lanfant, John B. Allcock, and Edward M. Bruner, 205–223. Sage Publications, London.

D'Altroy, Terence N.
    2002   *The Incas*. Blackwell Publishing, Malden, MA.

Douglas, Mary
    1966   *Purity and Danger*. Routledge, London.
    1972   Deciphering a Meal. *Daedalus* 101:61–81.
    1983   Culture and Food. In *The Pleasures of Anthropology*, ed. Morris Freilich,
    [1977]   74–102. Mentor, New York, and Scarborough, Ontario.

Fiddes, Nick
    1991   *Meat: A Natural Symbol*. Routledge, London.

Gorry, C., F. Adams, S. Boa, V. Boone, K. Dydynski, P. Hellander, C. Hubbard, J. Noble, D. Palmerlee, and R. Rachowiecki (editors)
    2002   *South America on a Shoestring*. Lonely Planet Publications, Melbourne.

Kolata, Alan L.
    1993   *The Tiwanaku: Portrait of an Andean Civilization*. Blackwell Publishers, Cambridge, MA.

Kolata, Alan L. (editor)
    1996   *Tiwanaku and Its Hinterland: Archaeology and Paleoecology of an Andean Civilization*. Smithsonian Institution Press, Washington, DC.

La Barre, Weston
    1947   Potato Taxonomy among the Aymara Indians of Bolivia. *Acta Americana: Review of the Inter-American Society of Anthropology and Geography* 5:83–103.

Levi-Strauss, Claude
1963   *Totemism*. Beacon Press, Boston.
1969   *The Raw and the Cooked: Introduction to a Science of Mythology*, Vol. 1. Harper and Row Publishers, New York.
1978   *The Origin of Table Manners: Mythologiques*, Vol. 3. Harper and Row Pub-
[1968] lishers, New York.

Lyon, James, Wayne Bernhardson, Robyn Jones, Andrew Draffen, Leonardo Pinheiro, Krzysztof Dydynski, Maria Massolo, Conner Gorry, and Mark Plotkin (editors)
2000   *South America on a Shoestring*. Lonely Planet, Melbourne.

MacCannell, Dean
1976   *The Tourist: A New Theory of the Leisure Class*. Schocken Books, New York.

Mamani, Mauricio
1981   El Chuño: Preparación, Uso Almacenamiento. In *La Tecnologia en el Mundo Andino: Runakunap Kawsayninkupaq Rurasqankunaqa*, ed. H. Lechtman and A. M. Soldi, 235–246. Universidad Nacional Autonoma de Mexico, Mexico D.F.

Mangan, Jane E.
2005   *Trading Roles: Gender, Ethnicity, and the Urban Economy in Colonial Potosí*. Duke University Press, Durham.

McCorkle, Constance M. (editor)
1990   *Improving Andean Sheep and Alpaca Production: Recommendations from a Decade of Research in Peru*. University of Missouri–Columbia Printing Services, Columbia.

Messer, Ellen
1997   Three Centuries of Changing European Tastes for the Potato. In *Food Preference and Taste: Continuity and Change*, ed. H. Macbeth. Berghahn Books, Oxford.

Mintz, Sidney W.
1996   *Tasting Food, Tasting Freedom: Excursions into Eating, Culture, and the Past*. Beacon Press Books, Boston.

Murphy, Alan
2000   *Footprint Bolivia Handbook*. Footprint Handbooks, Bath, UK.

Nash, Dennison
1996   *Anthropology of Tourism*. Elsevier Science, Oxford.

Orlove, Benjamin S.
1987   Stability and Change in Highland Andean Dietary Patterns. In *Food and Evolution: Toward a Theory of Human Food Habits*, ed. M. Harris and E. B. Ross. Temple University Press, Philadelphia.

Read, James
    2002   *The Rough Guide to Bolivia.* Rough Guides, London.

Salaman, Redcliffe N.
    1949   *The History and Social Influence of the Potato.* Cambridge University Press, Cambridge.

Sammells, Clare A.
    1998   Folklore, Food, and Seeking National Identity: Urban Legends of Llama Meat in La Paz, Bolivia. *Contemporary Legend* 1:21–54.
    1999   Making the World "Authentic" for Tourists: The Transformation of Llama Meat into Bolivian Food. Master's thesis. Department of Anthropology, University of Chicago, Chicago.
    2009   Touristic Narratives and Historical Networks: Politics and Authority in Tiwanaku, Bolivia. Ph.D. dissertation. Department of Anthropology, University of Chicago, Chicago.

Sammells, Clare A., and Lisa Markowitz
    1995   La carne de llama: Alta viabilidad, baja visibilidad. In *Waira Pampa: Un sistema pastoril camélidos-ovinos del altiplano árido boliviano*, ed. D. Genin, H.-J. Picht, R. Lizarazu, and T. Rodriguez. ORSTOM/IBTA, La Paz.

Sinclair, Upton
    1906   *The Jungle.* Grosset and Dunlap, New York.

Smith, Valene L. (editor)
    1989   *Hosts and Guests: The Anthropology of Tourism*, 2nd ed. University of
    [1977]   Pennsylvania Press, Philadelphia.

Swaney, Deanna
    1988   *Lonely Planet Bolivia: A Travel Survival Kit.* Lonely Planet Publications, South Yarra, Australia.
    1996   *Bolivia: A Lonely Planet Travel Survival Kit.* SNP Printing, Singapore.
    2001   *Lonely Planet Bolivia.* Lonely Planet Publications, Footscray, Australia.

Swaney, Deanna, and Robert Strauss
    1992   *Lonely Planet Bolivia: A Travel Survival Kit.* Lonely Planet Publications, Hawthorn, Australia.

Tambiah, S. J.
    1969   Animals Are Good to Think and Good to Prohibit. *Ethnology* 8(4):423–459.

Trouillot, Michel-Rolph
    1991   Anthropology and the Savage Slot: The Poetics and Politics of Otherness. In *Recapturing Anthropology: Working in the Present,* ed. R. G. Fox. School of American Research Press, Santa Fe, NM.

Urry, John
    1990   *The Tourist Gaze: Leisure and Travel in Contemporary Societies.* Sage Publications, London.

Valdivia, Corinne (editor)
  1992   *Sustainable Crop-Livestock Systems for the Bolivian Highlands: Proceedings of an SR-CRSP Workshop*. University of Missouri–Columbia Printing Services, Columbia.

Walvin, James
  1997   *Fruits of Empire: Exotic Produce and British Taste, 1660–1800*. New York University Press, Washington Square, New York.

Watson, James L. (editor)
  1997   *Golden Arches East: McDonald's in East Asia*. Stanford University Press, Stanford, CA.

Weismantel, Mary J.
  1988   *Food, Gender, and Poverty in the Ecuadorian Andes*. University of Pennsylvania Press, Philadelphia.

Wilk, Richard R.
  1999   "Real Belizean Food": Building Local Identity in the Transnational Caribbean. *American Anthropologist* 101:244–255.
  2006   *Home Cooking in the Global Village: Caribbean Food from Buccaneers to Ecotourists*. Berg, Oxford.

Zuckerman, Larry
  1998   *The Potato: How the Humble Spud Rescued the Western World*. North Point Press, New York.

CHAPTER SEVEN

Durian

The King of Fruits or an Acquired Taste?

Maxine E. McBrinn

Biographical sketch. Maxine McBrinn is an anthropological archaeologist who specializes in the arid lands hunters and gatherers of the western United States. While she has no formal background in the anthropology of food, she is an enthusiastic experimentalist of new tastes and cuisines. Maxine found her reaction to durian to be as complex as the flavor of the famed fruit itself.

Taste is one of the many ways to experience a new place. Enthusiastic visitors, including myself, seek out new foods and new dishes as part of being somewhere new. In an ideal scenario, the intrepid traveler tries the local cuisines and is rewarded by delicious or intriguing tastes. In the real world, however, squeamish eaters and sometimes even accommodating diners will find foods that repel them for one reason or another. In this manner, taste can also be a visceral and immediate indication that, to borrow from the *Wizard of Oz*, "Toto, I've a feeling we're not in Kansas anymore!" Yet there is something oddly satisfying about finding a repulsive new food, as it confirms that there are significant differences in eating habits and choices across the world. It would be disappointing if everyone everywhere ate the same things and yearned for the same flavors. There are foods that are highly sought after in one place but arouse immediate disgust in diners from other places. For example, ripe European cheeses can also be viewed as clotted, rotting milk, a view held by many Asians, who would never think of nibbling on such a thing. In turnabout, Asian delicacies such as kimchi and the so-called thousand-year-old eggs may be refused by suspicious Westerners. Some people are immediately repulsed by the idea of eating familiar (or not so familiar) animals, such as horses, dogs, snakes, or snails—meats that are enjoyed elsewhere. Many of the foods that arouse such divergent views are from animal sources, such as meat or dairy foods (Harris 1985; Simoons 1994), but there are also plant foods that are unappreciated by some diners. Many people, for example, dislike okra because of its texture when completely cooked, which some malign as "slimy" and for which the formal term, mucilaginous, suggests a comparison to mucus. One of the risks and rewards to traveling is to try these foods for oneself.

The joy of being in a new place is to try as many local culinary favorites as possible. Much of what is available to eat day in and day out can get boring, but new foods and new spices may reawaken our enthusiasm. But more than this, food is a shortcut into experiencing new worlds and new lives. Food informs us about the environment, about the plants and animals that live in the area (Messer 1984, 1989; Mintz and Du Bois 2002). For example, while it is appropriate to find fresh seafood near the ocean, catfish, trout, and other freshwater fish would be expected at inland locations. Cuisine also tells us a lot about the history of the place: about how and when nonnative foods arrived and how they became incorporated into the local customs (Sokolov 1991). In this way, local foods encapsulate the relationships among history, the environment, and outside influences. One of the surprises from a visit to Kenya was the frequency that cabbage and potatoes were offered, legacies of that country's colonial past. Food also informs us about economics and cultural training. For example, tortillas are portable and widely used when people travel to their workplace, whereas soups imply local diners. Woks use less energy to heat, for when fuel is scarce, and hot tea warms chilled bodies and cold fingers. Through food, through tastes and textures, visitors absorb some of that place into their bodies and make it a part of themselves.

Within any given society, some foods are considered to be especially suitable for men, or for women, for children, or for elders, for healthy young adults, or for invalids (Messer 1984, 1989; Mintz and Du Bois 2002; McKay 1980; Wilson 1975, 1980). There are foods that are considered bad for pregnant women, and foods that will boost the immune system. Some foods will heighten sexual desire and others will encourage sleep. There are foods that are eaten in a homemade meal, others that are more often eaten in restaurants, snack foods suitable for popular leisure activities, and other foods that are consumed privately or even in secrecy. These food categories are culturally constructed although there is also a wide degree of individual choice in the foods actually consumed.

Food and our responses to it are complex, in part because food selection offers a unique window into many aspects of human societies. There is a large body of literature on the anthropology of food and a wide diversity of theoretical approaches that can be used (for good review articles, see Messer 1984, 1989; Mintz and Du Bois 2002). Individual food choice is affected by a wide range of physical and sociocultural factors, including local ecology, economic status, gender, age, class, personal health, religious belief, and so on. Accordingly, anthropologists can choose a similarly wide array of approaches to study the topic, including ecological, ethnographic, economic, biocultural, nutritional, and ethnoscientific studies (Messer 1989). Those factors that lead to people classifying foods as "edible" or "inedible" are particularly interesting for the diner confronted by a new food that challenges their previous conceptions, the topic that unites the chapters in this volume. Food preferences are influenced by both sensory and cultural factors, by the taste, smell, look, texture, and source of the food as well as by the meaning assigned to those attributes. In other words, our cultural training influences how we interpret a potential food. Durian, the subject of this chapter, is an excellent example of a food that is loved, even immoderately desired, by some, yet reviled by others.

DURIAN FACTS

Durian is the fruit of the durian tree (Figure 7.1), *Durio zibethinus*, thought to have originated in Borneo and now cultivated in much of Southeast Asia, including Malaysia, Indonesia, Thailand, and the Philippines (Morton 1987; Rolnick 2003; Veevers-Carter 1984) *Duri* in Malay means "spike," prominent features of the large fruit (Figure 7.2) (Dunne 2002). The term *zibethinus* is derived from the Italian word, *zibetto* (civet cat or skunk), and notes the similarity of the odor of the fruit to that of the cat (Soegeng-Reksodihardjo 1962).

While not all members of the *Durio* genus produce edible fruit, a number of species do (Kostermans 1992; Soegeng-Reksodihardjo 1962; Veevers-Carter 1984), although only *Durio zibethinus* is commonly commercially cultivated. Durian grows wild or semi-wild around established villages (Morton 1987) and can even be used as a marker of previous settlements (Peluso 2003). There are hundreds of durian varieties, with more than 300 named varieties in Thailand alone (Morton 1987). Of these, somewhat less than a dozen are grown commercially. Durian grows best in jungle conditions, requiring lots of water and consistent warmth, especially for young plants becoming established

7.1. Durian tree. (DRAWING BY MAXINE MCBRINN)

(Morton 1987). Despite the fact that the trees do not fruit for five to ten years after being planted (Rolnick 2003), the amount of durian under cultivation has increased in at least some parts of Indonesia (Peluso 2003). New research on durian cultivars has focused on diminishing some of the characteristics that some find distasteful, including eliminating the odor (Fuller 2007; Sullivan 2007). Whether this will extend the appeal of the fruit to new markets remains to be seen.

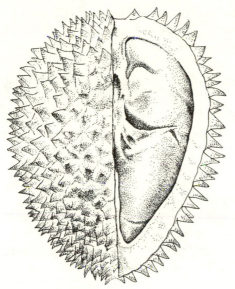

7.2. Durian fruit. (DRAWING BY MAXINE MCBRINN)

The durian fruit is also reputed to be prized by frugivorus animals. A Thai maxim says: "[T]he first to note the malodor is the elephant, which shakes the tree to bring down the fruit. After the elephant noses open the fruit with its tusks, the tiger fights the elephant for the fruit. Rhinoceros, wild pig, deer, tapir, monkey, beetle, and ant follow the tiger. The human must be very quick to get the durian" (Rolnick 2003). Perhaps to forestall not getting any fruit at all, villagers are reported to camp near trees with ripe fruit (Howell 1984:22; Morton 1987; Peluso 2003; Veevers-Carter 1984:42), ready to collect the harvest. Care must be taken, however, as the durian trees are tall, and the fruit heavy and covered by large, sharp spikes (Morton 1987; Wallace 1856). In some places, traps placed in the area add meat as well as durian to the diet by taking advantage of the game drawn by the durian scent (Morton 1987). The animal attraction for the scent of durian led E.H.J. Corner to posit his "Durian Theory," which states that the earliest fruiting trees used endozoochory (animals carrying seeds to new locations in their stomachs), rewarding the animals who dispersed the seeds with rich foods (Corner 1976; Veevers-Carter 1984:43–45). Corner believes that the durian is an outstanding example of a primitive fruiting tree.

VIEWS ON DURIAN

In Malay society, as in much of Southeast Asia, durian is highly esteemed. In fact, durian has been declared "The King of Fruits" (Dunne 2002; Rolnick

2003:541; Walsh 1999) and there are people who become fixated on all aspects of the fruit. Currently, there are large Web sites featuring many, many pages of discussion, advice, facts, photos, cartoons, recipes, and overall celebrations of durian.

Selling durian is a significant cash source for some groups, providing up to half their cash income (Peluso 2003:206–207). Southeast Asia has a number of aboriginal societies, some that traditionally focused on foraging (Brosius 1999; Endicott 1999a, 1999b; Howell 1984; Van der Sluys 1999) and others that have customarily cultivated swidden gardens of rice, maize, cassava, vegetables, fruit, and sometimes rubber trees (Dentan 1968; Peluso 2003:190). In Malaysia these groups are known collectively as the Orang Asli, which translates as "The First Peoples" (Endicott 1999b; Van der Sluys 1999).

At least one Orang Asli group, the Chewong, think so highly of durian that they move to live near the trees in harvesting season (Howell 1984:22). In addition, durian is one of the useful plants that are believed by the Chewong (Howell 1984:133) to have consciousness and a desire to help the people. In fact, durian has a starring role in the Chewong origin story, being the fruit stolen from Earth Six to feed the peoples of this earth (Howell 1984:74).

Among the Indonesian Dayak (Peluso 2003), durian also has an important economic role. Durian trees are long-lived, surviving perhaps up to seven human generations (Peluso 2003:191, 203–205). Once they have begun to fruit, they are individually named. Tree names most often honor the planter but sometimes refer to the quality of the fruit or some other distinctive attribute (Peluso 2003:184–185). Because of the high value of the fruit, once the planter and spouse have died, durian harvests are divided among the heirs according to how many generations removed they are from the planter (Peluso 2003:184–185), the heirs' residence, and other factors.

The Dayak (Peluso 2003:202), like many others, do not pick durian but rather wait for the fruit to fall naturally (also McCarthy 2005:69, but see Roseman 1998:110 for an example of durian being picked). This ensures that the fruit will be at its flavorful peak and that it will bring a good price if sold. Some towns and villages enforce this rule through social shame (McCarthy 2005:69) or fines (Peluso 2003:202) if residents pick underripe fruit, as this diminishes the value of all the fruit harvested in the community in the eyes of outsiders. A reputation for this practice could limit the price paid for future harvests.

Durian season lasts a couple of months, requiring an extended time when people must stay near the trees to collect the fruit and to keep animals and other people from taking it (Peluso 2003:202–203). Durian season, moreover, requires even greater logistical maneuvering. The fruit must be sold very soon after it falls and should be consumed within four or five days (Peluso 2003:202;

Soegeng-Reksodihardjo 1962; Wilson 1986), a challenge to people who live some distance from the roads or boats used to carry fruit to market.

Durian is considered a powerful aphrodisiac, as the Malay saying "When the durian falls, the sarong falls" (Rolnick 2003:542) implies. Perhaps love, or maybe just lust, follows, because when eating durian, the diner is reported to become heated and may start to sweat (Laderman 1981:474; 1983:44; Manderson 1986:132; Wilson 1986). Some of this heating effect may be caused by the high fat content of durian, second among fruits only to avocado, or perhaps by the similarity of durian's final chemical breakdown products to alcohol (Laderman 1981:474; Wilson 1986:264–265). This heating effect, and the resulting increase in attraction, may also explain why durian is considered an excellent make-up gift after marital discord. Instead of flowers or chocolates, Malay or other Southeast Asian men might choose to sweeten the relationship with durian.

The Malay belief that durian is heating reflects a complex ordering of food, drink, and medicine beyond classification as protein, fat, or carbohydrate or the commonly stated "good for me" or "bad for me." Like many Southeast Asians, Malaysians classify foods and other ingested substances as "hot" or "cold" (Laderman 1981, 1983:35–72; Manderson 1986; McKay 1980; Messer 1984, 1989; Wilson 1975, 1980, 1986). These terms signify intrinsic qualities that direct individual and group food use. The classifications are independent of temperature or spiciness and are linked to medicinal values and humoral conceptions of health and illness. Individuals in good health exhibit an appropriate balance of hot and cold in their bodies, while illness may be caused or exacerbated by a poor balance of these qualities. The specifics of these classification systems vary across Southeast Asia, both in qualities assigned to specific foods and in how they are applied to dietary and health practices. The Malay classification of durian as heating probably acknowledges its high calorie content and is an exception to the common ascription of fruits as cold.

Some Westerners, too, have fallen in love with durian. One of the most famous of those who learned to appreciate the odoriferous fruit was Alfred Russel Wallace, who said:

> The pulp is the eatable part, and its consistence and flavour are indescribable. A rich custard highly flavoured with almonds gives the best general idea of it, but there are occasional wafts of flavour that call to mind cream-cheese, onion-sauce, sherry-wine, and other incongruous dishes. Then there is a rich glutinous smoothness in the pulp which nothing else possesses, but which adds to its delicacy. It is neither acid nor sweet nor juicy; yet it wants neither of these qualities, for it is in itself perfect. . . . In fact, to eat Durians is a new sensation worth a voyage to the East to experience. . . . If I had to fix on two only as representing the perfection of the two classes, I should

certainly choose the Durian and the Orange as the king and queen of fruits. (Wallace 1856:229)

Wallace was not alone. A friend of Edmund Banfield was quoted as reporting,

> I have been spending a small fortune in durians, they are relatively cheap and very good this season in Singapore. Like all the good things in Nature ... durian is indescribable. It is meat and drink and an unrivalled delicacy besides, and you may gorge to repletion and never have cause for penitence. It is the one case where Nature has tried her hand at the culinary art and beaten all the CORDON BLEUE out of heaven and earth. (Banfield 1911: chapter 5; capitalization follows the original)

Banfield adds the note that his friend was not an enthusiast in regard to tropical fruits (Banfield 1911:chapter 5), making his rapture all the more remarkable.

Despite these rave reviews, though, it is extraordinarily easy to find quotes from Westerners who did not like the odor or flavor of durian. Many of their descriptions use a death, decay, or scatological reference to describe the experience. Sir Stanford Raffles, founder of Singapore, told friends that when confronted by the smell, he held his nose and ran away (Rolnick 2003:541). The nineteenth-century naturalist Henri Mouhot said, "On first tasting it, I thought it like the flesh of some animal in a state of putrefaction" (quoted in Rolnick 2003:541). Bob Halliday, a food writer based in Bangkok, said, "To anyone who doesn't like durian it smells like a bunch of dead cats" (quoted in Fuller 2007: n.p.). Rob Walsh, a self-proclaimed veteran food writer who had successfully eaten a wide range of odd foods, was taken aback by his response to durian: "[T]he smell of rotten eggs is so overwhelming. I suppress a gag reaction as I take a bite" (Walsh 1999:76–77).

That gag reaction is a physiological manifestation of disgust, a culturally conditioned response to certain situations, including the thought of eating smelly foods (Rozin et al. 1997; Schiefhövel 1997). While the origins of disgust are in distaste, the latter is a purely physical reaction, whereas the former is a conceptual rejection of the food in question (Schiefhövel 1997; Rozin et al. 1997.) Walsh (1999:76–77) quoted Paul Rozin as saying, "this aversion [to a rotten smell] is not innate. I believe the disgust reaction comes from a universally acquired aversion that is probably taught in the toilet training process." Foods that resemble feces in smell or texture become disgusting through that socialization process. Yet, as Rozin points out (in Walsh 1999), in many cultures, a few rotten-smelling substances become favored foods. European aged cheeses, Inuit rotted whale meat, Southeast Asian fermented fish sauces, and durians are all examples of these culturally significant exceptions. Rozin posits that part of the enjoyment from eating these foods is the struggle between mind and body, where the mind tells the diner that it is okay and the body says no. Because the taste is much better than the smell, there is a payoff to this thrill-seeking. Rozin compares the strong appeal of this situation to riding a roller-coaster and other actions that are initially off-putting.

The popular guides for visitors traveling to Malaysia generally discourage tourists from trying durian. For example, a recent edition of *Frommer's Guide to Malaysia* says:

> Dare it if you will, the fruit to sample—the veritable king of fruits—is the durian, a large, green, spiky fruit that when open, smells worse than old tennis shoes. The "best" ones are in season.... In case you're curious, the fruit has a creamy texture and tastes lightly sweet and deeply musky. (Eveland 2005:98)

The Rough Guide to Malaysia, Singapore and Brunei is even more discouraging, stating:

> [o]ne of the most popular fruits in Southeast Asia, durians are also, for many visitors, the most repugnant, thanks to their unpleasant smell.... flesh, whose flavour has been likened to vomit-flavoured custard. (de Ledesma et al. 2006:66)

The *Lonely Planet* guide, often chosen by more adventurous travelers, is a bit more encouraging. It says, "Hold your nose and let your taste buds discover the reason for all the fuss about durian" (Richmond et al. 2007:20) in their mention of durian as one of the "Top 10 Eating and Dining experiences to try." On the whole, the lack of strong statements encouraging people to try durian as part of their travel experience is surprising. Being exposed to the new—new people, new customs, new smells, new places, and new foods—is an intrinsic aspect of the travel experience. This should make trying durian especially attractive simply because the flavor of this fruit is distinctly alien to a Western palate.

Durian is so closely associated with Southeast Asia by Europeans that the name graces the titles of a memoir (Wynward 1939) and at least two novels (Keon 1960; Linehan 1996). Both novels are set in Malaysia, and the memoir, while principally focused on the author's experiences in neighboring Thailand, also recounts visits to Malaysia.

TRYING DURIAN

I visited Malaysia (Figure 7.3) to attend a family wedding, but as an anthropologist, I was eager to see and experience as much of the local culture as possible. Noting that Malaysia promised a wonderful selection of new foods to try, I gratefully learned that most of peninsular Malaysia has reliably purified public

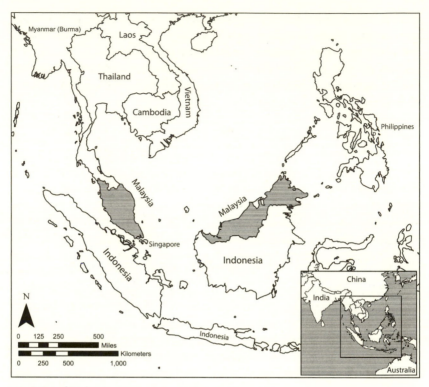

7.3. Map of Malaysia. (MAP BY MAXINE MCBRINN)

water. This is a boon for all tourists and is especially fortunate for adventurous eaters.

Malaysia is a food lover's delight. Because of its location and history, Malay, Indian, Chinese, and Thai cuisines are all easily and abundantly available. Most of these cuisines offer strongly flavored and spicy dishes. Malay food, in particular, uses chilies, lemongrass, coconut, and lime leaves and features a generous use of shrimp paste and dried fish. *Sambal*, a chili paste, is used in many dishes. Most towns have one or more areas where food venders congregate every evening in parks or markets with steam carts, creating a large temporary food court. Malay dishes like *asam kaksa*, a spicy noodle soup; *mee goring*, fried noodles; and *nasi lemak*, coconut-flavored rice served with greens and *sambal ikan bilis*, made from chilies and dried anchovies, are common and delicious.

Southeast Asia offers a wonderful and varied array of fresh fruit that can be bought in markets, and fruit juice venders at the food courts will squeeze fresh fruits to order. While many of the available fruits were familiar, like star fruit, lychee, banana, mango, papaya, passion fruit, watermelon, and pineapple, others, like jackfruit, mangosteen, rambutan, and pomelo were new to me. Rambutan was a special favorite. I could buy a bag of the red, fuzzy little fruit at street markets and then stroll along, using my thumbnail to loosen the peel and popping the fruit into my mouth. Even Malay desserts were an adventure. For example, *ais kacang* is made from shaved ice and red beans, often served with other toppings in luridly bright colors.

My husband, Ken, and I tried as many different dishes as we could find, dining at small local restaurants and from the ubiquitous food carts and playing many rounds of a favorite game that we call "menu roulette." To play, you point to any item on the menu that you do not recognize, and when it is served, you try it, no matter how it looks or smells. My cousin and her new husband looked on with a mix of excitement, enthusiasm, and disgust as we dined our way through many foods that they had not tried in more than a year in the country. The one Malaysian food that we were especially eager to try was durian. For that experience, we were prepared to make a special effort.

One evening, my cousin, Mary-Lyn, and David, her husband, drove us to an outdoor market in Petaling Jaya, the Kuala Lumpur suburb where they lived. Because of its pervasive odor, whole durian is not sold at most indoor markets or grocery stores, although prepackaged sections are often now available in many shops. Unbeknownst to us at that time, there is a ritual to buying a fresh durian. Interested buyers might examine the stem of the fruit to determine how long it had been separated from the tree—a dry stem means that the fruit is too old—or listen for the seeds moving inside when the fruit is shaken, or make sure the thorns are still sharp, another sign of freshness (Teo 2006). Buyers may demand a taste of the fruit they select as promising. The seller we watched took a small core from the flesh of the fruit, offering it to the customer for evaluation. If all is satisfactory, the seller and buyer negotiate an acceptable price. A couple was buying a durian from the fruit-seller when we found him, so we waited until they had finished and watched the transaction. We chose not to sample the fruit first ourselves, in part because we did not know how a durian should taste. Mary-Lyn, who is proud of her ability to find a good deal, had enthusiastically taken to bargaining during her stay in Southeast Asia, even dickering with shopkeepers in situations that I initially thought were not negotiable. She had become a fierce and skillful negotiator. Seeing that her skills were needed, she took the lead and bargained for a minimal price. As a piece of fruit, durians are quite expensive but not outrageously so. The cost of a durian at that time was comparable to the price of a casual dinner, although coveted varieties can be considerably more expensive (Teo 2006).

Once the transaction was complete, the seller handed us the durian in a plastic bag, and we headed back to the apartment, eager to taste our prize. Closed up in David's automobile, we were unaware of the increasing intensity of durian odor. We stopped briefly so that Mary-Lyn could make a quick purchase, with the rest of us staying in the car. When she returned, though, she could smell how the car stank and insisted that all the windows be opened—and left open for the rest of the trip home. In fact, she voted then and there to throw the durian away. Luckily for us, David agreed with our argument that we had to try it while we were in Malaysia. After more than a year in the country he also wanted to taste it, so we made it to their apartment with our durian treasure. Once we left the vehicle, however, the rest of us could detect the durian's scent, which was strongly reminiscent of a natural gas leak. It was not an appetizing scent, but we had been warned and were determined to persevere. Mary-Lyn forcefully told us that she would not try anything that smelled so disgusting, and so the durian eaters were reduced to three. On the way to the apartment, I absentmindedly swung the bag that contained the fruit and the thorns sticking through the plastic carved a few bloody scratches into my thigh before I realized the danger. Durian seemed even more formidable!

The fruit we had bought had been reduced in price because of a natural split in the hull, a good sign if the fruit is newly fallen as it indicates full ripeness but a bad omen if the fruit has sat too long. Being durian innocents, we were not aware of this subtlety, knowing only that the split created a bargain and would make it easier to break open the thick, hard rind. We carefully pried open the fruit, exposing the soft, pale-yellow flesh nestled around the large seeds. When open, a typical durian has five sections, each with flesh surrounding stones in the center (Rolnick 2003). Not sure how to proceed, we spooned the flesh off the seeds as they lay in the rind. The flesh was creamy and smooth with a strong flavor of something like garlic or onion. It had the texture of a ripe avocado and the flavor of onion ice cream. It was not bad, but was not immediately delicious, so that several mouthfuls were plenty. Our tongue and taste buds were saturated with the flavor and we did not want or need more. Mary-Lyn was still complaining loudly about the odor, so we regretfully threw the fruit over the balcony and into the drainage canal behind the apartment.

Then my newly married cousin kissed her husband and quickly backed away in horror. She said that David tasted just like the fruit smelled! Hmm, my husband and I thought smugly, it is a good thing that we both ate durian. Just as with garlic, having both partaken, we could not smell it on each other. We were sitting around the living room, catching up with family news when we realized that durian repeats badly. The first burp of what tasted like sewer gas was a rude surprise, and soon all three of us were belching distastefully. Having eaten the fruit apparently did not protect us from ourselves. Now we could smell and taste that durian scent, and there was no creamy texture or rich flavor to hide it. It was disgusting and continued far too long. We later learned that not everyone experiences this side effect, with perhaps only one in two suffering it, but all three of us did. At the time, it seemed clear that this was a standard result of eating durian.

Well, we thought, that was that. We had tried durian and were not impressed. But then we noticed durian-flavored ice cream for sale at the grocery store. Perhaps that would be better, perhaps it would not have the same side effects, and perhaps this time we would understand how people could be so enthusiastic about durian. The ice cream was delicious, since the richness of the ice cream strengthened that aspect of the durian flavor and muted the sewer-gas overtones. David and I were particularly greedy and each had a large serving, Ken had a smaller one, and Mary-Lyn once again declined. Again, however, we started burping a half hour or so after finishing. Regrettably the burps tasted just as bad as they had after the real durian.

A week later, during a visit to the Cameron highlands, my husband and I found durian-flavored hard candy for sale. Although the first two durian experiences had not been notable successes, how bad could candy be? It is sugar and fruit, and it is hard to go wrong with sugar and fruit. We bought a bag and eagerly sampled our treat. These sweets turned out to have what tasted like a sour molasses base with a durian overtone. The molasses flavor did not provide the creamy texture and flavor of the real fruit or the ice cream. Instead, the durian's natural-gas odor dominated the underlying bitter molasses taste. The candy was a great disappointment and our worst durian experience yet. And then came the crowning insult. The candies repeated, too, with that same sewer-gas effect! Three attempts to learn to love durian, three failures.

One redeeming feature of the candies, however, was that we were able to bring them home, so that we could share our durian experience with our friends. We were wickedly gleeful at the way people's faces screwed up with distaste; somehow their visible disgust justified our reaction. Unfortunately, once our friends were wise to us, we had a hard time giving away the remainder.

CONCLUSION

A fresh durian, unlike the candy version, has many flavors. A sample of some of the comparisons offered by others range from decayed onion, turpentine, garlic, limburger cheese, spicy resin (according to Otis Barrett as quoted in Walsh 1999 and Morton 1987:287), to Wallace's list of almond custard, cream cheese, onion sauce, and sherry wine (1856:435). Which flavors dominate the experience is probably the result of cultural training, training that also informs us which flavors are appreciated and which are repulsive. People who love durian find the aroma enticing (Fuller 2007; Sullivan 2007), probably the result of connecting the odor to the taste within. The reaction to both the taste and the smell of a durian will be the result of past personal experience and cultural training.

In addition, a truly fresh durian, one that is less than a day old, may offer a very different taste experience than one acquired in a city market, which may have been a number of days past perfection. Someday I hope to have the opportunity to try a fresh durian, which may offer more of the flavors I liked and less of the sewer-gas overtone. With practice I may be able to shrug off the durian-flavored burps as easily as I do the aftereffects of eating asparagus or garlic, or drinking coffee, all of which scent the body in one manner or another. I have not found the resultant odor a reason to not indulge in any of these foods, although some people in the United States abstain for just this reason.

I wonder if one of the reasons I did not immediately love durian is that it was always presented as a fruit, a classification that in the United States we reserve for sweet or sweet and tart fruits. The flavors of our fruits are acidic and refreshing rather than rich and complex, and we place non-sweet fruits, like tomatoes and avocados, in other food categories. This echoes Malaysians' classing durian as heating, while almost all other fruits and vegetables are considered cooling. Would my initial reaction have been more enthusiastic if I had not already formed a mental construct of durian as a fruit? What if I had thought of it as a new cousin to an avocado, which is similarly soft and oily? Would that have allowed me to concentrate on the more pleasing tastes within the wide range of durian flavors? I am disappointed with my reaction to this unique food. I know the value that Southeast Asians place on durian and badly want to be able to appreciate the fruit as much as they do. I continue to try durian when it is available but am honestly still mystified as to why it is so coveted. In the end, all I can say is that durian is an acquired taste, and I am still in the process of acquiring it.

REFERENCES

Banfield, Edmund James
    1911   *My Tropic Isle.* T. Fisher Unwin, London.

Brosius, J. Peter
    1999   The Western Penan of Borneo. In *The Cambridge Encyclopedia of Hunters and Gatherers,* ed. Richard B. Lee and Richard Daly, 312–316. Cambridge University Press, New York.

Corner, E.J.H.
    1976   *The Seeds of the Dicotyledons.* Cambridge University Press, New York.

De Ledesma, Charles, Mark Lewis, Richard Lim, Steven Martin, and Pauline Savage
    2006   *The Rough Guide to Malaysia, Singapore and Brunei.* Rough Guides, New York.

Dentan, Robert Knox
 1968   *The Semai: A Nonviolent People of Malaya*. Holt, Rinehart and Winston, New York.

Dunne, Niall
 2002   Durian: The Real Forbidden Fruit. *Plant and Garden News* 17:3 (Fall). http://www.bbg.org/gar2/topics/kitchen/2002fa_durian.html, accessed November 27, 2005.

Endicott, Kirk
 1999a   The Batak of Peninsular Malaysia. In *The Cambridge Encyclopedia of Hunters and Gatherers*, ed. Richard B. Lee and Richard Daly, 298–306. Cambridge University Press, New York.
 1999b   Introduction: Southeast Asia. In *The Cambridge Encyclopedia of Hunters and Gatherers*, ed. Richard B. Lee and Richard Daly, 275–283. Cambridge University Press, New York.

Eveland, Jennifer
 2005   *Frommer's Singapore and Malaysia*. Wiley Publishing, Hoboken, NJ.

Fuller, Thomas
 2007   Fans Sour on Sweeter Version of Asia's Smelliest Fruit. *New York Times* April 8, 2007. http://www.nytimes.com/2007/04/08/world/asia/08durian.html, accessed October 3, 2007.

Harris, Marvin
 1985   *The Sacred Cow and the Abominable Pig: Riddles of Food and Culture*. Simon and Schuster, New York.

Howell, Signe
 1984   *Society and Cosmos: Chewong of Peninsular Malaysia*. Oxford University Press, New York.

Keon, Michael
 1960   *The Durian Tree*. Simon and Schuster, New York.

Kostermans, A.J.G.H.
 1992   An Important Economical New *Duro* Species from Northern Sumatra. *Economic Botany* 46(3):338–340.

Laderman, Carol
 1981   Symbolic and Empirical Reality: A New Approach to the Analysis of Food Avoidances. *American Ethnologist* 8(3):468–493.
 1983   *Wives and Midwives: Childbirth and Nutrition in Rural Malaysia*. University of California Press, Berkeley.

Linehan, Fergus
 1996   *Under the Durian Tree*. Macmillan, London.

Manderson, Lenore
 1986   Food Classification and Restriction in Peninsular Malaysia: Nature, Culture, Hot and Cold? In *Shared Wealth and Symbol: Food, Culture, and*

Society in Oceana and Southeast Asia, ed. Lenore Manderson, 127–143. Cambridge University Press, New York.

McCarthy, John F.
2005   Between Adat and State: Institutional Arrangements on Sumatra's Forest Frontier. *Human Ecology* 33(1):57–82.

McKay, David A.
1980   Food, Illness, and Folk Medicine: Insights from Ulu Trengganu, West Malaysia. In *Food, Ecology and Culture: Readings in the Anthropology of Dietary Practices*, ed. J.R.K. Robson, 61–66. Gordon and Breach Science Publishers, New York.

Messer, Ellen
1984   Anthropological Perspectives on Diet. *Annual Review of Anthropology* 13:205–249.
1989   Methods for Determinants of Food Intake. In *Research Methods in Nutritional Anthropology*, ed. Gretel H. Pelto, Pertti J. Pelto, and Ellen Messer. United Nations University Press, Tokyo.

Mintz, Sidney W., and Christine M. DuBois
2002   The Anthropology of Food and Eating. *Annual Review of Anthropology* 31:99–119.

Morton, Julia F.
1987   Durian. In *Fruits of Warm Climates*, ed. C. F. Dowling, 287–291. New-CROP, Center for New Crops and Plant Products, Purdue University, West Lafayette, IN. http://www.hort.purdue.edu/newcrop/morton/durian_ars.html, accessed April 14, 2006.

Peluso, Nancy Lee
2003   Fruit Trees and Family Trees in an Anthropogenic Forest: Property Zones, Resource Access, and Environmental Change in Indonesia. In *Culture and the Question of Rights: Forests, Coasts, and Seas in Southeast Asia*, ed. Charles Zerner, 184–218. Duke University Press, Durham, NC.

Richmond, Simon, Damian Harper, Tom Parkinson, Charles Rawlings-Way, and Richard Watkins
2007   *Malaysia, Singapore and Brunei*. Lonely Planet Publications, Oakland, CA.

Rolnick, Harry
2003   Durian. In *Encyclopedia of Food and Culture*, Vol. 1: *Acceptance to Food Politics*, ed. Solomon H. Katz, 541–543. Scribner, New York.

Roseman, Marina
1998   Singers of the Landscape: Song, History, and Property Rights in the Malaysian Rain Forest. *American Anthropologist* 100(1):106–121.

Rozin, Paul, Jonathan Haidt, Clark McCauley, and Sumio Imada
1997   Disgust: Preadaptation and the Cultural Evolution of a Food-Based Emotion. In *Food Preferences and Taste: Continuity and Change*, ed. Helen MacBeth, 65–82. Berghahn Books, Providence, RI.

Schiefhövel, Wulf
 1997   Good Taste and Bad Taste: Preferences and Aversions as Biologic Prin-
         ciples. In *Food Preferences and Taste: Continuity and Change*, ed. Helen
         MacBeth, 55–64. Berghahn Books, Providence, RI.

Simoons, Frederick J.
 1994   *Eat Not This Flesh: Food Avoidances from Prehistory to the Present*, 2nd ed.
         University of Wisconsin Press, Madison.

Soegeng-Reksodihardjo, Wertit
 1962   The Species of *Durio* with Edible Fruits. *Economic Botany* 16(4):270–
         282.

Sokolov, Raymond
 1991   *Why We Eat What We Eat: How the Encounter between the New World
         and the Old Changes the Way Everyone on the Planet Eats.* Summit Books,
         New York.

Sullivan, Michael
 2007   Ooh That Smell: Designing a Stinkless Durian. National Public Radio
         Weekend Edition, May 12, 2007. http://www.npr.org/templates/story/
         story.php?storyId=10016534, accessed October 3, 2007.

Teo, Pau Lin
 2006   Durian King. *The Strait Times Stomp*. ST Foodies Club. Singapore. http://
         www.stomp.com.sg/stfoodiesclub/taste/03/index.html, accessed October
         21, 2007.

Van Der Sluys, Cornelia M.
 1999   The Jahai of Northern Peninsular Malaysia. In *The Cambridge Encyclopedia
         of Hunters and Gatherers*, ed. Richard B. Lee and Richard Daly, 307–311.
         Cambridge University Press, New York.

Veevers-Carter, W.
 1984   *Riches of the Rainforest: An Introduction to the Trees and Fruits of the Indo-
         nesian and Malaysian Rain Forests.* Oxford University Press, Singapore.

Wallace, Alfred Russel
 1856   On the Bamboo and Durian of Borneo. From a letter to Sir Jackson Hooker
         and printed in *Hooker's Journal of Botany*, vol. 8. http://www.wku.edu/
         ~smithch/wallace/S027.html, accessed October 3, 2007.

Walsh, Rob
 1999   The Fruit I Can't Get Past My Nose. *Natural History* (September) 108(7):
         76–78.

Wilson, Christine S.
 1975   Nutrition in Two Cultures: Mexican-American and Malay Ways with
         Food. In *Gastronomy: The Anthropology of Food and Food Habits*, ed. Mar-
         garet L. Arnott, 131–144. Mouton Publishers, Paris.

1980   Food Taboos of Childbirth: The Malay Example. In *Food, Ecology and Culture: Readings in the Anthropology of Dietary Practices*, ed. J.R.K. Robson, 67–74. Gordon and Breach Science Publishers, New York.

1986   Social and Nutritional Context of "Ethnic Foods": Malay Examples. In *Shared Wealth and Symbol: Food, Culture, and Society in Oceana and Southeast Asia*, ed. Lenore Manderson, 259–272. Cambridge University Press, New York.

Wynward, Noel

1939   *Durian: A Siamese Interlude.* Oxford University Press, London.

CHAPTER EIGHT

MSG and Sugar

Dilemmas and Tribulations of a "Native" Ethnographer

Lidia Marte

Biographical sketch. Lidia Marte obtained her Ph.D. in cultural anthropology in 2008 from the University of Texas at Austin, and is currently an adjunct instructor at St. Edwards University. Her research focuses primarily on place-memory, gender, and migration in the Afro-Hispanic Caribbean and its diasporas in the United States. Marte is also a photographer and visual artist who had been engaged with informal fieldwork in Latin America and the United States for decades before she became an anthropologist.

Even though I got initiated as an anthropologist by eating durian and spicy Mexican grasshoppers (my academic adviser offered these "exotic" foods to me in Austin, Texas, as we were discussing my future dissertation project), the most challenging eating events happened while doing fieldwork research on food, memory, and narratives of "home" among Dominican communities in New York City. My body is sensitive to MSG (monosodium glutamate, a potent food additive) and to refined sugars. When I eat MSG, my eyelids grow heavy, my eyes cross, and my muscles grow weak. I feel overwhelmingly sleepy, and I am completely unable to think clearly. Refined sugars also make me sleepy, although in a slightly different way. A brief vignette can illuminate my condition. I had just eaten a hearty and delicious meal at the home of one of the participants in my study. I left her place in the Bronx and walked to the train station. And there I was, again, cross-eyed, befuddled, and sleepy, having missed my stop for the second time on the Brooklyn bound "A" train. Limbs slightly numb, breaking into spontaneous laughter (dutifully ignored by the passengers), in my semi-stupor I fantasized; why hadn't I proposed to study community gardens in Austin, or food sharing among vegans, or even better, the etiquette of coconut consumption in the Dominican Republic?

Of course when my mind cleared a few hours later, I remembered perfectly why I was not studying something safe in Austin, a new "home" I found by chance while attending graduate school there. I was born and raised in the Dominican Republic, but I spent most of my adult life in New York City. As a visual artist, I used to consider myself a citizen of the world, struggling to transcend the social categories that conditioned my existence. But after the death of my mother in 1996, I felt the need to question my multiple experiences, my family history, and, especially, my recently discovered "ethnic" identity as an immigrant in the United States. Finding my visual arts and random critical readings insufficient tools for such a task, I embarked for Texas to enroll in a cultural anthropology program. I wanted to understand the practices and worldviews of a population that shaped my cultural history and my own place in the world. As a native speaker of Dominican Spanish, I am also in a good position to understand Dominican behaviors and ways of speaking in a way that might be more difficult for an outsider. My profound interest in Afro-Caribbean food practices and the lack of research done in such areas combined well with my commitment and desire to conduct ethnographic field research among Dominicans, but I had not factored my food sensitivities into the equation.

This chapter explores how I negotiated (as a Dominican American) the delicate dilemma of accepting/rejecting meals while researching food practices within my "own" communities, that is, social networks with whom I share not only a cultural history but of which I was part when I lived in New York City. Sharing my eating excursions will serve also as portal to question the challenges, benefits, and implications of ethnographic practices for "native" (or insider) anthropologists, especially for those engaged in food studies.

Two months into my dissertation fieldwork (once my brain started functioning again) I knew I had to reconsider my level of rapport and sincere engagement with my research collaborators. I had already realized shortly after I arrived in New York City that Dominicans today use both MSG and refined sugar in amounts that my body could not tolerate without consequences. I had long since forgotten this because, eating alone and with little variety, I had managed to change my diet, and it became possible for me to avoid MSG and refined sugars rather easily. Because of my strong reactions to these items, I probably would not survive the rest of fieldwork without some changes in my consumption of such substances, which are present in most Dominican food staple dishes.

The routine of fieldwork at seven Dominican households (located in Manhattan, Brooklyn, and the Bronx) was taking a severe toll on me. Sensitivities aside, I was always full (having accepted food everywhere I went, regardless of whether I had already eaten), nervous and slightly shaky from so much delicious sweet black coffee, with frequent mood swings preventing me from taking field notes, and with slight resentment and a desire to get the job done as fast as I could in order to escape to my refuge in Austin, Texas. Under the effects of brain fog, I forgot to be present and to pay attention to what was causing my discomfort. I forgot for almost two months my past ordeal and struggle to discover and eliminate my allergies, and I forgot that I had the experience and strategies to—literally and symbolically—reawaken myself to health again.

FIELDWORK RESEARCH IN AN URBAN JUNGLE

I went to New York City for a year in 2006 to do my dissertation fieldwork research on food, memory, and narratives of "home" among Dominican communities. My research focused on the food-centered migrant cultural histories of seven Dominican families, exploring the transformation of their gendered food practices, how they create and narrate new forms of communities, and how food practices and narrative memories help immigrant women create a sense of place and home in a society new to them.

Central to my methodological approach for this project was the tracing of food maps of each family (tracking how individuals navigate place through food relations), particularly through the perspectives of each household cook. This involved participant-observation and image-based documentations of both domestic and public food sites present in their daily food cycles. Home cooking with MSG was daily fare. Moreover, for some participants, Dominican restaurants were a daily part of their food paths, and such restaurant cooking is also loaded with MSG. I did not refrain from eating their cooking or from accompanying them to eat at such places, but after a while, I became careful in choosing which items on the restaurant menu were safe for me to consume through my familiarity with Dominican foods and through diverse delicate social negotiations.

Even though I was familiar with my field site and the Dominican population and was acquainted with most of the participant families (I knew these

8.1. Views of Dominican food ready to eat (*left*), and coffee greeting (*right*), in the Bronx, New York City. (PHOTOS BY LIDIA MARTE)

families through my visual arts and grassroots work with Latino organizations in New York City), this was my first fieldwork research as an ethnographer. During my three exploratory pilot projects from 2003 to 2005, my social interactions were more informal and I was perceived as a casual visitor who occasionally took some photos or asked questions about cooking. However, during a full year (with scant funding and the pressure to produce data for a dissertation) I became much more focused on exploring kitchens, households, and public foodscapes armed with all my media gadgets. In such garb, I explained to participants my timetable for the project and began performing my role as a researcher with specific purposes for my social interactions.

My challenges were associated with not only avoiding the allergy-causing substances during a long period of fieldwork but also the delicate etiquette and food manners of not refusing foods from my Dominican collaborators. One is always served food and coffee wherever one goes, and one is not supposed to refuse; to do so can be perceived as insulting. This is a particularly strong practice in working-class households. A visit to one of my women collaborators might proceed as follows. You are greeted effusively, and right away you are offered food. You refuse once ("no thank you, I have eaten"), and then the host asks for a second time ("how much do you want?"). You say, timidly, "*Bueno, está bien, un chin na' más*" ("Well, okay, only a little bit"), and then you can approach the person serving you to make sure that they do not fill up your plate, as is typically done.

Before or after meals (depending on the time of day) you are also offered coffee, espresso style, without milk, with a hint of fresh nutmeg and lots of sugar. A coffee offering is an implicit invitation to conversation, confidentiality, and more intimate talk, as if saying "let's gossip a bit." If you wish to establish rapport and to show you not only like the host but also wish to hear stories, then it is wise to accept. Now the aroma spreads, filling the kitchen, and memories of your previous associations with coffee arise (Figure 8.1).

The coffee is served and you are asked how many spoons of sugar you want. Usually a batch of coffee is prepared in exact quantities by calculating how many people will be served (in this case, two). Sugar is then put into each of the cups before they are offered to each person. You manage to say, in a low voice, "None, please," but it is too late; there are three spoonfuls in your cup already. *Yo no queria azucar* ("I didn't want sugar"), you murmur to yourself. The host hears something and, feeling sorry (*¡ay, perdón!*—"I am sorry!"), says, "I can make another batch." You, of course, do not wish to impose more work on her and refuse, drinking your delicious, strong sweet coffee and preparing, in my case, for an involuntary nap relatively soon.

EMERGENCE OF DOMINICAN FOOD SYSTEMS

The Caribbean region where the Dominican Republic is located (sharing Hispaniola Island with Haiti) is one of the most diverse areas of the planet. Dominican cuisine took shape within Caribbean regional food systems born out of the ecological and sociocultural colonial encounters of Europeans, indigenous societies, African groups, and Middle Eastern people, not to mention a wide variety of plants and animals (Ortiz-Cuadra 2006; Mintz 1997).

Indigenous populations on the island were decimated by disease and Spaniards within fifty years of occupation and slavery (roughly by 1560), but their agricultural practices and some food staples were quickly appropriated by the conquerors and their descendants as well as by enslaved Africans, whose descendants survive in Hispaniola until the present. Spaniards introduced a variety of new plants, such as bananas and large green plantains (both *Musa spp.*), coconut palm, mango and orange trees, along with Old World herbs and spices, and new animals, such as sheep, pigs, cows, and chickens. From Asia and Africa other items were introduced, such as sugarcane and coffee, which became key mono-crops in the slave plantation economy. Africans forced into migration as slaves probably managed to bring some yams, rice, spices, and seeds, as well as their agricultural expertise and culinary knowledge.

From this entanglement of local and global forces a shared "regional food system" (Ortiz-Cuadra 2006) developed in the Hispanic Caribbean from which an assortment of local foodways emerged. Some of the main Dominican staples such as *la bandera* ("the flag," made of rice, beans, and sometimes meat), *mangú* (boiled and mashed green plantains), and *sancocho* (meat and roots stew) carry ecological, linguistic, and cultural flavors as well as the varied meanings and power struggles of that mixture. It is from these geopolitical, economic,

8.2. View of environment in Dominican Republic (*left*); New York and Dominican Republic maps and produce (*center*); and view of New York City subway. (PHOTOS BY LIDIA MARTE)

and sociocultural negotiations in the Dominican Republic that Dominican immigrants' food practices were shaped in the past and continue to transform in New York City today (Figure 8.2).

For a variety of economic, socioeconomic, and political reasons, Dominican migration to the United States grew considerably from 1960 to 2000. Today the Dominican population in the Unites States is approaching more than 1 million (Torres-Saillant and Hernandez 1998) of which the majority lives in New York City. Like many other immigrant groups that preceded them, sectors of the Dominican population integrate and earn a living through food businesses such as grocery stores, restaurants, street-food vendors, and more recently supermarkets. Economic and cultural networks and consumer demands for such products come from Dominican customers who still prepare Dominican staples in their households and, more generally, from other Latino groups. In New York City approximately 43 percent of food businesses are owned by Latinos, and of these Latino-owned businesses, almost 50 percent are owned by Dominicans (Ricourt and Dana 2003).

Dominican shipping companies transfer not only remittances of money and letters but also boxes with food, which are exchanged by families and fictive kin between New York City and the Dominican Republic. These individual, group, and community food-centered survival networks extend also to the cultural meanings and uses of food in domestic and public spaces, becoming also sites of cultural memory and re-inventions of a sense of home with translocal implications.

DOMINICAN FOOD PRACTICES IN NEW YORK CITY

Dominican cooking practices among my collaborators were healthy; in the Dominican Republic, even in urban areas there are *colmados* (grocery stores) with plenty of fresh produce. In New York City, female cooks also go to great lengths to procure fresh ingredients but usually on a weekly rather than a daily basis; they explore which food stores in their neighborhoods offer the best produce, and if not available nearby, they travel by bus or train to another city borough. In the case of oregano, it was procured directly from the Dominican Republic, through friends or family, or else through Dominican specialty stores located only in Washington Heights. The cooks expressed explicitly in their food narratives how important fresh ingredients were to their Dominican flavors. Unlike the commonly held impression that Latino foodways are greasy and unhealthy, not all domestic cooks fry their foods or use lard. In fact, most of the participants used few greasy-fatty-fry methods, apart from adding small amounts of olive or corn oil to beans and using some of the fat already present when preparing meat dishes and soups. My collaborators emphasized this about their foods (contrasting them to the ones served in restaurants), which are clean and cooked well, with freshly chopped condiments and plenty of fresh salads. They use fresh or dried beans, not canned; they wash the long-grain rice and cook it in filtered water, adding a tiny bit of corn oil and salt when cooking it; and they wash and marinate their meats with plenty of lime, garlic, and cilantro (Figure 8.3).

I witnessed these seasonings firsthand as I documented food preparations, yet there was another oft-used ingredient, which was found in the chicken bouillon (or other powdered seasoning mixes of both "Latino" and "gringo" brands): MSG. While the dishes were simmering, they would add the bouillon or other powdered seasoning to the fresh condiments. Unknown to them, however, MSG was plentiful as an additive in such mixtures. For my research I was paying special attention to the preparations and meanings of three iconic Dominican staples: rice and beans, sancocho, and mangú; the first two dishes are seasoned with chicken bouillon or powdered seasoning.

The cooks also used refined white sugar for breakfast meals such as *café* (black espresso-style coffee), chocolate (hot chocolate), *majarete* (sweet maize-based hot soupy drink, similar to atole), and *avena* (hot oatmeal) and for *habichuela con dulce* (sweet beans cooked with cinnamon, cloves, and evaporated milk), a holiday dish prepared once a year exclusively for Semana Santa (Easter) in the Dominican Republic (which now in New York City is sold by street vendors year-round). As I conversed with cooks and during oral history recordings I asked them to explain why they used certain ingredients. Most of them did not mention what they call *sopita* (bouillon), but I asked about it as subtly as

8.3. Dominican woman preparing fresh seasoning in Brooklyn, New York City.
(PHOTO BY LIDIA MARTE)

possible. Some told me that their foods would not taste the same without the chicken bouillon or that they use it instead of salt.

Adding these kinds of seasoning to beans, stews, and meat preparations was not a new Dominican practice acquired in New York City. Brands such as Knorr and Lipton were introduced in the Dominican Republic (and in much of Latin America and the Third World), along with cereal brands, in the 1960s and 1970s as the first supermarkets selling processed foods were introduced and through food relief shipments. A wide assortment of commercial brands of processed foods became available to working-class populations, creating entire regions of new consumers. Before this phenomenon, most households used separate herbs and spices plus raw sea salt to cook their main meals. Increasingly, fresh foods were replaced by canned products (at a faster rate in urban areas) and by fast and convenient processed products to season beans, stews, fish, and meat dishes, maybe partly due to advertising and changing "labor-time patterns" (Mintz 1985). This ubiquitous practice, however, did not take hold in all rural areas or in all kitchens, since these items were initially expensive luxury products. Refined sugar (fine-ground white) was also a relatively recent development since the 1950s in the Dominican Republic. Before the widespread development of sugarcane refineries, raw and brown sugar, molasses, and honey were widely used by most of the population; white sugar was also the cheapest.

MSG AND SUGAR

I cannot discuss at length here the pharmacology of MSG and its disputed effects. Current research on this issue is both problematic and controversial (Geha et al. 2000a, 2000b). I only offer some pointers to clarify the nature of my sensitivity to these substances and how they affected me during fieldwork. MSG is the industrial flavor enhancer number D621. Free glutamate has many natural occurrences (including in our bodies), but the industrial varieties are obtained by fermentation from sugars and through bacterial secretions. The debate about MSG in clinical studies, Food and Drug Administration regulations, and the media is complicated and it has not yielded any general agreement about MSG's effects on health. More updated studies are needed about its effects and the experiences of people who are seriously affected by it, although the politics of its production and profit also merit examination.

MSG is a kind of "meaty" flavor to which humans seem to become quickly addicted. It has been classified as the fifth taste, or umami (de Araujo et al. 2003; Xiaodong et al. 2002). Industrial free glutamate (MSG) appears in a wide range of fast food and processed foods, including table-salt mixtures; seasoning mixtures; vegetable, chicken, and beef bouillon; potato chips, the sauce of ramen noodles, other dried-soup packages, and canned soups. It is sometimes hidden under the generic name of "spices," "natural spices," or another term buried in a disconcertingly long list of other suspicious ingredients. Beside Latino (also called "Hispanic" or "Spanish") restaurants, Chinese, Thai, and Japanese restaurants in New York City use it widely, as well as many street food vendors and small eateries. Few cuisines, especially restaurant cuisines, do not use some form of free industrial glutamate in one of its myriad forms, even if they claim that they use no MSG.

The addictive qualities of both MSG and highly refined sugars make them hard to judge without emotional connotations. Since not everyone is affected the same way (effects range from a mild to a strong sedative effect, among other things), the effects of MSG may be dismissed or may pass for digestion-related lethargy ("I ate too much; I need a nap"). Among some of the side effects that have been documented are obesity, alteration of cholesterol levels, elevated blood sugar, depression, and neuro-toxicity (Nemeroff 1981; Olney 1984). In my experience the last three effects were the most visible and disconcerting.

As with MSG, highly refined sugars are a drug-food that became widely used relatively recently with the growth of the food-processing industries.

Refined sugars appear in countless items in supermarket shelves, in a variety of hidden forms (refined sugarcane, high fructose corn syrup, etc.)—even in salty items such as canned soups. In my field site it was added in great quantities to coffee, desserts such as cakes and pastries, breakfast preparations such as hot oatmeal, majarete, hot chocolate, and other beverages.

I remember that it was only after my family emigrated to Puerto Rico in the 1980s that my mother could afford to buy processed foods, including, unfortunately for me, plenty of chicken bouillon, Adobo Goya seasoning, and Lipton soups. A scene comes to mind of me around fourteen years old, wearing a yellow dress and lying on a brown sofa in a lethargic paralysis, literally knocked out for a period of hours and brain-fogged for a whole day. In Puerto Rico, my mother's beans, which I had adored in the Dominican Republic, left me feeling sleepy, unable to do my homework or concentrate most of the day (and feeling guilty, thinking I was just lazy). I remember also feeling sleepy and weak after ingesting refined sugars. These effects were scarier to me before I knew what was causing them. Now, if I happen to consume a dish with MSG or sugar, I know what may happen and wait patiently or find a way to reduce the effects.

Before I even considered becoming an anthropologist, I had undergone many struggles with health issues while living in New York City. I was eating a lot of take-out Chinese food, pizza, and cheap packaged foods, such as ramen noodle soups. I also occasionally visited my sisters, who were living in the Bronx and Brooklyn, where I enjoyed eating their delicious Dominican foods. It took me many years to realize that MSG and sugar were affecting me drastically in health and general well-being (i.e., depression). At one point I thought I had chronic fatigue syndrome. After no doctor could diagnose my condition and none were able to help me (and because I had no health insurance), I decided to take my health into my own hands.

I began researching my symptoms and alternative healing systems. I carefully recorded my food intakes and physical reactions in a food journal. I proceeded to eliminate ingredients and processed food items one by one as I noticed their effect on my overall energy levels, digestion, and mood swings. My mind regurgitated memories of times and contexts of earlier periods of lethargy, stretching back to my depressive moods since early adolescence, and at a certain point it suddenly became clear to me: MSG and refined sugar were the culprits. Once I realized the unmistakable effect of these substances, I needed to break my addiction to these ingredients. To ease my withdrawal, I decided to eliminate one processed or street food at a time, starting with Chinese food, then ramen noodles, and finally any canned products. The pizza? Well, it stayed, but I had to ration it to once a week or less. I introduced daily intakes of vitamin C and one multivitamin (for the first time in my life) and substituted copious amounts of unsweetened green tea for the coffee with sugar I had been drinking. Even after only half of these changes became a regular routine, I felt awake for the first time in decades. I began to read all labels on food packaging. Unfortunately, as most of us now know, not all ingredients are listed clearly, and deceitful labeling can refer to MSG as "spices" or "natural flavor" and refined sugars as "high fructose corn syrup." It took me awhile to become a keen expert at spotting these disguised ingredients, and sometimes I did not find out they were present until after I had consumed them.

With the help of my sisters, I learned how to cook my beans and soups at home, omitting the chicken bouillon. In time I cleaned my kitchen of all canned and processed foods. I learned to eat out only on rare occasions, choosing carefully from the menu. Not consuming these substances as part of a regular diet had a tremendous effect on my energy levels and sense of well-being, and even if later by accident or chance I occasionally ate something containing MSG or indulged on some ice cream, my body was better able to recover.

SURVIVING THE FIELD: TO CONFESS OR NOT TO CONFESS

Fast forwarding to my fieldwork, I had to consider carefully if I should speak to my collaborators about what was happening. If I did, what might be the reactions and the consequences? In Dominican food interactions, especially if one is a guest (which I clearly was, in spite of my "insider" status, because I did not live in New York City anymore), one is not supposed to reject food; it is considered offensive and impolite and can be interpreted in a number of negative ways. Some may interpret the refusal to share foods as a suspicion on my part concerning the taste (the flavor of each person's beans, for example, has implications for their personal reputation as cooks) or the cleanliness of their cooking. Even more important, rejecting items like coffee or the elaborated *sancocho* may be interpreted as a refusal to engage in more intimate conversations. A high price to pay, indeed.

As often happens during fieldwork, things seem to work themselves out by chance. I already had agreements with the five families that I needed for my study, but because of scheduling conflicts, some days I made appointments that were not kept and I was left with no household to visit. Thus, I began spending more time with two of my older sisters (who also live in the city) on days when I could not work with the other families. It took me a few weeks to realize that my sisters were not only giving me their family love but, with patience and humor, answering my questions, serving me their delicious foods, and reminiscing with me about their memories of Dominican Republic.

I accompanied them to grocery stores, supermarkets, and restaurants and helped them with their jobs and housework. I soon realized that they were not only Dominican but first-generation working-class migrant women that still cooked the main staples of their home country. It seemed dishonest and unfair not to consider the home spaces and life histories of my sisters as another intersecting field site. They also seemed eager and excited to share in my research (since I have seemed to them odd and un-Dominican for most of my life). Their food practices also provided contrast data and a rich backup source when the other families were not available.

In these more intimate spaces that I shared with my sisters, I could consider expressing my allergy concerns. I, however, was still reluctant to interfere with anyone's cooking practices. The ethical dilemma for me was that it felt inappropriate to interfere with the way people season their foods, especially since I was an ethnographer trying to understand their perspectives and practices, not trying to change them. So I could not refuse foods. My sister F. understood and accepted my reactions and refrained from using chicken bouillon when I visited her in the Bronx. But she refused to believe that her Adobo seasoning had MSG (the jar listed onion, garlic, cilantro, and "other spices") or even that MSG could be an allergen. One day in Brooklyn, my sister R. noticed my lamentable state after one of her meals. She kept asking, and I finally confessed there were some ingredients in the food that affected me. We talked about it; she was at first skeptical, as any good Dominican would be, which I understood. I asked her to observe how she felt next time we ate beans, meat, or soup, particularly to note how her body and muscles felt. I already had noticed how a siesta was an invariant result of her lunch meals and Sunday sancochos (Figure 8.4).

In a week, a welcome episode helped R. realize the power of MSG through one of her delicious Sunday sancochos, in which she did not use chicken bouillon but instead added two spoonfuls of the Adobo brand "Latino" powdered seasoning mix. Those two spoonfuls forced me to change my plans to work with another family that day, and I could not even concentrate on my field notes. R. was not able to do her laundry or even watch her telenovela on TV. Her husband, laughing at what he thought were women's imaginary reactions, refused to recognize any effects (even after R. noticed her own reactions and decided to rid her cooking of such seasonings), in spite of him being a diabetic, a condition that MSG and sugar tend to aggravate. These ingredients, as I well remember, are quite addictive, so R.'s husband (the diabetic) would rush to the supermarket to get chicken bouillon to add to his food, asking my sister (about me), "Is she coming to visit today?" As R. began noticing a difference in the way she felt after eating, she asked me to help her get rid of unnecessary processed foods in her kitchen that contained MSG and refined sugars. We did a major cleanup and filled a garbage can (Figure 8.5).

R. told me that she thought she needed the chicken bouillon even for cooking chicken, as she laughed at how illogical that sounded. She had been

8.4. View of R.'s *sancocho* prepared in Brooklyn, New York City. (PHOTO BY LIDIA MARTE)

influenced by the advertising industry, as have many others, to be an uncritical, passive, and good consumer. She was still worried that eliminating this product would affect the taste of her foods, yet to our amazement (and to my considerable relief), her beans and stews tasted as delicious as before, or even more so since we were both awake to comment on the taste and to continue our day's routines. This episode gave me at least one "safe" household. My sister F. did not change her seasonings; she was under a lot of stress about her housing situation so I did not attempt any further discussion about MSG. I kept eating her foods, in small quantities, and her elimination of chicken bouillon in her beans whenever I visited reduced considerably the detrimental effects of the small amount of Adobo she used.

I did not feel it was appropriate to mention my allergic reactions to MSG and refined sugar to the other five families unless they expressed a curiosity and interest in finding out more. Therefore, I decided that I would not refuse foods, but I would find ways to diminish my exposure to the offending substances. Because these Dominican foods not only were important for my study but also had a sacred association for me and my collaborators (in addition to being really delicious), I continued eating them and just paid attention my reactions. Since I was tracing the food paths that each cook followed in the city, many

8.5. MSG clean-up day in R.'s kitchen, Brooklyn, New York City. (PHOTOS BY LIDIA MARTE)

times I had to eat at Dominican restaurants that they visited frequently in their neighborhoods. I continued accompanying them to these establishments, but I ordered tubers, white rice, or other foods unlikely to contain MSG or sugar.

I drank my sweet coffee and consumed with glee their delicious beans and stews, but I told them that I had just eaten or took only a small portion. This way, when I needed to film, take photographs, record audio narratives during food preparations, or draw maps with them, my brain was clear. I was able to focus the camera, and my hands were not shaky. On my way to the train after visiting one of these families, I would stop at a grocery store to buy a cup of hot water and put a strong black or green tea bag in it with powdered Vitamin C, before continuing my journey. This decreased the risk of missing my subway stops because of drowsiness or of being unable to move before the subway train doors closed.

Between meetings, I reinforced my immune system with herbal tinctures. Additionally, I took one day off a week, camping at the "MSG free zone" at my sister R.'s apartment in Brooklyn. By these varied means, I was able to continue to ride the trains, maintain my appreciation of their cooking, survive the rest of fieldwork, and more important regain a renewed passion and excitement for the work I was doing.

EATING IN THE FIELD AND THE PREDICAMENTS OF NATIVE ETHNOGRAPHY

After I began to manage my allergies, I did not have major obstacles finishing my research, although it was intense and demanding as people have hectic lives in New York City, especially working-class individuals engaged in constant struggles for basic survival. I managed to do my "deep hang-out" for as long as it was possible, without intruding too much on people's privacy, unless they invited me to shadow them (in such cases I would stay in particular homes sometimes for a few days). Most routines—ours and that of our collaborators—get rearranged during the fieldwork process; plans usually do not stick for long. The field is alive with countless interactions, and we are all surviving in that messy soup of the everyday.

I did not insist on clarifying the MSG issue with my Dominican collaborators during fieldwork because it could have changed the whole dynamic of our interactions, and I could not risk that ethically, ethnographically, or personally. (I have since shared my concerns with three of the women, since I wish to continue working with them.) In fact, I did not ask any of them to remove anything, nor did I ever refuse foods. In the case of my sister R., I confessed my condition because she openly asked me and seemed concerned. She then volunteered to see how her cooking tasted without chicken bouillon or, as she calls them, *polvitos* (small powdered seasoning packets). She was also curious as to how she would feel after eating. It would have been hypocritical not to accept her agency in deciding if she wanted to make changes.

My ethical considerations were not the result of an illusion of "objectivity" and the role of detached observer (elements of critique that my research approach addresses) or because I was unaware that our mere presence affects the social dynamics in anything we do. (I knew this already through my work as a photojournalist and with grassroots community organizations.) I was concerned about what right I had to question their choices, especially if they did not think MSG had any ill effects on them. Moreover, questioning their seasoning choices could have been perceived as a power gesture by an educated outsider. It could have also undermined the trust they had in my appreciation for the importance of their creative cooking labor and, in consequence, draw into question their personal worth in my eyes.

One of the most troubling discoveries through this experience for me was that participants in my study (and most other Dominicans that I have casually asked about MSG) ignored the name MSG and its potential effects and even dismissed their own reactions after eating foods that contained it. What bothered me was not necessarily that they could have unhealthy personal and collective habits but rather the lack of information available to them about processed food items that might have allowed them to consider the consequences of their choices. It is notable that the media have sometimes provided misinformation and even outright lies through advertising (a good example is the investigation and public exposé of the tobacco industry and the repercussions this had on consumer patterns of smoking).

People have a right to make choices, yet if they are unaware of or ignore the effects of their choices, how freely are they making such choices? The food politics that allows some to profit from people's consumption of products that might put their health at risk seems to me ethically wrong. There is a need for studies that question the spatial-racialized politics of food availability, since most processed food items are consumed by marginalized populations (who seem to be also specific targets of these products' advertising campaigns) living in particular urban sectors whose choice of foods are constrained by what is offered—usually at higher prices—in their local supermarkets.

An open intervention in my collaborators' cooking practices would have meant a whole debate, reeducation, and discussion about MSG and the evidence for its effects and would have become another project, one that I am now seriously considering doing in the future. It seems ethically wrong not to share this information, because it may offer some relief for someone in those families (especially the children) suffering MSG and refined-sugar allergies. Such a project will require serious consideration about how to proceed, and it may move my assorted ethnographic methods into more explicitly feminist action research.

I learned important lessons through these episodes, such as that as an ethnographer, I was willing to make sacrifices for my research. I also realized that, regardless of my cultural history as a Dominican, I was indeed an outsider. And, finally, I learned that I was still allergic to MSG and refined sugars. The design of my dissertation research (which took me years to clarify and find the most appropriate tools and approaches) and the field-guide document I created to bring with me took into consideration not only the balancing acts of native anthropology but also the inflections and politics of feminist ethnography. I paid attention to ethical, methodological, and theoretical issues that were important in the way I practice ethnography with my commitment to collaborative and critical research. However, even though it was in the back of my mind, I did not give much consideration in my design to my personal health—and to the potential tensions and ethical issues it might provoke—until I realized how it was affecting me during fieldwork in the performance of my work.

The politics, poetics, and ethics of eating in the field for native ethnographers have many ramifications, but they reside specifically in the ethical dilemmas of people's rights to information about their food habits, the political negotiations of social interactions with our collaborators in acceptance and respect of their practices, and the paradoxes of appreciating and wanting to inscribe in our studies their culturally specific worldviews, regardless of whether we agree with their ideologies and practices. Being an "insider" researcher has tremendous advantages but also puts in evidence our privileged positions as scholars, even when (as in my case) one may belong to the same class, race, and gender as our collaborators.

Concepts such as "strange" and "familiar" are filters we use to delineate not only the boundaries that preexist but also those that are created on the ground through interactions. Assuming that our shared history, language, and cultural understanding with participants in our research make us instant "natives" is a naïve and uncritical posture that may create social tensions. It can also blind us to significant differences and meaningful contradictions that exist not only between "ordinary" people and scholars but also among networks and individuals within the same "ethnic" group with whom we are working. Being mindful that our conceptual tools are representational filters and not actual constitutive elements of social phenomena and that the "field" is an extended shifting map of relations is surely more productive than assuming dichotomies.

To negotiate field engagements and the implications of this kind of insider ethnographic practice, a researcher needs to explore and define (preferably before long-term social interactions begin) their own cultural specificity and situated personal history in relation to the communities they will be working with, placing emphasis on potential issues that may bring friction and also questioning the familiarities that may blind us. This self-calibration is a good recommendation for all ethnographers, but for insider anthropologists, just like refusing familiar foods, there may not be a choice. Remembering the writings of the anthropologist Renato Rosaldo (who lost his wife while doing fieldwork), I realized the implications of fieldwork at a deeper level, confirming that the boundaries of the "field" that we draw can be illusory (Rosaldo 1984; see also Abarca 2006; Gupta and Ferguson 1997) yet at times concrete, delicate, and problematic, especially for "native" ethnographers (Kondo 1990; Narayan 1993; Visweswaran 1994).

For me the field did not begin or end with that year in New York City, but I have regained (from a different perspective) a stronger connection to working-class Dominican communities. These new common grounds were generated by overcoming my challenges while eating in the field and through the gift of time and new friendships that my research collaborators nurtured through their foods and memories, and even through the encounter of our differences.

REFERENCES

Abarca, Meredith E.
  2006   *Voices in the Kitchen: Views of Food and the World from Working-Class Mexican and Mexican-American Women.* Texas A&M University Press, College Station, TX.

De Araujo, I.E.T., M. L. Kringelbach, E. T. Rolls, and P. Hobden
    2003   Representation of Umami Taste in the Human Brain. *Journal of Neurophysiology* 90:313–319.

Geha, Raif S., Alexa Beiser, Clement Ren, Roy Patterson, Paul A. Greenberger, Leslie
    C. Grammer, Anne M. Ditto, Kathleen E. Harris, Martha A. Shaughnessy, Paul
    R. Yarnold, Jonathan Corren, and Andrew Saxon
    2000a   Multicenter, Double-Blind, Placebo-Controlled, Multiple-Challenge Evaluation of Reported Reactions to Monosodium Glutamate. *Journal of Allergy and Clinical Immunology* 106:973–980.
    2000b   Review of Alleged Reaction to Monosodium Glutamate and Outcome of a Multicenter Double-Blind Placebo-Controlled Study. *Journal of Nutrition* 130(45):S1058–S1062.

Gupta, Akhil, and James Ferguson
    1997   *Anthropological Locations: Boundaries and Grounds of a Field Science*. University of California Press, Berkeley.

Kondo, Dorinne K.
    1990   *Crafting Selves: Power, Gender, and Discourses of Identity in a Japanese Workplace*. University of Chicago Press, Chicago.

Mintz, Sidney W.
    1995   *Sweetness and Power: The Place of Sugar in Modern History*. Viking, New York.
    1997   Time, Sugar and Sweetness. In *Food and Culture: A Reader*, ed. Carole Counihan and Penny Van Esterik, 357–369. Routledge, New York.

Narayan, Kirin
    1993   How Native Is a "Native" Anthropologist? *American Anthropologist* 3(2): 95.

Nemeroff, Charles B.
    1981   Monosodium Glutamate-Induced Neurotoxicity: Review of the Literature and Call for Further Research. In *Nutrition and Behavior*, ed. Sanford A. Miller, 177–211. Franklin Institute Press, Philadelphia.

Olney, John W.
    1984   Excitotoxic Food Additives: Relevance of Animal Studies to Human Safety. *Neurobehavioral Toxicology and Teratology* 6(6):455–462.

Ortiz-Cuadra, Cruz Miguel
    2006   *Puerto Rico en la Olla, ¿somos aún lo que comimos?* Doce Calles, Spain.

Ricourt, Milagros, and Ruby Danta
    2003   *Hispanas de Queens: Latino Panethnicity in a New York City Neighborhood*. Cornell University Press, Ithaca, NY.

Rosaldo, Renato
    1984   Grief and a Headhunter's Rage. In *Text, Play, and Story: The Construction and Reconstruction of Self and Society*, ed. E. Bruner, 178–195. Waveland Press, Prospect Heights, IL.

Torres-Saillant, Silvio, and Ramona Hernandez

    1998   *The Dominican Americans*. Greenwood Press, Westport, CT.

Visweswaran, Kamala

    1994   *Fictions of Feminist Ethnography*. University of Minnesota Press, Minneapolis.

Xiaodong, Li, L. Staszewski, Hong Xu, K. Durick, M. Zoller, and Elliot Adler

    2002   Human Receptors for Sweet and Umami Taste. *Proceeding of the National Academy of Science* 99:4692–4696.

Table Manners and Other Rules to Eat By

CHAPTER NINE

Eating Incorrectly in Japan

James J. Aimers

Biographical sketch. James Aimers grew up in Toronto and he completed his B.A. and M.A. at Trent University in Peterborough, Ontario. He obtained his Ph.D. in Maya archaeology at Tulane University (New Orleans) in 2002 and has taught at Southern Illinois University, Miami University (Ohio), and the Institute of Archaeology at University College London. In 2008, he accepted a permanent position in anthropology at SUNY Geneseo.

[E]ach man calls barbarism whatever is not his own practice . . . for we have no other criterion of reason than the example of idea of the opinions and customs of the country we live in.

MONTAIGNE (1978, IN GEERTZ 1984:264–265)

In 1989 I finished my undergraduate degree in anthropology and was accepted to the Japan Exchange Teaching (JET) program, a cultural exchange program sponsored by the Japanese Ministry of Education that brought people under thirty-five years of age from eight countries to Japan to assist in language instruction in public schools. For a twenty-three year old with little experience outside of Canada and no teaching experience or knowledge of the Japanese language, this was the ultimate in cultural immersion. In August 1989 I found myself in the historic city of Kyoto, working as the only non-Japanese person in a large high school and living on the grounds of a Buddhist temple.

I was prepared for the difficulties posed by not speaking or reading Japanese, but I was somewhat startled by the number of serious issues that emerged regarding food. Language and food—things we take for granted every day—suddenly became stress-inducing, time-consuming quagmires. Try grocery shopping without reading labels sometime. Imagine my consternation after biting into a peanut butter and lard sandwich (impossible to tell lard from butter without being able to read . . . or ask). I cannot recall how many time I bought a delicious-looking chocolate pastry to find the "chocolate" was azuki bean paste. The Japanese love the stuff. I do not.

Fortunately, I quickly made some wonderful friends who were warm, fun, and unfailingly helpful. One of these friends I'll call Mr. Sato. Mr. Sato was a physical education teacher and an energetic, funny, outgoing man. He had visited the United States and Europe and was one of the few Japanese friends I made who seemed to have a real sense of the strengths and weaknesses of those places without either idealizing or demonizing them.

While he was a man with a real curiosity about the world, he was also fiercely proud of Japan, its history, and its culture. He loved to show me and my friend Mike (also a Canadian) the rough and tumble world of Japan, the small bars and working-class restaurants of the back streets of port cities like Kobe and Osaka. These are places I might never have seen without Mr. Sato, and they added depth—and plenty of fun—to my experience there.

In one of these places Mike and I tried eating raw intestine. Early on in Japan we had both resolved, in the spirit of anthropological relativism, to eat whatever was offered in Japan, no matter how horrifying. That night we reached a classic Japanese compromise and barbecued the intestine. Mr. Sato liked it raw and found it amusing when we begged him to let us cook it.

THE INCIDENT

On this same night occurred one of the most awkward incidents of my entire stay in Japan. Mike and I were happy to let the fluent Mr. Sato order the food while we focused on the delicious Japanese beer. Another policy I had adopted when eating was not to ask what a food was before I tried it, but we had just eaten intestine and I could see that the mischievous Mr. Sato was up to something, so I asked.

One of the questions Japanese people often asked me was, "Do you like Japanese food?" The frequency of this question, I think, draws attention to the fact that although the Japanese are proud of their cuisine, they are also aware that is distinctive, and thus it is a significant way they distinguish their culture from that of others. I always enthusiastically (and honestly) replied yes. Years later, when I have a choice, I will inevitably choose a Japanese restaurant over any other type. But knowing that North Americans often have what they considered to be odd food preferences, people in Japan also frequently asked if there were foods I would *not* eat. Mr. Sato had certainly been through this with both Mike and me and he knew that I would not eat whale. It was, in fact, the only food that I had ever specifically named. I never even mentioned *natto*, a fermented soy bean that, to my palette, had the texture and appeal of mucus. I would eat natto (sparingly, and with carefully concealed horror) if it was offered, but not whale, and I had said so.

So when Mr. Sato replied that he had ordered whale, I was flabbergasted. I said something like "Mr. Sato, you know I'm opposed to killing and eating whales," to which he replied along the lines of "This is Japanese culture. You said you want to learn Japanese culture so you should eat whale like we do." I replied that whale was endangered and therefore should no longer be eaten. He asked what was the difference between killing a whale and killing a mosquito (a very Buddhist question, by the way). I said "quantity." From there it went downhill and the details are foggier, but the end result was the following statement by me: "Our friendship is suspended until that whale is off the table."

This put Mike, who worked with Mr. Sato, in an awkward situation. Mike tried to talk our way out of it through humor and diversion, but there were several endless minutes of stony silence from me. Finally, Mr. Sato gave in and the whale was removed from the table. The conversation slowly resumed and the night ended normally . . . at least as far as I remember given the quantity of beer involved.

RELATIVISM IN ANTHROPOLOGY AND IN LIFE

I have thought about this incident often in the ensuing years because it was such a challenge to my idea of cultural relativism. Relativism in anthropology is a methodological position through which we try to suspend cultural bias by interpreting beliefs and actions in their specific cultural context. Cultural relativism was first promoted by Boas and his students, who were attempting to avoid ethnocentrism: the application of one's own cultural standards in value judgments about the behavior and beliefs of others.

For me and many of my Western friends in Japan, it was practically axiomatic that one should do what the Japanese do and eat what the Japanese eat. Every oddly textured, unpleasant food I ate in Japan became a small anthropological triumph when a Japanese person commented approvingly. These everyday events were important ways for me to establish my identity in Japan.

Many of the comments I got about my eating habits led me to believe that I was gaining trust and approval and that one day I might actually "fit in." When so much of my daily life was filled with stress related to not being able to do simple things (like read a bus schedule or buy a stamp). this openness to food quickly became an important part of my persona in Japan.

I had refused to eat whale because I was aware of an international ban on whaling established by the International Whaling Commission (IWC) in 1982. The IWC was formed in 1948 to help preserve whale stocks and thus maintain the whaling industry. In subsequent decades, however, as more non-whaling states joined (Day 1987) and the global environmental movement gained momentum, the IWC's focus shifted toward conservation of whales (Hirata 2004:184). The IWC's ban of whaling in 1982 was meant to be a five-year moratorium so that whale stocks could be examined and the issue recon-sidered in 1990. However, that review did not occur and the ban has held ever since, a decision the Japanese government questions.

My discussion here is not intended to resolve the Japanese whaling issue, which one of the reviewers of this volume called "one of most horribly vexed and contentious issues in world politics." There are constant new developments in the controversy and as an archaeologist involved these days primarily in the study of ancient Maya ceramics, I am simply not qualified to offer reliable con-clusions about what is true and what is not true or who is right and who is wrong in a debate rife with emotion and exaggeration on nearly every front. My goal is to provide a basic background to the complexities of the debate and my personal reflections on it when I lived in Japan and since.

WHY DO THE JAPANESE STILL EAT WHALE?

In the spring of 2005 the Australian newspaper *The Age* reported that whale was still on the menu in Japan and was being promoted as a healthy food for children at 280 schools (Cameron 2005). Why is there this insistence on eating whale when it is so bad for the Japanese image abroad? Kalland and Moeran (1992) argue that whaling contributes little to the Japanese economy (the industry employs only a few hundred people) and has been a blot on Japan's international reputation. Questions have also been raised about just how healthy whale is, given high levels of substances like mercury and PCBs in samples (Alcock 2002).

The Japanese have claimed for some time that the whale they eat is simply a by-product of scientific study of whales. The World Wildlife Fund suggests that whale diet and health can be studied through skin samples and biopsy darts without killing them (see Lambertsen 1987), but the Japanese counter that they do more than 100 tests that in sum require the whales to be killed, and even the IWC notes a lack of consensus on lethal versus nonlethal methods (Hogarth 2007; see also Morell 2007). In any case, since 1987 about 600 whales (reports vary) have been caught each year in the Southern Ocean and North Pacific. This does seem to be a larger sample than can be justified scientifically. The fact that the meat is then sold and eaten suggests that this is at least in part a commercial enterprise, an argument made persuasively—and emotionally—by Greenpeace on its Web site. The Japanese government claims that selling the meat to private processors simply covers its scientific expenses (Strieker 2001).

Another important strand in this debate is DNA evidence from Japanese supermarkets that showed that meat from some endangered species of whale was making its way into the Japanese diet, despite claims by the Japanese that they focus on non-endangered species (Baker et al. 2000; Dalebout et al. 2002). The Japanese claim to hunt only minke, Bryde's, sperm, and sei whales (CBS News 2002) but the DNA evidence makes this claim questionable. Baker and colleagues found evidence of "eight species of baleen whales, as well as sperm whales, beaked whales, killer whales, dolphins, porpoises, domestic sheep, and horses, among nearly seven hundred 'whale' products purchased in Japanese markets from 1993 to 1999" (2000:1695).

One explanation, the one that Mr. Sato offered, is that the consumption of whale is a long cultural tradition. The earliest known reference to whale consumption in Japan is in one of the earliest Japanese books, written somewhere between the seventh and tenth centuries (Chamberlain 1981 [1919]), and there are frequent accounts of Japanese whaling by at least the seventeenth century. However, many reports note that whale was only widely consumed in the hungry decade following World War II, when modern ships and harpoon guns became available (Kirby 2005). Some historians have argued that the Japanese in fact have a traditional aversion to eating whales as they were considered divine (Hirata 2004:190), and even today, many shrines, local festivals, and religious rituals focus on the whale. In an interview with *The New York Times*, a man dining at a whale restaurant demonstrated that this idea is still alive: "We may eat the whale, but we also revere it. . . . How can a total stranger tell us not to hunt whales without knowing how much this meat means to us?" (Sims 2000:A1). Nevertheless, whale meat is probably not a popular food in Japan for reasons to do more with taste than politics or religion. I have read and heard that the meat has a pungent flavor that generally requires heavy ginger seasoning or other techniques to mask its taste. It is also very expensive, about 50 percent more than beef, which is already expensive in Japan. Although its price has been falling since 1999, demand for whale meat is still weak (Faiola 2005).

Although the motivations for the consumption of whale in Japan are not entirely clear, many Japanese find our refusal to eat whale irrational. Perhaps it is. Most of us choose to eat foods that have harmful impacts at least occasionally. Cattle ranching and soya production for beef are devastating the Amazon forests at a breathtaking rate. For the sake of the planet, all of us should stop eating beef since no matter where it is produced, it requires huge energy inputs for relatively little caloric value.

Furthermore, Japanese whaling advocates argue that they are not likely to hunt the whales to extinction given the amounts they catch, the size of the populations from which they hunt (minke whales are no longer endangered), and the fact that whale meat is still not that popular in Japan despite aggressive attempts to promote its consumption. Kalland and Moeran (1992) take the controversial position that we can now seriously question the argument that all whales are endangered. They believe that some whaling opponents have tacitly acknowledged this by shifting perspective to argue on ethical grounds that whales should be protected because they are unusually intelligent creatures, like dolphins or dogs (Friedham 2001). But pigs and llamas are smart and that does not stop many people from eating them.

FOOD AND IDENTITY

All of this is only superficially about whale. I think this is a debate about globalization, homogenization, and—ultimately—identity. For one thing, the Japanese think of whales as fish, and they are a fish-eating culture. There is a clear sense among some Japanese, one that Mr. Sato was able to articulate clearly, that this is just another example of the Western world telling everyone else what is right and what is wrong: in other words, cultural imperialism. To them it would be comparable to Indian Hindus demanding a worldwide ban on beef because it conflicts with their values or to the Japanese asking Americans to stop hunting deer, which the Japanese adore (see also Sims 2000). Hideki Mornuki of the Japanese Fisheries Agency objects to the way that the media focuses on bloody images of whale slaughter, adding to the implication that the Japanese are monsters for eating whale: "What if we show a scene of a cattle being slaughtered to people who eat beef everyday?" (Parameswaran 2007c).

Hirata (2004) argues that, ironically, the efforts of activist groups like Greenpeace against whaling have been motivating factors in the Japanese government's protection of it. This reminds me of a saying I heard often in Japan: "The nail that sticks up gets hammered down." One thing I think is fair to say about the Japanese as a whole is that they generally dislike direct confrontation, which is a major part of the strategies of groups like Greenpeace.

It is ironic, then, that the Japanese reaction has itself been unusually aggressive and confrontational. In that sense, it challenges Western perceptions of the Japanese as deferential. Maybe the Japanese are simply reacting in a typically

Western way—drawing a line in the sand to make a point with Westerners. There *is* a double standard here in that some North American aboriginal communities are allowed to hunt species of whales that are in fact endangered. There is thus at least some hypocrisy in the U.S. government's position, of which the Japanese are acutely aware (McGuinness 2002). They are also concerned that banning other sorts of fishing (e.g., tuna) may also be on the Western agenda (Kirby 2005).

Hirata (2004) argues that the centralized, top-down nature of Japanese governmental bureaucracy also protects it from public protest, or whatever protest there is from a populace that is not generally all that interested in the whale issue. Political factors are also involved, in that funding for Japanese fishing agencies may be reduced if whaling is discontinued, whereas an increase in commercial whaling would likely increase the funding and power of these agencies. Furthermore, the Japanese media tend to "mince their words" on the subject, according to Takaaki Hatori, a professor at Rikkyo University in Tokyo (Parameswaran 2007c). He compared it to the muted discussion of dog consumption in some Asian countries because it as seen as "barbaric" elsewhere. For a variety of reasons, therefore, the debate about eating whale within Japan is minimal.

This is also another example of how, in a seemingly contradictory way, a more interconnected, "globalized" world can provoke new and quite aggressive expressions of cultural identity to protest perceived outside threats to cultural unity. Nevertheless, Japan is acting in a very traditional way by seeking a compromise: the *limited* ability to hunt whales. The IWC was set up, recall, not to ban whaling but to manage it sustainably. The Japanese also argue that since whales eat large numbers of fish, whales that are at sustainable levels should be harvested to protect fish stocks (Sims 2000). No one wants to hunt whales to extinction but, the Japanese say, why not hunt whales in a sustainable way?

I saw the urge to compromise in almost all my negotiations with the Japanese, who would much rather say maybe than no. Yet in this debate the Japanese find themselves pitted against the classic Western yes-or-no, all-or-nothing, take-it-or-leave-it dichotomy. They are asking for "maybe," a middle ground, but we hear them saying no because that is the way that we think. After the 2007 IWC meeting, a spokesman for the Japanese delegation said, "We had a spirit of compromise at this meeting and the anti-whalers just can't help themselves but to pass hate resolutions" (Parameswaran 2007a). This animosity may be because many people doubt the Japanese have a truly sustainable concept of sustainable fishing (overfishing of bluefin tuna is sometimes cited, among other examples). Again the debate becomes more about cultural mistrust and misunderstanding than about whales. In this case, opponents see no real compromise in the pro-whaling Japanese position.

The Japanese continued to lobby for an end to the two-decade-old moratorium on commercial whaling, including motions at the 57th International Whaling Commission meeting in South Korea in June 2005 (Faiola 2005). There were plans at that time "to almost double 'scientific whaling' of Antarctic minke whales from 440 to more than 850, and to undertake fresh kills of humpback and fin whales for the first time in decades, according to diplomats familiar with the proposal" (Faiola 2005:A19). I was unable to get exact numbers by species over several years, but it is clear that, overall, the Japanese have taken more whales every year since 2001, from 598 in 2001 to 1,320 in 2006. Of the six countries for which I could find data (Norway, Iceland, Japan, Russian Federation, United States, and Denmark), Japan has taken the most whales in that period (5,304), nearly 2,000 more than Norway, which also hunts whales commercially (Morell 2007).

RECENT DEVELOPMENTS

The year 2007 was not a particularly good year for Japan in this debate. In April, the Greenpeace ship *Esperanza* was blocked for entry into Yokohama harbor for several days through tactics of the Japanese sailor's union, a move that hardly won the hearts and minds of conservationists.

At the end of May, at the IWC, Japan made a claim that the whaling ban was causing unnecessary hardship for four economically struggling whaling communities (Abashiri, Ayukawa, Wadaura, and Taiji). Japan proposed that small vessels be allowed to catch minke whales "exclusively for local consumption" (anonymous 2007:1). A press release from Wednesday, May 30, 2007, on the IWC Web site noted that "there was no consensus on the issue," which was left open.[1] Japan withdrew the proposal rather than forcing a vote, noting that it did not wish to provoke confrontation and further divide the IWC.

At the same meeting, the IWC reviewed the issue of special permits that have allowed Japan and other countries to kill whales for scientific study. According to the commission's Web site, "Under the lethal component of the programme in 2006/07, 505 Antarctic minke whales and 3 fin whales were caught. Japan also has a North Pacific programme under which a total of 195 Common minke, fifty Bryde's, 100 sei, and six sperm whales were caught in 2006." During the meeting a resolution was adopted by the IWC that called upon Japan to indefinitely discontinue its lethal aspects of its scientific study (Morell 2007:532). The Sea Shepherd Conservation Society, a more radical offshoot of Greenpeace, trumpeted the resolution, claiming that Japan got "trounced" at the meeting.[2]

Then in June 2007, Japan (along with Iceland) proposed a review of the endangered status of all great whales species at the fourteenth meeting of the signatories to the Convention on International Trade in Endangered Species (CITES) in The Hague, Netherlands. This motion was defeated fifty-five to twenty-eight (with thirteen abstentions) (Hood 2007). CITES members also voted to stop an evaluation of finback whale stocks even though it had been approved in committee. In striking contrast, another proposal by Australia, that scientific review *not* be permitted while the commercial whaling ban was in place, was accepted with sixty votes for, twenty-three against, and thirteen abstentions.

Relations between Japan and Australia seem to exemplify Japan's increasingly isolated position on the whale issue. Japan's interactions with Australia are now seriously strained over Japanese hunting of the humpback whale, which migrates along the Australian and New Zealand coasts to the Pacific, and this threatens to sour their diplomatic relationship more generally. Whale watching is a multimillion dollar industry in Australia (Parameswaran 2007b). Although the Japanese have stated they will kill only fifty whales, this is rarely mentioned in reports, perhaps in part because people simply do not believe it.

On its Web site, Sea Shepherd argues that had the Japanese proposal for review been accepted, it "would have led to the immediate resumption of international commercial trade in whale products for the first time in more than twenty years." Similar claims are made by Sue Fisher of the Whale and Dolphin Conservation Society: "Not only do pro-whaling countries want to lift the ban on whaling, but they also aim to lift restrictions on international trade in whale products—which, if allowed, would once again fuel an uncontrollable slaughter" (Hood 2007). The language here suggests a certain amount fear-mongering, but the debate has become so heated and contentious even among scientists and anthropologists that it is hard to know what to think. There seems to be little agreement on anything about whaling, including issues of sustainability and cultural rights.

From my position outside the debate as an interested observer, it seems to me that if an animal is not endangered, its hunting is traditional (as it is in Japan), and such hunts can be monitored, then this should be considered. This is the case in the United States and the Russian Federation. Japan has been consistent and clear that it has no intention of wiping out whale stocks as some conservationists claim. In fact, they have always argued for management of stocks. But mistrust of Japanese intentions seems so entrenched and the facts so contentious that it is hard to see where the debate is going, if anywhere. One thing seems clear though: this dichotomized, good-guy/bad-guy discourse makes for good headlines and taps into a feeling of moral superiority among well-meaning people who, like me, rarely have the time to examine the issues in depth.

Japan is aware of these contradictions and at the end of the 2007 meeting claimed that the IWC had lost sight of its original mission to manage whale stocks. One of the Japanese delegates, Akira Nakamae, noted that "Japan upholds the principle of using all living marine resources" and may start a new organization with like-minded countries. Some reports claim that there are up to thirty nations that might join Japan in forming a supposedly management-oriented organization that would challenge the IWC's role, which currently appears to be oriented toward ending whaling. If Japan withdraws from the IWC, that organization would not only become ineffectual but could in fact collapse. Eugene Lapointe, former secretary general of CITES, put it plainly: "If Japan leaves, the IWC is dead" (Parameswaran 2007b).

Why this dangerous standoff? Japanese delegates have noted that much of the debate is now framed by emotion, not science. I agree that this is not about managing resources in a rational way, and as IWC member Joji Morishita noted, "This hypocrisy leads us to seriously question the nature by which Japan will continue participating in the forum" (Parameswaran 2007b). The science is by virtually all accounts contested, and so for now it seems that emotional arguments are leading the debate. Somewhere along the line this debate has become reminiscent of Orwell's *Animal Farm*, in which "all animals are equal, but some animals are more equal than others."

Apparently some science is more equal than others as well. It was on the basis of "sound science" that the United States was able to secure unanimous support for subsistence hunts of Western Arctic bowhead whales by the Inupiat and Siberian Yupik Eskimos. This victory was based primarily on sustainability of the whale stocks but also on an appeal to the notion of traditional lifeways. It is odd to me that similar arguments about traditional lifeways in Japanese coastal communities have not been successful. I wonder how Japanese scientists can get it so wrong, and why traditional Japanese lifeways are seen to lack the substance of traditional Eskimo ones. Perhaps their proposal to allow the capture of whales for local subsistence was tainted by their practice of selling whale meat from scientific study. In the broadest sense, the fact that there is a debate at all highlights the subjectivity of even "hard" science like whale population assessment.

Currently, the IWC is split between pro-whaling nations, led by Iceland, Japan, and Norway, and anti-whaling members, including Australia, Brazil, Britain, New Zealand, and the United States. Because neither group has the 75 percent majority needed for policy change, there is little hope that these issues will be solved there, and this is a debate that seems to get hotter all the time. In Norway, activists from a group calling themselves Agenda 21 sunk an unoccupied whaling ship while it was docked at port in 2007. Also in 2007, the Sea Shepherd Conservation Society threw acid on the Japanese whaling ship the *Nisshin Maru*, injuring two sailors. Greenpeace denounced Sea Shepherd's action, but the Japanese government went farther, labeling the group "terrorists." Japan is now considering unilaterally allowing some of its coastal communities to whale. This conflict is clearly far from over.

CONCLUSION

How little I knew of all of this that night with my friend Mr. Sato! And how like the global debate on whaling were our positions, although I certainly did not know that then. Back then I was self-righteous but not particularly well-informed and a momentary anti-relativist, willing to challenge Mr. Sato on this issue with little background knowledge. Having taken some time to look into these issues nearly twenty years later, I see no clear right and wrong as I did then but subtlety and frustrating ambiguity even in matters of biological science. This sort of process is familiar to most anthropologists, but the recognition of ambiguity and an interest in compromise are even longer traditions in Japan.

Anthropologists routinely claim to admire and appreciate diversity. But what kind of diversity? Diversity on whose terms? Can we accept the consumption of whale in Japan as a reasonable goal under some as-yet-undefined agreement and set of circumstances? Seventeen years after the incident maybe I can. Would I eat whale now? Probably not—mostly because the conservation issues are still not clear to me. But to be honest, I realize now that my refusal to eat was also a way for me to assert my cultural values during a year when I had to constantly accept those of others. My refusal was a stubborn expression of my identity, a refusal to be "hammered down" by another culture, and an attempt to take the moral high ground. The defense of whaling by some Japanese—clearly not by all or even most—is similar but, in my experience, has been less moralistic, hypocritical, and un-relativistic than the Western response. In that sense, Mr. Sato's position was at least as rational as my own, and perhaps I owe him an apology.

NOTES

1. See the IWC Web site at http://www.iwcoffice.org/meetings/meeting2007.htm for more information.

2. For more information about this group and the issue, see http://www.seashepherd.org/news/media_070607_1.html.

REFERENCES

Alcock, Selene
  2002   Whale Meat in Japan. *Radio National*. Australian Broadcasting Corporation. June 22.

Anonymous
  2007   Proposed Schedule Amendment to permit the catching of minke whales from the Okhotsk Sea–West Pacific Stock by small-type coastal whaling vessels. Proposal by Japanese delegation to IWC. http://www.iwcoffice.org/_documents/commission/IWC59docs/59-9.pdf, accessed May 24, 2010.

Baker, C. Scott, G. M. Lento, F. Cipriano, M. L. Dalebout, and S. R. Palumbi
  2000   Scientific Whaling: Source of Illegal Products for Market? *Science* 290 (5497):1695.

Cameron, Deborah
  2005   Whale on Japan's School Lunch Menu. *The Age* (Australia), May 21.

CBS News
  2002   Japan Remains Firm on Whaling. May 9. http://www.cbsnews.com/stories/2002/05/09/tech/main508442.shtml, accessed December 15, 2005.

Chamberlain, Basil Hall
  1981   *The Kojiki.* Tuttle, Boston.
  [1919]

Dalebout, Merel L., Gina M. Lento, Frank Cipriano, Naoko Funahshi, and C. Scott Baker
  2002   How Many Protected Minke Whales Are Sold in Japan and Korea? A Census by DNA Profiling. *Animal Conservation* 5:143–152.

Day, David
  1987   *The Whale War.* Douglas and McIntyre, Vancouver.

Faiola, Anthony
  2005   Reviving a Taste for Whale: Japan Introduces Meat to Children as It Fights Moratorium. *Washington Post Foreign Service,* June 19, p. A19.

Friedham, Robert L.
  2001   *Toward a Sustainable Whaling Regime.* University of Washington Press, Seattle.

Geertz, Clifford
  1984   Distinguished Lecture: Anti Anti-Relativism. *American Anthropologist* 86: 263–278.

Hirata, Keiko
  2004   Beached Whales: Examining Japan's Rejection of an International Norm. *Social Science Japan Journal* 7(2):177–197.

Hogarth, Bill
  2007   Chair's Summary Report of the 59th Annual Meeting, Anchorage Alaska, May, 2007. http://www.iwcoffice.org/_documents/meetings/ChairSummaryReportIWC59.pdf, accessed August 5, 2007.

Hood, Marlowe
    2007   Japan Fails in Back Door Whaling Move at Wildlife Trade Forum. http://
            www.terradaily.com/reports/Japan_Fails_In_Back_Door_Whaling_
            Move_At_Wildlife_Trade_Forum_999.html, accessed June 6, 2006.

Kalland, Arne, and Brian Moeran
    1992   *Japanese Whaling: End of an Era?* Curzon Press, London.

Kirby, Alex
    2005   Japan Pushes Whale Meat Revival. *BBC News.* June 19, 2005. http://news.
            bbc.co.uk/2/hi/asia-pacific/4106688.stm, accessed November 1, 2005.

Lambertsen, Richard H.
    1987   A Biopsy System for Large Whales and Its Use for Cytogenetics. *Journal of
            Mammalogy* 68:443–445.

McGuinness, Padraic P.
    2002   Whale-Hugger's Case Is Up the Spout. *Sydney Morning Herald*, May 28, p.
            13.

Morell, Virginia
    2007   Killing Whales for Science? *Science* 316(5824):532–534.

Parameswaran, P.
    2007a   Vote Boycott over Japan Mars Whaling Talks. http://www.terradaily.com/
            reports/vote_Boycott_Over_Japan_Mars_Whaling_Talks_999.html,
            May 30.
    2007b   A Whale Of A Problem For Japan At Home And Abroad. http://www
            .terradaily.com/reports/A_Whale_Of_A_Problem_For_Japan_At_
            Home_And_Abroad_999.html, June 1.
    2007c   Whaling passions muted in Japan. http://www.terradaily.com/reports/
            A_Whale_Of_A_Problem_For_Japan_At_Home_And_Abroad_999.
            html, June 1.

Sims, Calvin
    2000   Japan, Feasting on Whale, Sniffs at "Culinary Imperialism" of U.S. *New
            York Times.* August 10, p. A1.

Strieker, Gary
    2001   Japan Finds Whaling Moratorium Unappetizing. March 28. http://
            archives.cnn.com/2001/TECH/science/03/28/whale.japan/index.html,
            accessed May 25, 2010.

CHAPTER TEN

No Heads, No Feet, No Monkeys, No Dogs

The Evolution of Personal Food Taboos

Miriam S. Chaiken

Biographical sketch. Miriam Chaiken received her Ph.D. in cultural anthropology in 1983 from University of California at Santa Barbara. She has conducted research and worked in international development in Southeast Asia and east and southern Africa for more than twenty years and has a permanent position as a professor of anthropology and department head at New Mexico State University. She has served as the president of the Society for the Anthropology of Food and Nutrition and is primarily interested in combating hunger and improving the conditions of health and nutrition for children in the developing world.

Every fledgling anthropologist who is preparing to conduct first fieldwork is formally trained in research methods and informally prepared by the anecdotes shared by friends and mentors who have already successfully navigated the rite of passage that fieldwork represents in the discipline. My training was no different than this scenario. While a graduate student at University of California–Santa Barbara, I took research methods from the esteemed Paul Bohannan (then president of the American Anthropological Association) and classes on theory from other faculty. I delved into Southeast Asian cultures with Donald Brown (and previously as an undergraduate with James Eder at Arizona State). All of these professors set the bar high for us, challenging us to do excellent qualitative and quantitative fieldwork and to continue this important tradition of anthropologists. The informal transmission of knowledge needed during this apprenticeship was shared by the senior grad students, who had returned from "the field" full of wisdom and amusing tales of what not to do in conducting fieldwork, stories that remain vivid in my memory even now, decades later. Nowhere in all of this excellent preparation did anyone warn me about chicken-head soup. But I get ahead of myself.

In the early 1980s I began to prepare for dissertation field research in Southeast Asia, and ultimately Palawan Island in the Philippines was the destination for my work. Palawan was an ideal choice because many of my interests could be pursued in this one locale. I had become interested in the process of spontaneous relocations of populations, which was happening all over Asia, paralleling a process of government-managed relocation schemes that were also moving people from areas of population density to frontier regions. I had originally envisioned exploring this issue in Indonesia, where the government-planned "transmigrations" were well established and well documented, but political difficulties in that nation at the time made this a problematic location. There was a smaller-scale process underway in the Philippines, and Palawan Island was the site of a notoriously badly managed relocation project near the town of Narra. Both of these conditions factored into my choice of Palawan for research. But the real reasons for the selection of this site boiled down to personal choices. My friend and undergraduate mentor, Jim Eder, had been working in Palawan for many years and generously provided contacts and networks to help establish plans for my working there as well. Secondly, my then boyfriend and now husband, Tom, went to Palawan in 1979 to scout for possible locations for both of our dissertation research projects. While my intent is not to expose my romances indiscreetly, my encounter with chicken-head soup was a direct result of my attachment to Tom.

During the summer that Tom was in Palawan, he received a great deal of support from a family I will call the Flores, who had been great friends of Jim. This couple generously gave Tom advice and a place to stay while he scouted locations for our fieldwork. They knew that Tom was unmarried at the time, and although he referred to me and indicated I would be joining him when it came time for our full stint of fieldwork, Mrs. Flores apparently thought she had a better plan for his future. She had an unmarried friend from a prominent local family who she thought would make an ideal wife for Tom, and the chance to live in the United States was a welcome prospect for this woman. In spite of her valiant efforts, Mrs. Flores's matchmaking efforts were unsuccessful. When Tom returned to begin fieldwork in 1980 with a wife (me), she was obviously disappointed that her friend was not destined to be betrothed to the handsome American anthropologist.

All of this is a roundabout introduction to the chicken-head-soup encounter. When we arrived in the Philippines, after months of preparation, we spent the first few days living in luxury with good friends Bob and Gina Cowell, who were working at the International Rice Research Institute (IRRI) on the Philippines' main island of Luzon. This was a way to make an easy transition to the heat and humidity and to begin our tentative efforts to speak the national language, Tagalog. While our visit to IRRI was wonderful in many ways, we also experienced our first episode of food poisoning, ironically from a lavish country-club-style party at IRRI. We left Luzon and arrived in Palawan still wobbly from that illness.

The morning we arrived in Palawan we traveled to the Flores' home, where Mrs. Flores had prepared lunch for us that she called chicken noodle soup. Although my constitution had not yet adjusted to the high heat and humidity and I was still reeling from the IRRI illness, the thought of the Philippine version of my grandmother's "Jewish penicillin" sounded like just the right meal. As we sat down to eat our chicken soup, I noticed something peeking at me from my bowl, partially obscured by a fat noodle. Upon brief exploration it became apparent that Tom's bowl contained noodles, chicken pieces, and broth, and mine contained a chicken head (or, more precisely, rooster as the cockscomb clearly indicated) and two chicken feet, as well as my share of noodles. Hmmm, what to do? To this day I do not know whether my bowl contained those body bits just by chance or Mrs. Flores thought these were special and intended to share them with me . . . or whether this was her expression of displeasure of my role in botching her matchmaking plans. Even after two years of fieldwork in Palawan, I am not sure how to interpret the body bits in my bowl. Although most families include heads and feet in the cooking pot, it is odd that I would receive them all in a random portioning of soup. Heads and feet are not special delicacies that I was singled out to receive, so what was the symbolism of my soup?

As I was new to the practice of ethnographic fieldwork, I was concerned about not offending my host, but I was also pretty sure I could not bring myself to chew on a chicken head, and so I sipped broth and ate a few noodles, but I kept some in the bowl to hide the remnants of the soup I had not been able to bring myself to eat. In that first meal in Palawan, I had discovered the first two of the food taboos that I would later codify for myself: no heads, no feet.

A few days after our arrival we had located a house in the village of Napsaan, on the remote and isolated west coast of Palawan, where we settled in for our fieldwork. Palawan has long been considered the Philippines' frontier, as it is remote, sparsely settled, and the destination for prospectors and pioneers seeking to claim lands and a new life. The west coast of Palawan where we lived is the most inaccessible area of the island, where most travel is still done on foot or by boat along the coast of the South China Sea. The coastline is dotted with small villages of subsistence farmers who cultivate upland rice in slash-and-burn fields. The mountainous terrain and relatively easy access to land have permitted this traditional system of cultivation to flourish, and little area has been developed into the irrigated rice paddies that are commonly found elsewhere in Asia.

The village where we lived was only about thirty-five miles as the crow flies from the capital city of Puerto Princesa, but it was worlds away in a practical sense. Access was difficult at all times, and impossible during the worst of the rainy season as getting to Napsaan required driving through several big rivers, the largest located in the middle of the island in the Iwahig penal colony. If weather permitted, once or twice a day a jeepney, converted weapons carriers that were remnants of World War II, made the bumpy journey to Napsaan carrying people and cargo in each direction. One's journey was equally likely to be shared with live pigs and chickens as with fellow passengers, and we soon learned the maxim that there is no such thing as a full jeepney; there is always room for another person or two. On a good day, the journey from Napsaan to Puerto took about two and a half hours, on a bad one the journey could take as long as seven hours, depending on the number of breakdowns and flat tires. Given the difficulty and relative expense of travel for our meager research budget, trips to Puerto were fairly rare, but welcome, respites from life in our village.

Our house was a typical rural Philippine house on stilts, with bamboo slats woven into panels for the walls and widely spaced slats for the floor. Complete with thatch roof, this house was like a giant basket, and the loosely woven walls and slats in the floors allowed the air to circulate and the whole building to breathe. We soon adjusted to life in our village; made friends with our neighbors; learned to sleep soundly with a mosquito net that prevented bats, mice, and lizards from sharing our bed; and learned how to manage in a house lacking both electricity and running water.

Over the next two years in the field, we encountered many wonderful foods. I learned to use many exotic ingredients that I had never encountered growing up in suburban Phoenix, but we also had a few challenges in the food department. We quickly, and fortunately, learned that local people were familiar with the concept of allergies, and when food that was offered was too far out of our comfort level, a claim of being allergic to said food gave us a gracious way to refuse. Tom's polite fiction of being "allergic" to shellfish, which he really dislikes, was usually greeted with other people recounting the food allergies that they or a family member had experienced. We invoked the allergy excuse quite rarely, as most of the foods we encountered proved to be tasty and enjoyable treats. Although I had never cleaned and prepared a whole fish prior to my life in Palawan, I eventually learned how to grill over an open fire the incredibly fresh fish we could sometimes buy from neighbors who had been fishing in the sea. This produced some delicious meals of grouper and red snapper, although my first effort at cooking fish was disastrous and resulted in tossing it out in the woods for cats to scrap over in the night. In general, our consumption of protein largely rested on neighbors' success at fishing.

Much of the fieldwork we have conducted over the years was in communities like Napsaan, where obtaining fresh food was a big challenge. In our isolated village on Palawan that was because of the absence of a market. The few local *sari-sari* stores, windows in the wall of someone's home where we could purchase items, stocked only basic durable and dry goods such as matches, kerosene, sugar, and instant coffee. Every household grew its own vegetables, most of the men went fishing occasionally, and people gathered shellfish during low tides. Surplus foods, such as extra fish that were caught, were processed at home for storage and consumption at a later date, usually by packing them in salt and air drying. We compensated for the difficult access to food by buying rice in bulk, which was our staple three times per day, as was the local custom. We would purchase dried, salted fish or fresh fish from neighbors when they had some to spare, and we occasionally splurged and bought a chicken for the pot. When we visited the capital city, we would purchase a few canned goods to provide occasional relief from the monotony of our rice-based diet.

A few months into our stay we began to grow a vegetable garden, but our inexperience resulted in poor yields of everything except zucchini and yellow squash (*kalabasa*), so this was only marginally successful in bringing home dinner. During one three-week period during the rainy season, the seas were too rough for local men to venture out fishing, and our diet during that time consisted *only* of rice and yellow squash for three meals a day. Once back in the United States, it was many years before I could face yellow squash with any enthusiasm. We also tried raising our own chickens and found our skills with animal husbandry were as pathetic as our farming. One hen was enticed away into the forest by the wild roosters that inhabited the hinterland; another was killed in the night by a snake and her chicks were scattered and lost. Clearly, we were not cut out to be subsistence farmers like our neighbors. During our two years in Napsaan, it was frequently difficult to count on access to foods to provide the *ulam*, or savory side dish to accompany rice.

As part of my research involved collecting data on household food consumption and child nutrition, I was well aware that the diet of most locals was far better than what we were consuming. Despite this awareness, we had neither the time nor the skill to become full-time subsistence cultivators, and so we had to make do with the limited food resources at our disposal. There were a few important interludes that gave us a respite from our dietary monotony, the most common of which was when someone had reason to throw a party. In rural Palawan, the person who has a birthday is not treated by their friends and family to a celebration; rather, the person who has the birthday celebrates by throwing a party, preparing lots of food, and inviting everyone around to help them mark the occasion. Poor families had modest celebrations that involved only their closest family members and consisted of noodles cooked with vegetables (*pancit*) or tinned mackerel in sauce. Wealthier households mark the occasion by slaughtering a pig as the centerpiece of the feast. Both the best and worst dishes we encountered were served at these feasts.

Slaughter of a pig for cooking at a party necessitated cooperation by people from neighboring households, as the butchering process was complicated and no part of the pig was allowed to go to waste. The butchering was usually performed by the men, who would collect the blood and offal and turn it over to the women for preparation, while the men built a spit and started a low fire to slowly roast the whole pig to prepare the famous dish *lechon*. In this preparation the meat remains succulent, as it is naturally basted by the rendering fat of the pig as it cooked, and the outer skin became a crispy counterpoint to the meat. Preparing lechon was expensive and time consuming, as the properly prepared pig required hours of slow roasting and rotation to be ideal. It represented the finest in Philippine cooking and was a dish highly anticipated by all guests at a party.

The second-most popular dish that was usually served at parties was made from the innards of the pig cleaned and prepared by the women. This dish was known as *dinuguan*, from the root word *dugo*, or "blood." In a nutshell, dinuguan was pigs' intestines cooked in pig blood with vinegar to prevent the blood from coagulating. While this is a local favorite, and a dish that I ate on many occasions, I never learned to share my neighbors' love of this concoction. I may have been channeling my Jewish grandmother when I faced this dish with revulsion, as I imagined my kosher-keeping grandmother rolling over in her grave at the though of eating something so *treyf* (unclean).

In addition to birthday parties or celebrations of saint's days, smaller gatherings of men were occasionally held during which they would typically drink and play cards. Women were not normally included in these parties, but if they happened to be close at hand they were invited to share whatever food the men had prepared. There was a special classification for food served at these events: *pulutan*, which are finger foods to be eaten while drinking. Instead of the store-bought chips or pretzels that might be the fare for such occasions in the United States, pulutan was generally a strongly seasoned meat or seafood dish that counterbalanced the flavor of the beer or *ginebra* San Miguel, a Philippine gin. I have had pulutan that consisted of squid cooked in soy sauce and vinegar (*adobo*-style) and also strongly seasoned fried chicken, both delicious treats, but on one memorable occasion I was offered pulutan that led to my third food taboo.

In some parts of the Philippines, notably in the north of Luzon Island, far from Palawan, eating dogs is considered a delicacy. In Palawan, dogs were not common fare but nor were they coddled house pets. Most dogs were fairly mangy beasts that largely fended for themselves but were kept by households with the expectation that they provided protection. For this reason, dogs were given names that made them sound ferocious, such as Matapang (which means brave or fierce) and, notably, Hitler. The risk of rabies in dogs was also well known, and this too led to ambivalent attitudes toward keeping dogs in the home.

There were a few households that seemed to treat their dogs more like the family pet that I had grown up with, where the dogs lived in the house and were shown affection by their owners. One such exception was the household of Jose and Linda Alvarez, a couple who ran a small sari-sari store and several small businesses. Jose and Linda became our good friends, and as their store window was in the central part of the village, it was a frequent gathering place for people as they walked through the area. I recall many happy conversations on the benches outside the window of their store, and many language lessons as local people coached me to become proficient in the national language, Tagalog. Another reason I liked to visit Jose and Linda was because their friendly black dog, Perla, would greet all comers with a wagging tail and plea to be petted. This was a couple I could relate to.

One day well into my second year in Palawan, I walked by the Alvarezs' store and saw Linda sitting outside, obviously in a foul mood. Jose and his companions were close by, sitting on the verandah of their house, very inebriated and in high spirits as a rousing card game was underway. I was invited to come to join them, and as I greeted them they offered to share their pulutan, which was on a platter in the middle of the table. Linda then piped up, with alarm, that I should not eat this pulutan as Jose had killed and cooked Perla and was serving her to the guests. She was clearly very angry with Jose and was upset about what he had done to Perla, a dog who was her faithful companion at home while she tended the store. Linda was not about to share in partaking of this pulutan. Obviously, I was not alone in my shock at the prospect of eating the family pet! In fact on earlier occasions, I had heard my neighbors refer to northerners disparagingly as "dog-eating people," so I came to learn that my taboo against eating dog (especially Perla) was considered acceptable by many people. In Palawan eating dog is a guilty pleasure that usually only men engage in, and eating dog as pulutan has macho qualities. My polite refusal to share the dog meat was generally ignored, and I joined Linda outside to sit in silence, reflecting on the fate of the friendly black dog.

The fact that Jose and his *barkada*, or pals, could blithely eat Perla may not be attributable to insensitivity so much as the scarcity of meat and animal protein. Although fish was consumed when available and on special occasions families would cook a chicken, meat was rarely consumed because it was rarely available. Lacking a butcher or meat market, everyone felt pangs of "meat hunger," as Richard Lee so poignantly discusses among the San people (Lee 1993).

Many families raised pigs, but these were intended as investments to be sold for profit when they reached maturity. These pigs were shipped to Puerto Princesa to be sold at market for a better price than they could ever fetch in the village. Other livestock were intended as working animals; there were a few oxen and water buffalos that were used to pull plows in cultivating irrigated rice fields or to pull a sledge or a cart. Unless an animal died of natural causes, such valuable animals would never be considered fair game for the cooking pot. Meat consumption was a rare and special treat.

In some ways it is ironic that meat was so seldom available, as Philippine cooking is replete with recipes that effectively preserve and season meat in the absence of refrigeration. Efficiently using a pig butchered and sold locally would not have been a problem. Perhaps the most famous national dish, *adobo* (different from Spanish and Latino versions of the same name) blends soy sauce, rice wine vinegar, and lots of garlic and black pepper into a marinade and preservative for raw meat. Even very tough cuts of ancient animals become tender and delicious prepared in this way. Other preservation involved slicing meat into thin strips and smoking it over a fire, resulting in a bacon-like flavor, or salting and drying it in the air, similar to the preparation of hams and cured meat found in so many cultures.

The only occasions when meat might be available to purchase were when someone had luck with hunting—with either conventional weapons or a "pig bomb." Our time in Palawan coincided with President Ferdinand Marcos's imposition of martial law, and guns and bullets were illegal. While a few households might have owned hunting guns, these were kept under wraps and never used to my knowledge. Hunting was a macho affair, as groups of men would track and kill a formidable wild pig in the forest, using a traditional spear as a weapon. Hunting was only successfully carried out by a few men, all of whom were members of the ethnic minority Tagbanua people, who had a stronger hunting-and-gathering tradition than the majority population of lowland Filipino farmers. When these Tagbanua men returned to the village carrying the carcass of a wild pig, everyone, including the local anthropologists, would line up to try to buy some of the precious meat to satisfy their "meat hunger."

The other strategy to obtain wild pig involved an ingenious explosive device called a "pig bomb," borrowing the English words to name this device. These were perhaps the original improvised explosive device (IED), not intended for targeting enemy Humvees but rather marauding wild pigs. For farmers who planted upland rice close to the forest margins, protecting the crop from the threat of wild pigs was a constant challenge. Pigs would root around these fields just as the rice was ripening, and one pig's nighttime raid could do tremendous damage to a farmer's annual harvest. To combat these porcine threats, many farmers rigged pig bombs, made of a mixture of extremely ripe mashed bananas and shards of broken glass wrapped in banana leaves. The smell of ripe bananas attracted the pigs to these baited bombs, and as they bit into them, it set off a detonation. The homemade detonators were made from phosphorous scraped from match heads as the incendiary material, as gun powder was illegal under martial law. The shards of glass would be propelled through the pig's face and head, killing the animal. Most pig bombs detonated just before dawn, and we recall waking up with the sound of the explosion during the pre-harvest season and happily anticipating the first light when we could go inquire whose pig bomb had been successful and whether there was any fresh meat to purchase. Pig bombs were generally only used during the few weeks before and during the rice harvest, as these were the only times the wild pigs were lured out of the remote forests by the promise of cultivated foods to ravage.

The other wild animals that threatened to wreak havoc on farmers' fields were the monkeys and birds that also lived in the forests. Birds were only active during daylight hours, so for the few weeks of the harvest season, many families would build a lean-to in their fields and camp there for the duration of the season. Children were out of school during this harvest holiday and were put to work in the fields, scaring birds by waving their arms and using slingshots to pelt birds with pebbles.

Monkeys, like pigs, were active during the night hours and presented a more serious threat to the harvest. We found monkeys to be ingenious when it came to experimenting with human food, and they routinely raided the farm fields to feast on ripening rice. Once while we were hiking on another island, a curious monkey found Tom's backpack sitting on the ground, unzipped it, and helped himself to a peanut butter sandwich that was wrapped in plastic. Local farmers had equally ingenious ways to combat these monkeys, as they devised snares that were baited with the ripening rice. The bait was placed on top of a long pole cut from a variety of thorny tree, which the sensible monkeys would not climb as they would be impaled. The snare was placed on an adjacent pole that the monkey could climb, and as he reached out to grab the rice, it tripped a counterweight and noose, snapping the poor monkey's neck.

Some local people, as with the eating of dogs, found these snared monkeys acceptable game for the cooking pot. Others, however, commented that they too closely resembled humans and so they had qualms about eating them. Thus, I was safe in my fourth food taboo as they understood some people's reticence to partake of monkey meat.

Other wild animals did not rate dietary deference as far as I was concerned. On one sojourn we traveled on foot a long day's walk away to the more remote village of Bubusawen, also on the west coast of Palawan. Bubusawen was one of the coastal villages settled by lowland Christian farmers who were homesteading land not occupied by one of the indigenous ethnic minorities of Palawan. We were accompanying our friend who was the parish priest, and he had planned to visit Bubusawen to say Mass in this remote community, which had no formal church, in celebration of a saint's day. We were joined on our adventure by a number of young people who volunteered for the local church and by our landlord/father-figure/neighbor Mang Luis, who was a Tagbanua. We camped on the floor of local porches for the few days that we were in Bubusawen and were well cared for by the local villagers. They were pleased to have visitors, as this was a rare experience. As we shared the festivities and honors intended for our friend Father Erning, we sat down to a dinner of rice and a flavorful stew. As we chatted over dinner my husband thanked our hosts and commented that the chicken was delicious, to which I replied, "I've cut up a lot of chickens; these are not chicken bones." As the conversation continued, we were informed that we were eating a stew of monitor lizard, a huge lizard common in the area that often exceeded four feet in length. Mang Luis dropped his plate and looked appalled. He said that for the Tagbanua people, monitor lizard was strictly taboo and that he could not continue eating this food that clearly now repelled him. While sympathizing with Mang Luis's reaction, we did not share his dislike of eating lizards. To the delight of our hosts, we happily cleaned our plates. This was a little lesson to us: to each her own food taboos.

Acknowledgments. I am grateful to our editors for helpful suggestions in revising this chapter and to many students over the years who have been regaled with our tales of adventures in eating. I received helpful feedback and comments on this chapter from James and Pia Eder, Gina Cowell, Billy Garrett, David Brokensha, and my aunt and prolific author Miriam Chaikin.

REFERENCE

Lee, Richard
  1993   *The Dobe Ju/'hoansi.* Harcourt Brace College Publishers, Fort Worth, TX.

CHAPTER ELEVEN

Buona Forchetta

Overeating in Italy

Rachel Black

Biographical sketch. Rachel Black received her Ph.D. in 2006 from the Università degli Studi di Torino, Italy, specializing in European history, food studies, and gastronomic history. She is currently a professor of anthropology at the Open University of Catalunya, a private Internet-centered open university based in Barcelona, Spain. She is also the coordinator and a founding member of Slow Water, a nonprofit organization created in 2008 to share information and knowledge about water resources and water management techniques.

Shortly after I first moved to Turin, Italy, I was invited to dinner to meet my fiancé's family; this would be my first meal in an Italian household. I was nervous about meeting Alberto's family, but I was also excited about having an authentic home-cooked meal. Back in North America, Italian cuisine had always been a favorite. I had even worked in an Italian restaurant. Going into this experience I felt I had a pretty good knowledge of Italian food; I was confident I could navigate my way around the table despite my shaky and rudimentary grasp on the Italian language. However, I encountered a number of surprises during my first truly Italian meal.

In 2001 I moved to Turin to pursue a doctoral degree in cultural anthropology at the University of Turin. Although I am Canadian, I had been living in France and moving to Italy did not cause me too much culture shock. Nevertheless, I was caught off guard by the little differences that I sometimes failed to notice initially. Often for anthropologists, going into the field can mean a radical shift in everyday practices. However, for those doing ethnographic research at home or in Western countries, this is not always the case. While doing fieldwork in Italy I had to be careful not to let familiarity cloud my observations; I was afraid I would misinterpret exchanges and miss important points of analysis because of my inability to spot cultural differences.[1]

This became apparent from my first meal with Alberto's family. When I sat down at the table, I did not realize the importance of this meal. Later, Alberto would explain to me that a young person does not take a boyfriend or girlfriend home to meet his or her parents unless that is the person they are likely to marry. In North America I had brought many friends home to meet my parents and thought nothing of what I expected to be a rather informal family meal. In time, I learned that Northern Italians tend to be particularly guarded about their private space, and rarely are non-family members invited for meals in the home.

After introductions, we were seated at the small table in a room where Alberto's family usually eats their daily meals (the more formal dining room was reserved for special occasions such as birthdays and Christmas lunch). Alberto's parents, two sisters, and brother seemed happy to squeeze together to make room for me, the newcomer. Vivi, Alberto's mother, disappeared into the kitchen and came out with the first course (*antipasto*), *vitel tonné*, a classic Piedmontese starter that consists of thinly sliced veal with a tuna sauce. It sounded bizarre but it tasted great. As a guest, I was served first as all the members of the family anxiously awaited their servings. Alberto and his siblings were all good eaters and avid fans of their mother's cooking. I would learn later that there was a pecking order in the food service, especially when it came to something sweet. When Vivi asked me if I would like seconds, I happily nodded for more. I had not had a home-cooked meal in a long time and my appetite was whetted by this appetizer.

Vivi disappeared once more and after a miraculously short while, she made her entrance with a large bowl of pasta, *tajarin al ragù*. Tajarin or *tagliarini* (the name is derived from the verb *tagliare*, "to cut") are a ribbon-shaped long pasta from the Piedmont region. Traditionally, this type of pasta was made by rolling out pasta dough and cutting it carefully into strips using a knife or wire. Most home cooks these days buy their pasta at a *pastaficio* (pasta shop) or make their own at home using a pasta machine that cuts the pasta into uniform strips. *Ragù* sauce has little to do with the bottled variety that North Americans can find in their local grocery stores. I discovered that nearly every region has its own variation on the theme of ragù, but all tend to be some sort of meat sauce. Ragù is an excellent example of the regional variety in Italian cooking; my experience of Italian-American cuisine had not prepared me for this regionalism at all. In Piedmont, ragù consists of a base of carrots, celery, onions (finally diced, these three ingredients are called a *soffritto*, known as *mirepoix* in classic French cooking), lean ground beef, local pork sausage, red wine, and stewed tomatoes (which are often canned at home during tomato season at the height of summer). This is one of the first recipes that Vivi taught me. Learning to cook Piedmontese dishes grounded me not only in the local culture but also in Alberto's family.

Once again, Vivi asked me if I would like another serving of pasta: "*Non farmi complimenti!*" (literally, "Don't make me any compliments," or don't be overly polite). I had never had a sauce this rich and delicious. I happily nodded for more. I was starting to get full, but I figured this was the last course, and I did not want to offend my hosts by refusing more. I was eager to make a good impression. My plate was piled high with pasta and Alberto grated a nice portion of *Parmigiano-Reggiano* cheese over my lovely ragù. I smiled and dove in once more until I had finished every last tajarin. Vivi looked on approvingly as I, like everyone else, cleaned my dish with a piece of bread. Everyone called out "*Scarpetta!*" Alberto explained that this literally meant "little shoe" but referred to the practice of cleaning up your plate with bread, which showed a hearty appreciation for the food and the cook. However, in more formal dining situations, scarpetta is considered rather uncouth.

I eased back in my chair a little and wished I had worn an elastic waistband. As the plates were cleared, I began to wonder what was for dessert but then another, unexpected course appeared. How could this be possible? In North America, pasta is usually the main course. I was finding out the hard way that Italian meals are not structured in quite the same way. Lunch and dinner often consist of an *antipasto* (appetizer), *primo* (a first course of pasta or soup), *secondo* (a meat course) accompanied by *contorni* (vegetables that need to be ordered separately in restaurants), and then *dolce* (dessert). There are other variations as well that might include a salad after the main course or some cheese, often instead of dessert. When Alberto's mother came out carrying a roast followed by several vegetable dishes, there was little I could do to contain my surprise. It all looked so good but I was nearing full capacity. I smiled and chewed my food plenty, taking my time. I sipped my red wine in hopes it would help digestion. I do not think I had ever eaten so much in my life.

Once the main course was cleared, a plate of *pasticcini* (finger-sized pastries) came out, and Alberto's siblings immediately attacked the platter. I was pleased that my lack of enthusiasm went nearly unnoticed. Alberto's father,

Renzo, brought out a bottle of *grappa* (an alcohol made from grape skins and stems) and some thimble-sized glasses. How could I refuse? Renzo explained that grappa is the perfect way to end a copious meal because it aids digestion. I am not sure if that is true, but it was exactly the cure I was looking for and I wanted to believe it.

I survived my first meal with an Italian family but I realized I had a lot still to learn about Italian cuisine and culinary culture. I think I made a fairly good impression on Alberto's family but I also became known as a *buona forchetta* (literally, a good fork). This expression is used to refer to someone who enjoys good food. To my North American way of thinking, I thought this made me sound a little gluttonous; however, Alberto assured me that in Italy being a buona forchetta is a positive attribute and much appreciated in a country where the table is the center of family life and sociability.

It may seem like I moved to Italy just to eat (that was only part of the reason), but in reality I was doing research. For three years, I had done research on open-air markets in Turin and Lyon, France. When I lived in France I frequented the many open-air markets in Lyon and I was fascinated by the social and culinary interactions taking place at these age-old institutions. At the market, I made all kinds of friends and learned local recipes while brushing up on my French. When I moved to Italy, the first thing I did was find the neighborhood market. In fact, this is where I learned to speak Italian. I would point at the produce and the vendors would kindly hold up the requested vegetable and say its name, encouraging me to repeat after them. At times it was lonely being a foreigner in these two cities where few people spoke my native tongue (English), but the market offered me an important moment of sociability each day. The more I shopped, ate, and learned Italian, the more I understood the importance of the market and food in everyday life in Europe. This is where people went to be together; it was not just a place to buy fresh produce each day. The social aspect of the market was just as important as its economic side.

Shopping in Canada is quite different from shopping in Italy. I grew up in North America and always went to supermarkets. When I moved to Italy, I was amazed that many Italians shop each day at markets. In Canada, I had grown up in a house with a large refrigerator and freezer. I was surprised to find that most Italian households had miniscule fridges. This is another reason that Italians grocery shop more frequently. This was decidedly different from stockpiling once a week at the supermarket. Daily shopping places an emphasis fresh and seasonal produce, which is reflected in regional Italian cuisine. In Italy, it would be nearly unthinkable to eat asparagus in October. I started to appreciate the seasons that I found on my plate and I really enjoyed that not all produce was available year-round like at home. Eating strawberries became an early summer celebration. I ate as many berries as I could (often until I was ill), knowing they would not last long at the market stalls.

Although markets are still important social spaces, more and more Italians are shopping at large supermarkets. This is largely the result of the increased entry of Italian women into the workforce. Italy's domestic structures are undergoing a major transformation as women and families struggle to find a balance between work and domestic life (Counihan 2004; Helestosky 2004). This can be seen in the changes to the types of meals that are prepared in the home. Not all working members of the family come home for lunch like in the past and multi-course meals are usually reserved for special occasions.

Breakfast has never been a substantial meal in most areas of Italy. From my experience, breakfast often consists of milk, coffee, and sweet pastries or cookies. In cities, many people stop by their local bar for a *caffè latte* (coffee with a generous amount of warm milk) or a *cappuccino* (coffee with a *cappuccio* [hood] of foamy warm milk that is almost never drunk after lunch), which are often consumed standing up at the bar. Bars are important social spaces where people stop in alone or with friends to enjoy a coffee or cold drink. In Italy, bars are not necessarily associated with drinking alcohol and minors are certainly not prohibited from entering. The bars in Turin are well known for their *aperativi*. An *aperativo* is a drink, anything from Campari and soda to Prosecco (a dry, sparkling white wine from the Veneto region), consumed after work (usually from 6:00 PM to 9:00 PM). Many Turinese bars lay out impressive buffets of finger food that patrons snack on while milling about the bar with their drinks. This is another occasion where food and drink encourage socializing.

More and more Italians are starting to eat their lunches in bars, restaurants, and cafeterias. This was not always the case: in the past people often lived a short distance from work and returned home for lunch. Not only do Italians now commute farther to work but working hours are increasing and less time is dedicated to lunch. In addition, fewer women have the time to shop and prepare for the elaborate lunches that were typical in the past. Schoolchildren still frequently come home for lunch but the types of meals being consumed at midday are changing. Previously, lunch was the main meal of the day and it included an antipasto, primo, secondo, and dolce. This is quite rare now but there are those who still have a three-course meal outside the home at lunch (Parasecoli 2004).

For most Italians, dinner has become the main meal. This is an important time for family to come together around the table. However, this may not be quite as idyllic as it sounds or all that different from typical North American eating habits. Although most families eat at the same time and eat the same food, there was one participant that I did not imagine. The first time I had dinner in an Italian household, I was surprised when the television was turned on; my stereotypes of Italian commensality were shattered. I thought everyone would just zone out and watch the TV. This was not entirely the case. Most Italians watch the *telegiornale* (TV news) during meals. The television blared in the corner and the people around the table talked together, occasionally commenting on something that was said on the television between bites. It was as if the television was another person sitting at the table. I was never really sure what to make of this behavior and I found myself getting in the habit of flipping on the news during meals.

Italian dinners tend to be more substantial than lunch these days. Although most Italians still eat dinner at home, more money is spent on dining out as the country becomes increasingly affluent. You can go to a restaurant and have a four-course meal but *pizzerie* are probably by far the most popular choice for Italian diners. Pizza is quick, filling, and inexpensive. Originally from Naples, pizza is one of the more homogenized and ubiquitous foods in Italy, although most Italians agree that the best pizza is made in Naples (Neapolitan pizza tends to have a thicker crust and simple toppings). Another restaurant trend in Italy is an increase in the ethnic cuisines available. Other than Chinese restaurants, there were few dining options outside of regional Italian classics in the past. Recently, there has been a proliferation of Indian, Thai, Japanese, and African restaurants in major Italian cities. This trend is also related to the fact that Italy has become an important receiving country for immigrants over the past twenty years (previously, it was known as a sending country). This shift has not been without its growing pains; however, immigrants to Italy have brought their cuisines with them, and sometimes food is a first point of contact between Italians and foreigners. In fact, there have been many initiatives in cities like Turin to promote markets, such as Porta Palazzo, as multicultural spaces. Foreigners flock to markets to search for ingredients from home, to network with compatriots, and to find jobs and housing (Figure 11.1). In many ways, food is just the starting point for a number of complex relations.

Despite the increases in dining out and prepared food, culinary traditions are still strong in Italy; however, processed and fast food is also becoming an important part of the national foodscape. That said, not all Italians are rushing to McDonald's. Founded in Northern Italy, the Slow Food movement brings together people who are interested in supporting local culinary culture and identities, as well as biodiversity and sustainable food-production practices (Petrini 2004). Carlo Petrini originally founded the Slow Food movement in protest against Italians not taking the time to slow down and enjoy food and commensality. The first Slow Food happening took place in Rome in 1986 to protest the opening of a McDonald's in Rome's Piazza di Spagna. Petrini and other Slow Food protesters passed out slices of home-cooked pizza to passersby. Slow Food has grown from a small Italian group to an international

11.1. Moroccan women buying chickens at the Porta Palazzo market in Turin, Italy.
(PHOTO BY RACHEL BLACK)

movement that is working to maintain biodiversity throughout the world as well as encouraging people to eat food that is "good, clean and fair" (Petrini 2007). More generally, the success of the Slow Food movement in Italy demonstrates the centrality of food to local and national identity and health.

Slow Food may be gaining ground but the process of globalization and culinary homogenization is nearly unstoppable, even in a country like Italy.

Not only do restaurants like McDonald's threaten everyday culinary practices and Italian cultural heritage but the homogenization of Italian food has had an impact on local identity and social life. Admittedly, cuisine, like all cultural expressions, is in constant flux. However, the rise of Italian industrial food-processing plants has popularized dishes such as *lasagne al forno* and *pollo alla diavola*. These are the sorts of dishes that are ubiquitous on restaurant menus and in frozen food cases throughout Italy. Prior to the 1960s, these dishes would have been strictly regional and tied to the place where they were created. Regional Italian cuisine used to tell the story of local agriculture, showcasing the products of a specific region. Often we find the place-names erased from popular dishes and the variation of ingredients has become rather limited with local produce not always featured. This is not to say that industrial food production and large-scale food distribution have been entirely successful at creating a unified Italian cuisine: local food still exists, even if it is not always considered everyday food as it was in the past. For example, many villages in central Italy have a *sagra* (fair) that celebrates a local product. While living in Umbria, one of my favorite pastimes was to visit neighboring villages for a taste of the local specialty. There were *sagre* that featured sour cherries, deer meat, or chicory. Usually the town square or park would be transformed into a large dining area with long tables and basic lighting strung up between posts or hung in tents. Locals would pitch in to cook and provide the waitstaff for the event. These meals were usually accompanied or followed by accordion music, music by some sort of band, and ballroom dancing. Diners and dancers would come from all over the countryside; many towns have built their culinary reputations on these events. Italians tend to pull out all of the stops on food and wine for special occasions.

Italians have taken many steps to protect their culinary heritage; beyond popular cultural movements like Slow Food, Italy has a complex legal system that protects food appellations and traditional production methods. These sorts of legal systems are not without their politics and they tend to cause great tension at a local level; in most cases the creation of a *denominazione di origine protetta* (often referred to as a *dop* and translated as "protected geographical origin") means the protection of not only tradition but also local economic interests. Alison Leitch outlines the complex politics and economics of creating a dop in her ethnography of *lardo di Colonnata* (2003). As *lardo* (cured pork fat) becomes a protected food, local producers run up against modern European hygiene laws that give little consideration to traditional methods of food production. In Leitch's investigation of the case of lardo, it becomes clear that local identity and culinary traditions are not the only things at stake when the producers of the local pork delicacy try to limit the area and output of production of this product. At the same time, Italian legislation concerning

11.2. Culatello di Zibello, a dop product, curing in a cellar near Parma, Italy. The damp, humid fog in this area helps produce the mold that covers the salami and gives it a complex and unique taste. (PHOTO BY RACHEL BLACK)

the traditional and local production of food safeguard techniques that have been mastered and passed on through generations of producers. *Culatello di Zibello* (Figure 11.2), a dry-cured pork product from the Emilia-Romagna region, is also a dop product. Many producers outside the designated production zone have tried to copy the production technique, but none can compare because this special product is dependent on local know-how as well as the special microclimate of this area. Culatello cannot be made without the fog that invades this humid plain area. In this case, the dop recognizes the distinctiveness of Culatello di Zibello on many levels and protects this local specialty from commercial imposters looking to make profit off of its fame and limited availability.

One of the best ways to protect culinary heritage and traditions is to cook. Special occasions and religious holidays mean special dishes and long hours in the kitchen for most Italian women. All major Catholic celebrations have their own special culinary traditions that vary from region to region. My first Christmas with Alberto's family turned out to be an even greater test of my appetite compared to my first meal there. I had asked Alberto if I could help prepare Christmas dinner. He raised his eyebrows and explained to me that the main meal at Christmas was actually lunch on Christmas day. I realized I had come a long way but I still had a lot to learn. Vivi happily agreed to have me under her feet in the kitchen, and I eagerly signed on for my two-day apprenticeship in Piedmontese Christmas cooking. Our first job was to prepare the meat for the *pasta ripiena* (stuffed pasta such as *ravioli* and *plin*). Vivi had done the shopping at her favorite butchershop in the countryside and proudly unveiled a veal roast, slices of *prosciutto crudo* (dry-cured ham), and a *cappone* (capon). We began by roasting the veal and boiling the chicken. This seemed like a lot of food to me, but Vivi explained that we would use the chicken broth for the *pasta al brodo* (pasta in broth); the veal was for the pasta filling; and the chicken would be eaten as the secondo. We spent all day preparing the filling for the pasta dish and prepared a light meal for the *vigilia di Natale* (Christmas Eve). Because we were exhausted after cooking all day, it seemed like Christmas Eve would never arrive. I could barely keep awake as we waited to go to church for Midnight Mass.

The next morning, we woke to cups of rich hot chocolate made with chunks of melted dark chocolate, milk, and cream. After breakfast and the opening of gifts, we were back in the kitchen—we had pasta to make. Vivi created a huge mound of flour and proceeded to create a well. A dozen eggs were cracked into the center and they were slowly mixed into the flour until lustrous yellow dough was formed. This had to be kneaded at length, an exhausting job. Alberto stepped in to lend us some muscle. Now it was time to prepare the dough for rolling. The dough was worked into balls and kept under a damp tea towel until it was ready to be worked. Pieces were cut off and flattened before being fed into the hand-cranked pasta maker. In the past, the sheets of pasta would have been carefully rolled by hand; however, even with the pasta maker, it still takes a great deal of skill to make the pasta extremely thin (which makes all the difference). Each sheet was then cut up into rounds using a special cutter. A ball of filling was dropped in the middle; the pasta was folded in half; and with a quick movement of the hands, the sides were brought together to form a beautiful *cappelletto* (literally, "little hat"). Repeat hundreds of times. At first, I was all thumbs: my pasta tore and my little hats were far from elegant. However, after many tries, I was making passable cappelletti and Vivi gave me a nice flour-dusted pat on the back. It is in these instances that I think about how much of culinary mastery is about embodiment and that this type of knowledge is emic: it cannot be fully explained by a teacher; the student must learn from doing and feel the right way to cook. Getting dirty in the kitchen, with your hands in the dough, is a great way to learn to cook.

In Italy, until the rise of cookbooks and women's magazines in the 1960s, firsthand apprenticeship in the home was how most women learned to cook. This is still an important part of Italian cookery and many recipes are handed down from mother to daughter. At the same time, there are many young Italian women who do not cook. I have heard friends in their thirties explain that their mothers did not want them to cook because they saw it as a burden. Women now are often expected to work outside the home while also doing the majority of domestic duties. Many women who came of age in the 1960s and 1970s decided that they wanted their daughters' lives to be different from their own; they wanted them to become doctors and lawyers, not housewives and secretaries. Gender roles in the domestic sphere have been shifting slowly for the past thirty to forty years. I have also met many Italian men who pride themselves on their culinary skills. However, I found this male culinary bravado was often saved for special occasions rather than everyday meals.

As we sat down to Christmas lunch and I lifted my spoon to my mouth, I felt one step closer to understanding Italian culture and becoming part of Alberto's family. Food has a special place in Italian culture and most Italians will enthusiastically and expertly discuss food and wine with little prompting. By taking an interest in local culinary practices you are sure to endear yourself with your Italian host or informant.

Although I felt I knew a great deal about Italian food when I arrived in Italy, the more I ate and traveled around the country, the more I realized how much I still had to learn. It is common to feel a sense of familiarity when you enter a country that is similar to your own or where there is a comparable standard of living; however, this familiarity can be deceiving or even misleading. As an anthropologist, one must stay aware of small differences, particularly when it comes to eating, because they can be easy to overlook but potentially tell us so much about people's lives. At times I found that this false familiarity was even a cause of cultural misunderstandings.

Italy has one of the richest culinary cultures in the world, one that can provide an endless source of anthropological information. As you travel this country, I recommend the *buona forchetta* approach: eat and drink everything. Immerse yourself fully in Italian culinary culture, keeping in mind that beyond each hill is a new mouth-watering experience.

NOTE

1. For more on doing anthropology "at home," see Jackson 1987.

REFERENCES

Counihan, Carole
    2004   *Around the Tuscan Table: Food, Family and Gender in Twentieth-Century Florence*. Routledge, New York.

Helestosky, Carol
    2004   *Garlic and Oil: Food and Politics in Italy*. Berg, New York.

Jackson, Anthony (editor)
    1987   *Anthropology at Home*. Routledge, New York.

Leitch, Alison
    2003   Slow Food and the Politics of Pork Fat: Italian Food and European Identity. *Ethnos: Journal of Anthropology* 68(4):437–462.

Parasecoli, Fabio
    2004   *Food Culture in Italy*. Greenwood Press, Westport, CT.

Petrini, Carlo
    2004   *Slow Food: The Case for Taste*, trans. W. McCuaig. Columbia University Press, New York.
    2007   *Slow Food Nation: Why Our Food Should Be Good, Clean and Fair*, trans. C. Furlan and J. Hunt. Rizzoli International Publications, New York.

CHAPTER TWELVE

"No Thanks, I Don't Eat Meat"

Vegetarian Adventures in Beef-centric Argentina

Ariela Zycherman

Biographical sketch. Ariela Zycherman is a doctoral candidate in the Department of Applied Anthropology at Teachers College, Columbia University, in New York City. She has conducted fieldwork in Argentina and Bolivia and is interested in the relationship between household economics and culture in food choices. Before beginning graduate school, Ariela received her B.A. in anthropology with honors from SUNY Binghamton in 2004 and spent a year as an Americorps VISTA volunteer with the New York City Coalition Against Hunger.

In the summer of 2006 I conducted my first independent research project in the province of Tucumán in northwest Argentina. The project goal was to conduct pre-dissertation research and explore the ways people perceive and relate to their diet. This research would be instrumental for understanding the larger social and political issues, and the economic hardships, that contribute to regional risks of hunger and malnutrition, which became visible during the aftereffects of Argentina's 2001 economic collapse in the province of Tucumán. I set out to elucidate the typical Tucumán diet and to uncover the deep-rooted connections of people to their diet.

Before leaving for Tucumán I worried endlessly about what I would do about my own diet in the field. The Tucumán diet is beef-centric. I am a vegetarian. Actually, I am not a vegetarian but I do abide by similar dietary guidelines. I grew up in a Jewish kosher home and I feel attached to three specific kosher laws: I do not eat pork, I eat kosher-certified meat, and I do not eat meat and milk together. I do these things out of habit, but they are also meaningful to me because they are representative of my Jewish heritage. Over the years I have preferred to eat vegetarian rather than bring my own food where I know kosher meat is not available. I have been doing this for nine years, since I began my undergraduate education. I have remained vegetarian for up to an entire year at a time, only deviating from the diet for the sporadic holiday or to indulge in the occasional hot dog. I find it easier to describe my eating habits as vegetarian because I eat meat so rarely. When people probe further and ask why I am a vegetarian, I tell them that I grew up in a kosher home and am attached to a traditional diet, which is not available to me right now. As I prepared for my fieldwork in beef-obsessed Argentina, one professor told me to get over my "vegetarian-ness." He told me that a good anthropologist must totally engage and take part in as much of the culture as she possibly can. I understood what he was telling me, but it is hard to give up something that is ingrained in you and represents a part of who you are. I felt torn between giving up my traditions to study other traditions and missing out on what had potential to be important data. I did not resolve the answer until I got into the field and my nerves and lack of experience resolved it for me.

Luckily, my dietary restrictions actually allowed me to collect useful and interesting data. Throughout Tucumán, my position as a vegetarian promoted certain diet-centric discussions that might not normally have been heard. And at the first *asado* (Argentine barbeque) I attended, discussions revolving around my not eating beef turned to reflections on what beef eating symbolizes in Tucumán. My choice not to eat beef created a forum where people could discuss other scenarios where beef was not consumed. People talked about what the absence of beef feels like for them and the importance of beef in their everyday activities. I uncovered new and unexpected themes involving national identity, health, and family that shaped the remainder of my research and promoted a deeper understanding of what beef symbolizes.

David Sutton (1997), a vegetarian anthropologist who conducted fieldwork in Greece, had similar experiences. Prior to leaving for the field, Sutton received a message from a colleague warning him that if he did not eat meat in Greece, his "manhood" would be misunderstood. Similarly to my experience, Sutton's decision not to eat meat resulted in increased interest in him by the community, the opportunity to explore differences that are not often apparent, and the divulgence of themes embedded in food. My experience in Tucumán taught me that although great data can be acquired by participating fully in the lifestyle of your informants, it can also be collected by admitting to and maintaining differences. I adhered to my own traditions during my research period, creating a strong relationship with my informants rooted in respect for dietary customs. I emerged from the field with rich and interesting information.

ARGENTINA AND BEEF

Argentina is a country renowned for its beef, but this association is a relatively recent phenomenon. Like in the rest of the New World, in Argentina Europeans who were born away from their homelands came to be known as creoles or, in Spanish, *criollos* (Cara 2003; Civantos 2005). Originally referring to people, the meaning of "criollo" has expanded to include certain cultural traditions, including diet. As time advanced and criollos could no longer be considered newcomers to the land, those previously referred to as criollo began to be referred to as citizens of their particular country, that is "from Argentina" or "Argentine" (Cara 2003). This etymological change made the cultural traditions of the criollos the national signifiers. One of these cultural traditions was the consumption of beef.

Argentine national identity has been depicted as a beef-eating cowboy since the early days of Spanish settlement in the sixteenth century, when the Spanish brought cattle to the New World with their early settlers. The cows that escaped easily adapted to life in Argentina's heartland, known as the *pampas* (White 1945). On those grasslands they grazed and reproduced, breeding prolifically. The pampas became characterized by the wild cattle that were multiplying there in large numbers. Cowboys had always tended to the cattle, and by the late eighteenth century, the official criollo profession of *gaucho* was created. The gauchos, or the Argentine cowboys, tended to the expanding cattle industry, moving the heads across the plains and delivering them for slaughter (Bethel 1993; Cara 2003; Slatta 1983). The gaucho's role was to support Argentina's fairly undiversified market economy by supplying the main product for national consumption and export, beef. It was this process that helped to commence the first phase of the creation of the beef-centric culture of Argentina. The gaucho became a national and international symbol of Argentine rural values and traditions that coincided with its independence from Spain in 1816 (Montaldo and Nouzielles 2002; Sawers 1996). The gaucho represented the criollos' ability to survive and reap from the land (Delaney 1996). In addition to the supply of beef the gauchos offered, the beef diet and the manner of preparation (using all parts of the cow and cooking over a low grill on an open fire outside) that they maintained became something that non-gaucho Argentines could reproduce. Over the course of centuries, Argentina has remained true to its beef-eating criollo identity. Argentina now has the highest rate of beef consumption per capita in the world, weighing in at 149.6 pounds (68 kilograms) annually. In comparison, people in the United States consume an average of 67 pounds (30 kilograms) of beef annually (Davis and Linn 2005; Matos and Brandani 2002)

TUCUMÁN AND METHODS

Northwest Argentina, where Tucumán is located, is one of the top two beef-consuming regions in the country (Matos and Brandani 2002). People in the region are so attached to the Argentine beef-centric diet that in 2003, in the aftermath of the country's economic collapse in 2001 when the price of beef rose dramatically in comparison to incomes, there were deaths attributed to malnutrition and hunger. These deaths are particularly curious in Tucumán where a large variety of other foodstuffs is produced in large- and small-scale farming initiatives and is available for individual consumption. It seems, however, that no one wants to eat them. According to *La Gaceta*, the Tucumán local newspaper, people are so attached to beef that when it is not available, they are unwilling to replace it with other foodstuffs (La Gaceta 2005). This relationship to a particular food sparked my interest in the beliefs supporting such a strong attachment to a diet. I chose to study Tucumán because of its residents' reputation of having a strong attachment to the beef diet and because of the reports that the hunger and high malnutrition levels of 2003 resulted from this.

There are approximately 1.3 million people in the province of Tucumán. In Argentina it is the smallest province geographically but also the most densely populated. Tucumán's climate and terrain make it suitable for intense and personal farming, and thus, it is aptly nicknamed *el jardin de la republica* ("the garden of the republic"). Tucumán encompasses a variety of extremely different topographies. The providence is rich in ecological diversity and boasts the enormous Andean mountains, flat lands with subtropical weather, and even a desert mini-region. This study focuses on Tucumán east of the Andes. Currently, Tucumán has a large agricultural industry composed of citrus, sugar, and soy mostly grown for export, but even so, Tucumán is one of the poorest provinces in all of Argentina with an unemployment rate of 11.8 percent (Provincia de Tucumán, Datos Estadisticos). These statistics, however, only apply to the 770,000 people living in the greater metropolitan area of San Miguel de Tucumán. There are no statistics available for the rest of the province, but it is probable that the percentages of unemployed and underemployed people are higher.

The beginning of Tucumán's economic woes began in the mid-1960s when Tucumán's sugar-cane industry faced a major depression (Sawers 1996). World sugar prices fell and the *zafra*, Tucumán's traditional manner of sugar harvest, was no longer efficient (Cavallo and Mundlak 1982). The results of the sugar depression left Tucumán with increased poverty and high levels of social and economic disparity (Sawers 1996). This depression, coupled with the fall of Peron, who had promoted national industry (although not very successfully), made Tucumán a hot bed for guerilla activity against the military regime who had taken over the government in 1955 (Lewis 2001). The military coup that replaced the Peron government attempted to fight inflation and make the economy more efficient. They attempted to stabilize prices, which hurt the agricultural sector to which Tucumán was attached. During the 1970s and early 1980s, Argentina's infamous "Dirty War" took place in which guerillas tried to oust the current military government. Tucumán became the center of the battle between the military coup and the insurgents for control of Argentina, which left the province in shambles (Lewis 2001). In 1984 the violence began to subside and a new president was elected. But with the elections of 1989, Tucumán once again was subject to economic strife. In the 1990s Tucumán suffered greatly from President Carlos Menem's economic policies, which led to the pegging of the Argentine peso to the U.S. dollar and the large-scale privatization of the national economy, which ranged from water concessions to the national railroad system (Lewis 2001). While the whole country suffered from the poorly implemented privatization of their utilities, Tucumán, already a poorer region, experienced a disproportionate rise in unemployment.

The setbacks of the early 1990s, coupled with the preexisting fragile local economy, made the effects of the 2001 countrywide economic collapse particularly acute in Tucumán. This collapse is said to have been caused by frail politics, excessive borrowing, and the pegging of the local currency to the U.S. dollar (Armony and Armony 2005; Lewis 2001). After the collapse, the Argentine peso lost 70 percent of its value and the gross domestic product was reduced by 11 percent (Cruces and Woden 2003). According to the World Bank's 2002 report, the high rise in the poverty rate was caused in great part by the rising price of foodstuffs, which constituted a major portion of the expenditures of the poor. Food was an important export to Argentina, and prices rose drastically with the peso's devaluation (World Bank 2003:i). Currently, the region is rebounding from those tragic years and is acclimating to re-nationalized utilities.

In order to gain a more comprehensive view of the province and possibly expose differences in diet related to specific settings it was necessary to divide my time among three distinct places. I chose these locations because they offered a broad view of the region, each demonstrating different access to food via the availability of food for purchase, foods produced, and the ability to travel to obtain food. In addition to their distinct characteristics, these locations also offered me easier access and personal security as I did my research. Prior to arriving in Tucumán I was not concerned about crime or assault; nothing I read implied that Tucumán was a dangerous place. However, like many depressed or urban areas, there are certain parts that are more dangerous than others. As a single woman in a machista society, I heeded the advice of my local friends and stuck to areas where good transportation made it easy for me to come and go to areas that were known to be safe during the day and in the evening. I began my research in San Miguel de Tucumán, the fifth-largest city in Argentina. I focused specifically on the center of the city—"el Centro," as it is known—because that is where the major markets, large apartment buildings, companies, and other signs of global influence are located. As a comparison case to the urban center, I focused on a small farming town in the north of the province called San Isidro. San Isidro is characterized by subsistence farming and small agricultural business. The town is one hour's drive to the north of Tucumán by coach bus or car. As my final locus for research, I chose a small peri-urban village named Pacara. Pacara is located close to San Miguel de Tucumán, eleven kilometers out of the city, but in the center of cane fields and isolated from the city by poor transportation, poverty, and unemployment. Nevertheless, its proximity to the city offers people employment and shopping opportunities.

Despite my best efforts to create a well-formed comparison case with ethnographic data from different locations, Pacara became my main domain for exploratory research. I was able to do some ethnography in San Miguel and San Isidro as well, but I was not invited to participate or "hang around" to the same extent as I was in Pacara. People in Pacara easily opened their homes to me and were eager to invite me for a meal or have me interview them. I took advantage of the situation and conducted the majority of my initial ethnographic research in Pacara. This interest in my presence originated during my first visit to Pacara, when I told my hosts that I did not eat meat. My status as a guest who did not eat meat made me a curiosity. People wanted to spend time with me and understand me. Being a vegetarian made me interesting and granted me an opening into the community where I was easily able to meet new people and explore my research interests more intensely. I think people in Pacara were more interested in me than were the inhabitants of the other two sites because of Paraca's geographical space. Pacara is a village whereas San Miguel de Tucumán is a city and San Isidro is a spread-out rural community. Word travels quickly in Pacara, everyone knows everyone else, and people only need to walk ten minutes to get from one side of town to the other. Within this space it was easier for people to notice that I was there and get accustomed to my presence. When I visited one home, other neighbors often visited it too. Consequently, I was introduced to large networks of people and extended family members and friends. In the urban and rural settings I had to make appointments to see people, I was not as visible, and the buzz about me and my "vegetarian-ness" was quieter. I knew my time was short in Tucumán and I wanted to make the most of it, so I took advantage of my popularity and conducted all my preliminary investigations in Pacara. Later, I was able to use what I learned there to design interviews to compare interactions with and understandings of beef in all three locations.

I used ethnographic tools such as participant observation, archival research, semi-structured interviews, and structured interviews to record weekly food recalls, review of food shopping lists, dietary general histories, and food free lists, where my informants were asked to list all the things Argentineans eat. As a participant observer I partook in various events in all three locations. Mostly, I was invited for lunch, the largest family-oriented meal of the day, and I was able to assist in cooking, shopping, and food ordering. I attended birthday parties in two of three places and generally just "hung out" and socialized with locals. In addition to participant observation, interviews, and archival research, I spent time collecting information on prices and the availability of different foods in all three locations. I surveyed various street vendors, storefronts, wholesale and supermarket vendors to take notes on the variety of goods sold, their hours, and their prices. I also spoke to restaurant owners of both sit-down and take-out establishments about traditional foods and the history of eating in Tucumán. From my experiences I was able to compile a recipe booklet of popular regional cuisine.

BEEF EATING

The research demonstrated that what Tucumános ate was mainly beef and mostly at lunch time. Meat in general provides 65 percent of the protein intake of the average Argentine and 50 percent of that meat is beef (Navarro et al. 2003). Various forms of beef are served daily at lunch. The varying ways people include beef in their diets not only demonstrate the importance of this one food but also the exclusion of others. Vegetables, particularly green ones, are readily available in the region, but with the exception of potatoes, cooked tomatoes, carrots, and onions, they are almost completely avoided. Sometimes meals are served with a salad typically made from lettuce, tomato, and onion. This practice, however, is not seen in everyday eating but instead occurs in restaurants. Other types of vegetables are available in the region, although not in bulk and not always in good condition. Depending on where one lives, gaining access to a variety of vegetables ranges from fairly easy to extremely difficult. Researcher Alicia Navaro investigated the connection between health and the Argentine criollo diet in the nearby province of Cordoba in Argentina. Navarro explains that Argentines have a high rate of animal fat and protein consumption, mainly obtained from red meat, and this is coupled with a low consumption rate of fiber and fish. *La Gaceta*, the Tucumán newspaper, recently wrote that the majority of Tucumános do not eat the recommended daily amount of fruits and vegetables and that they eat them less than five times per week (La Gaceta 2007). The article also describes the vegetables that people do eat as "starchy ones," like potatoes and corn, and attributes the absence of green leafy vegetables to the lack of variety available in the marketplace (La Gaceta 2007).

People's decisions to consume beef reflect biological, cultural, and economic factors, which influence the local diet. Macbeth and Mowatt (2004:102) explain that "socially and culturally induced food preferences and aversions can become unconsciously integrated in the physiological reactions of the individual." On countless occasions people explained to me what an important foodstuff beef was for them and how vegetables made them feel disgusted or unwell in some way. A young woman named Marcela joked with me: "We live in such a culture of meat even the dogs are part of it. My dogs won't eat vegetables but will eat meat." An older woman told me she made a large dinner for her family the night before. It was a large soup with tripe and lentils. Her son would not eat it because he considered the lentils in the soup to be vegetables and they ruined the dish. The importance of beef in the Argentine diet is not simply relative to vegetables' lack of importance, but it stands on its own as a singularly important food. Dieters who remove beef from their diets attribute their hunger specifically to a lack of beef, even when replacing one protein for another. No other food is equivalent; without it, a meal is not a meal; and only once it is consumed will hunger be satisfied. One informant explained, "When I don't eat meat I don't feel like I am eating."

The beef-centric diet coalesces in the Argentine tradition of an asado. The tradition of an asado revolves around the beef itself and the process of cooking it. The asado is similar to a U.S. barbeque, but it is reminiscent of the gaucho experience of using a special grill, called a *parilla*, and takes advantage of many parts of the cow not popular in the United States. The parilla is a pit, usually filled with charcoal and covered with a heavy metal grate. The parilla is built low to the ground, and cooking on it is reminiscent of the gaucho practice of grilling over a campfire in the middle of the pampas. Special cuts of beef unique to Argentinean butchering are put on the grill, in addition to the intestines, liver, ribs, and other beef-based food items like chorizo and blood sausage (Figure 12.1). Argentine butchering is different than U.S. butchering in that for one large cut of American beef—the flank, for example—Argentines break that down into five or six cuts, all used for different, specific preparation and cooking methods (Matos and Brandani 2002). There are specific cuts of beef used for the asado including but not limited to *costillas* (a type of rib), *vacio* (a type of flank), *matambre* (flank steak), and *entraña* (like skirt steak).

12.1. An entire side of beef for sale in the butcher shop, a typical sight in Tucumán.
(PHOTO BY ARIELA ZYCHERMAN)

Despite the workweek constraints, the time-intensive asado still plays a major role in facilitating the traditional beef diet, providing a place, a time, and a manner of experiencing it. The asado typically takes place on weekends, usually on Sundays. The tradition of a Sunday asado is also not restricted to holiday weekends; rather, it is a weekly event. Entire extended families and friends gather together on weekends to eat and to share in each other's company around an asado. The length of cooking time required by the asado creates a social environment as family members or groups of friends spend time together and help as the meat grills over a slow fire. The process of making asado can take from two to four hours and the grill must be constantly monitored and more food cooked.

THE FIRST ASADO

While doing my fieldwork in Argentina I was invited to several asados. Attending asados was a great way for me to conduct research. It gave me a chance to talk to large numbers of new people, witness family dynamics, and, of course, focus on the beef. It was participant observation at its best. But as I

211

was once asked by a classmate, "If you are not eating beef at an asado, how are you participating?" As a researcher I participated as much as I could in their everyday lives, paying special attention to their meals and to their shopping. I was still able to note what was prepared, how it was prepared, what was eaten, and how it was eaten and to discuss the food and how they procured it. At the same time, I was honest about who I was, what I was doing there, and how I ate. At the asado I participated in the same ways; I was a guest, I mingled, I stood by the parilla, I helped cook, and I always found something to eat. However, at first it was not obvious to me how to be a vegetarian and participate at the same time. In the following story I will describe how my role as a participant observer and as an inexperienced, nervous, first-time anthropologist at my first asado fashioned my relationships with my informants and shaped the research I was embarking on for the next three months.

I arrived in Tucumán on a sunny and beautiful day in late May. The following day, after arguing with two network providers and dealing with an unexpected four-hour siesta that shut down the entire province, I managed to get my cell phone working. With my newly working equipment, I called a couple I had contacted before leaving for Argentina. As part of my preparation for this project, I had reached out to every nonprofit organization that was dealing with poverty and hunger in the province in order to find some informants who were working directly with the aftereffects of the economic collapse. Prior to my field experience I did not know anyone in Tucumán, my professors did not know anyone, and my contacts in Buenos Aires did not know anyone, so I hoped this method would increase my sample size. The couple who had responded, Lily and José, are the directors of a small not-for-profit organization that deals with development in poor rural regions of Tucumán. Their organization runs a small library, offers adult-education classes, and provides a free afternoon snack for the children of Pacara. When I called them, they invited me to a "meeting" on Saturday so I could tour the village. I, of course, accepted the invitation, not knowing what to expect.

At ten on Saturday morning I met Lily and José for the first time when they picked me up in a tiny red 1987 sedan. The car was already full with their two teenage nephews and two young sons. But to my surprise, they managed to squeeze everyone into the back and the seven of us drove off. We drove out of the city, past the recently familiar landscape of buildings and past the sugar fields. Suddenly we made a left and the car stopped in front of a store. I asked what we were doing there and José told me we were getting the supplies for an asado. Although I knew what an asado was in theory, I had never attended one. When I asked about the imminent asado, my friend José answered: "It's what Argentines do on the weekends. We eat lots of meat." Minutes later Lily returned to the car with three gigantic bags of various cuts of red meat. I thought to myself, "Crap! I am not ready to make a choice." I was taken off guard by my invitation to the asado and felt unprepared to make a decision as to whether I was going to be eating meat. Had I been invited on a Sunday, the typical day for the asado, and had our meeting been scheduled closer to lunchtime, I might have expected the event and made the decision whether to describe myself as a vegetarian ahead of time. Unfortunately, it was 10:00 AM on a Saturday and I was confused. On my first outing, in my first week, of my first field experience I was experiencing the age-old anthropological mantra, "things in the field do not always go as planned." I always thought I would be able to adapt to unexpected situations but I was still not accustomed to my surroundings in Tucumán and had not yet decided what I was going to do about my kosher/vegetarianism.

In my astonishment and nervousness I blurted out to my hosts, "Thank you so much for the invitation, but I don't eat meat." I regretted my choice the minute the words came out of my mouth, but to avoid confusion I did not take my comment back. I wanted to appear confident and decisive. At the same time, I was worried that their first impression of me was that I was rude and ungrateful. Luckily, Lily and José understood and told me not to worry because there would be other things to eat. José assured me that it was okay because they were "accustomed" to eating meat and I was not. I told them I was sorry and they should not go to any extra trouble. They assured me (although not convincingly) that they would not go to any extra effort.

We continued on our journey into and past the sugarcane fields where the village of Pacara is located. Another surprise was that everyone involved with the organization in Pacara was invited to the asado. More than twenty adults and many children were there to meet me when we arrived in Pacara, and word spread quickly that the U.S. visitor did not eat meat. Subsequently, the lunch discussion revolved around beef and what it meant to the individuals participating in the asado. People revealed intimate details about their health, impressions of health, and family negotiations about diet. At the asado there were four cuts of beef served: lomo (like tenderloin steaks), costilla (from the rib cage), ancho (like ribeye), and bife de chorizo (similar to sirloin but butterflied). The cuts of beef were constantly monitored on the parilla, and when the meat was served, someone remained outside with the parilla to continue cooking. There seemed to be an endless amount of beef and the guests took seconds and thirds. In addition to beef, tamales with chicken and empanadas stuffed with beef, onions, and eggs (prepared earlier) were warmed up on the parilla. Four salads were on the table: a lentil and tuna salad, Russian salad, purple cabbage salad, and a tomato and cheese salad. (Two salads were prepared when we arrived and the other two might have been prepared afterward.) Lemons and limes, common Tucumán condiments, were cut up and scattered over the table.

During the meal I had the opportunity to talk to many of the Pacara residents. I did not have to do much prompting to get them to talk about their diet. The simple fact that I was not eating the same thing as they were was enough to propel the conversation in that direction through the entire meal. My vegetarianism made people think and discuss what it was like for them when their traditional diet was threatened and acquiring beef was more difficult to achieve. Three specific topics emerged during that first asado that shaped the way I approached the why and how questions of my research in the subsequent weeks. These three themes were beef's role as a symbol of Argentine nationality, the consumption of beef as a symbol of both good health and poor health, and beef as a facilitator of strong family relationships. I took my hint, and Mars and Mars's advice to "follow my material" (2004:76), and I decided to pursue these three themes. Coupled with the preexisting poverty and economic disaster of Argentina, these premises created a colorful and explanatory picture of how the diet was understood and maintained by its partisans. Additionally, they added another cultural dynamic to the question of how hunger can occur in such a fertile place.

DOING THE RESEARCH AS A VEGETARIAN

My informants were not shy in asking me why I did not eat meat. In fact, it was their favorite question. When compared to the Argentine way of eating my diet seemed less nourishing and missing the most important part of the meal. Numerous people made comparisons between my size and health and their size and health, drawing conclusions from what they understood the caloric and nutritional value of their beef diet to be. For example, one person said: "All vegetarians are fat; they eat too much bread and not enough proteins. They have big round puffy bellies like starving people." They were not saying I ate too much or what I ate was fattening; rather, they thought I was eating in an unhealthy manner. People wanted to know why I did not partake in the same customs that they did. When I responded, I made it as clear as possible that I thought eating beef was okay and that it was my behavior that was weird. I further explained that it was my custom not to eat much meat when away from home, and then, if they were interested, I explained the kosher diet. When I answered that this was "my custom," I hit the jackpot. Argentines use the particular terms "custom" and "accustomed" to describe their everyday activities. The phrase "accustomed to beef" manifested itself over and over when people spoke about their diet. Just as José did on the day I met him, it was common for people to say to me: "In Argentina we are accustomed to eating lots of meat, and it's how we eat. In North America they don't eat that way." These conversations led to long commentaries of the importance of beef in their lives, the frequency in which they consumed it, and reflections on times when it was not available.

Conversations about the diet in general and beef specifically were enlightening, interactive, and explanatory, even though I did not partake in the actual eating of beef. I often came early to help prepare food, to learn how to cook, and to chat with the women (the cooks and shoppers of the house). The women welcomed my presence and were happy to let me help them prepare for any upcoming event (asado, birthday party, luncheon). Despite my not eating meat, the women were not shy about teaching me how to prepare and cook meat. My friend Carmela said to me, "Even thought you aren't going to eat meat, there is no reason my husband shouldn't." Then she insisted that it was also important that I learn to cook meat for my future husband. So alongside Carmela in the kitchen I learned to make a *milanesa* dinner for a family of eight, pounding each steak until it was flat, making the herbed egg bath for the meat, and frying it until it was perfectly crisp. I spent time with Carmela's extended family, learning to sauté the beef, make the dough, and stuff and fold the turnovers to prepare 300 beef empanadas for an enormous family party. From the local butcher I learned how to dismember a chicken and prepare it for sale and identify entrails for asados. Lastly, my friend Miguel Angel taught me how to diversify chicken feed so that the chickens produced intensely colored eggs. In his retirement, Miguel Angel decided to raise chickens mostly for their eggs and occasionally for their meat. He takes great pride in knowing each chicken's natural egg color. He showed me how his chickens produce lovely shades of pink, yellow, and green eggs and how he can recognize which chicken produced the egg by the egg's color. Miguel Angel has discovered how to intensify each chicken's egg coloration by feeding it different quantities of corn, store-bought feed, and a host of other dried plants. I was excited to learn his tricks, but I told him I was not sure I would be able to practice the technique at home because my superintendent does not allow animals in my New York City apartment building.

People made an effort to include me in their meals by making something additional, like a potato and cheese *bomba* (dumpling), a vegetable empanada, or fried zucchini. Other times they removed the meat from something they were serving or just did not serve me the meat. I did not want to be an imposition to my hosts and I constantly volunteered to come by for *maté*, a popular herbal drink, or after a meal instead. But people continually and repeatedly insisted that I break bread with them, which I was more than happy to do. I often helped out in the kitchen and tried to insist that whatever was being made on my behalf should not require too much extra effort.

I noticed, however, that nobody ate what I was eating, ever. I suspect two reasons for this: one was respect for the visitor and the other was dietary preference. I think that probably the latter is more correct. When I offered people cheese dumplings, they looked horrified. When I offered a vegetable empanada, they gagged. When I offered fried zucchini, they asked, "Don't you know we don't eat anything green?" These interactions gave me data on their meals, because everyone else seemingly continued to eat as they typically would, despite my eating something different. I was able to verify that these were characteristic meals, minus my plate, when I ate with less accommodating people or at restaurants with other informants. These meals also demonstrated the limits of how far from their standard diets people were willing to go. I was able to gather the consumption data on these subjects and simultaneously witness reactions to other foods that would not normally be served to them.

FURTHER UNDERSTANDING THE BEEF

That first asado and my unplanned experience of telling my informants I was a vegetarian proved to be the most beneficial accident of my trip.[1] The three topics that emerged from the meal helped me to be cognizant of certain embedded meanings in the practice of eating beef. As I "followed my material" and continued investigations in San Miguel and San Isidro, I noticed that these themes of nationality, health, and family were recurring and almost universal throughout the province. The data that emerged create a multilayered system of sociocultural values and rules in which eating beef becomes synonymous with you and your family being healthy, family-oriented Argentines.

When my informants discuss beef, they are often discussing how beef characterizes them as Argentine people. Mintz (1996) explains that a diet or a "cuisine" often comes to represent the identity of a group of people when that cuisine is something that they alone have and it is a commodity. Oknuki-Tierney (1993) writes about rice as an identifier of Japanese nationality. She explains that this metaphor for "us" and "you" often is reinforced when the staple food item is also related to the land. This behavior often creates strong food preferences where nationality and food are not detachable. Beef is a product unique in quality and quantity to Argentina and is historically significant as it is one of the first successful agricultural products in colonial Argentina. This theme of national identity came up repeatedly throughout the course of my research. Beef was used on numerous occasions as a tangible representation of the differences between "us," the Argentines, and "you," the American. During a conversation over dinner, one informant told me about the time that she had gone to Missouri to visit her daughter, who was there as an exchange student. She said that while she was there, she had tried to make milanesa for her daughter's host family. To shop for the meal she went to the supermarket but the market did not have any cuts of meat worthy of her dish. The only meat she found was in the freezer section, pre-wrapped and very expensive. My informant felt embarrassed about the event and felt she was out of place as an Argentine shopping in a U.S. grocery store. After she recalled this incident, her husband commented that he was not interested in traveling there if the meat was so bad. This "culture of meat," which incorporates not only a taste for the product but the knowledge of how to use it, is often referred to with pride as a unique quality of Argentine identity.

In Tucumán, people also expressed an attachment to the diet because of its association with health. Popular belief is that healthy adults are people who eat meat on a daily basis. On countless occasions people expressed to me how important eating meat was to their health and physical well-being. The idea of not eating beef is often associated with poverty, illness, and old age. Individuals who cannot afford to eat beef or are on diets often describe themselves as hungry or feeling ill. These negative associations with non-beef eaters keep many from deviating from this diet, despite the risks associated with such a high-fat, high-cholesterol diet. Many of my informants admitted seeing costs to their health because of their heavy beef-based diet and talked to me about the cases of malnutrition that plagued the country after the economic collapse. Others talked about more personal experiences; one informant told me both her mother and father had "suffered from everything: high blood pressure, hypertension, heart disease"; she claimed this was caused by this high-cholesterol diet. The idea of abandoning or adjusting her diet, however, was less appealing than risking illness. Almost half of my informants told me that one or more persons in the family were suffering from health problems related to a high-protein, high-fat diet, like obesity, heart disease, high cholesterol, and high blood pressure. All were advised by their doctors to completely eliminate red meat from their diet, but not one followed that direction. It is popular for many of my informants to replace beef with chicken for weekday meals. However, all of my informants who cited health problems as a reason they did not eat meat daily, or almost daily, told me that on weekends they always attend an asado. My informants could not accept the advice of their doctors completely because eating beef proved to be more important than such health concerns.

The consumption of beef is also synonymous with family relations in Tucumán; beef is almost always present as part of the meal when a family gathers together. Lunch is the main meal of the day and often features beef. Businesses in Tucumán close from 1:00 to 5:00 PM daily to observe siesta. Workers generally return home for lunch and the family eats together. While the work dynamic is changing in Tucumán with more women going to work, the importance of a large lunch remains the woman's responsibility. Many women are unable to cook time-intensive meals but buy frozen or take-out meals so that their family can gather together on a daily basis. A few women from San Miguel explained to me that the lunch specials in restaurants for take-out usually include a milanesa or lomo. In this way, they address the dietary preferences of their family and encourage family time, while simultaneously being employed outside the home. An informant who runs a popular empanada store that does heavy business on Sundays, selling his most popular item—beef empanadas—for asados, explained how food, or more specifically beef, in Argentine culture brings the family together. He used the example of the asado to drive home the connection between family and beef. The asado revolves around eating beef and the process of cooking beef, facilitating a time and a place for the whole family, including the larger extended family, to come together. For the opportunity to take part in an asado, individuals travel long distances, spend extra money, and put themselves at risk of health problems. Big lunch meals and weekend asados revolve around two things, beef and family. Argentines gauge their own familial connections and those of people around them by how they participate in these rituals.

CONCLUSION

I am glad I admitted at that first asado that I did not eat meat. This choice, conscious or not, enabled me to learn a few things about doing fieldwork that could not be learned at home. First, I learned that my informants could relate to others who stick to dietary customs in the same way they do. This mutual understanding that people have reasons for deciding which foods they will or will not eat can create a strong bond between researcher and informant. People felt comfortable talking to me about their food "hang ups" because they knew that I had my own. Second, I learned that just because I did not eat all of the foods other people were eating, I did not have to miss out on the opportunity to interact with those foods and with the people who prepared and consumed them. I gained significant hands-on experience shopping for, preparing, and cooking beef, as well as sitting at beef-centric meals with my informants. Once I made it clear that I was interested in what they were doing, they became interested in teaching me. Finally, I learned that even though the element of taste was missing in my research, it did not mean I could not understand how the diet is structured, what it means, what it represents, its history, and the social weight it carries. Participating in other ways, like visiting the family, drinking maté, coming to a party or dinner, and talking, can also generate data on the topic of food.

In Tucumán, I was lucky. The people were sympathetic to my diet. They realized early on, or so I hoped, that not eating meat was my own peculiarity as opposed to a criticism of their lifestyle. While my experience in Tucumán was good, I can imagine that in other situations the choice not to eat meat might not be as fruitful. In Tucumán, people are somewhat familiar with Jews, the United States, and the global food market and, therefore, are acquainted with people maintaining different patterns of eating. For young anthropologists like me, going into the field with dietary restrictions is worrisome and daunting. In my case I was torn between giving myself up entirely to the discipline and sacrificing a vital part of my research for my own culture. My decision to follow the latter came as a surprise even to me. As it turned out, however, I did not sacrifice anything. Instead, not eating beef and approaching food participant observation in a nontraditional manner opened other doors to what is often hidden information. I can never be sure of what I might have learned if I had eaten beef at the asado that first Saturday. But I do know that despite my nervousness and accidental admission that I was a vegetarian, my first field season was a success and I was able to collect useful data that not only began to answer my original questions but also divulged the complexity of the issue at hand.

NOTE

1. For a broader discussion of this section and the implications for these interpretations, see Zycherman 2008.

REFERENCES

Armony, Ariel C., and Victor Armony
  2005   Indictments, Myths, and Citizen Mobilization in Argentina: A Discourse Analysis. *Latin American Politics and Society* 47(4):27–54.

Bethel, Leslie (editor)
  1993   *Argentina since Independence.* Cambridge University Press, Cambridge.

Cara, Ana C.
  2003   The Poetics of Creole Talk: Toward an Aesthetic of Argentine Verbal Art. *Journal of American Folklore* 116(459):36–56.

Cavallo, Domingo, and Yair Mundlak
  1982   *Agriculture and Economic Growth in an Open Economy: The Case of Argentina.* International Food Policy Research Institute, Washington, DC.

Civantos, Christina
  2005   *Between Argentines and Arabs: Argentina Orientalism, Arab Immigrants and the Writing of Identity.* SUNY Press, Albany.

Cruces, Guillermo, and Quentin T. Woden
2003   Transient and Chronic Poverty in Turbulent Times: Argentina 1995–2002. *Economics Bulletin* 9(3):1–12.

Davis, Christopher, and Biing-Hwan Linn
2005   Factors Affecting U.S. Beef Consumption. USDA, Economic Research Service. http://www.ers.usda.gov/publications/ldp/oct05/ldpm13502/, accessed August 15, 2008.

Delaney, Jeane
1996   Making Sense of Modernity: Changing Attitudes toward the Immigrant and the Gaucho in Turn-of-the-Century Argentina. *Comparative Studies in Society and History* 38(3):434–459.

La Gaceta
2005   *La Dieta del Tucumáno Deja Mucho que Desear.* October 10. http://www.Lagaceta.com, accessed May 8, 2007.
2007   No Se Consume ni la Cantidad ni el Tipo de Verduras y Frutas Necesarias. April 11. http://www.Lagaceta.com, accessed May 8, 2007.

Lewis, Daniel K.
2001   *The History of Argentina.* Greenwood Press, Westport, CT.

Macbeth, Helen, and Fiona Mowatt
2004   Researching Food Preferences: Methods and Problems for Anthropologists. In *Researching Food Habits*, ed. Helen Macbeth, Helen MacClancy, and Jeremy MacClancy, 102–117. Berghahn Books, New York.

Mars, Gerald, and Valerie Mars
2004   Doing It Wrong: Why Bother to Do Imperfect Research. In *Researching Food Habits*, ed. Helen Macbeth, Helen MacClancy, and Jeremy MacClancy, 76–85. Berghahn Books, New York.

Matos, Elena, and Aldo Brandani
2002   Review on Meat Consumption and Cancer in South America. *Mutation Research/Fundamental and Molecular Mechanisms of Mutagenesis* 506–507:243–249.

Mintz, Sidney W.
1996   *Tasting Food, Tasting Freedom: Excursions into Eating, Culture and the Past.* Beacon Press Books, Boston.

Montaldo, Graciela, and Gabriela Nouzeilles
2002   *The Argentine Reader: History, Culture, Politics.* Duke University Press, Durham, NC.

Navarro, Alicia, Maria P. Diaz, Sonia E. Muñoz, Maria J. Lantieri, and Aldo R. Eynard
2003   Characterization of Meat Consumption and Risk of Colorectal Cancer in Cordoba, Argentina. *Nutrition* 19(1):7–10.

Ohnuki-Tierney, Emiko
1993   *Rice as Self: Japanese Identities through Time.* Princeton University Press, Princeton, NJ.

Provincia de Tucumán, Datos Estadisticos
2006   Informe Trimesteral Abril/Junio; Mercado de Trabajo. http://www. Tucumán.gov.ar/planeamiento/estadistica/inf206/mercadotrabajo01. htm, accessed February 15, 2008.

Sawers, Larry
1996   *The Other Argentina: The Interior and National Development.* Westview Press, Boulder, CO.

Slatta, Richard
1983   *Gauchos and the Vanishing Frontier.* University of Nebraska Press, Lincoln.

Sutton, David
1997   The Vegetarian Anthropologist. *Anthropology Today* 13(1):5–8.

White, C. Langdon
1945   The Argentine Meat Question. *Geographical Review* 35(4):634–646.

World Bank, The
2003   Argentina: Crisis and Poverty 2003; A Poverty Assessment, vol. 1:1–75. http://web.worldbank.org/WBSITE/EXTERNAL/TOPICS/EXT POVERTY/EXTPA/0,,contentMDK:20206723~isCURL:Y~menu PK:443285~pagePK:148956~piPK:216618~theSitePK:430367,00. html, accessed February 15, 2008.

Zycherman, Ariela
2008   To Beef or Not to Beef: Defining Food Security and Insecurity in Tucumán, Argentina. *Ecological and Environmental Anthropology* 4(1):28–37.

CHAPTER THIRTEEN

Eating with the Blackfeet

Who's Been Eating Whose Food?

Susan L. Johnston

Biographical sketch. Susan Johnston is a professor of anthropology in the Department of Anthropology and Sociology, West Chester University, West Chester, Pennsylvania. She was awarded her Ph.D. in anthropology in 1999 from the University of Pennsylvania. Johnston's areas of specialty within human biology are medical and nutritional anthropology, with her research thus far focused on native North American populations. Prior to returning to graduate school, Johnston was a physician assistant working in academic and various clinical settings; her undergraduate degree was in human ecology (an interdisciplinary major in anthropology, biology, and psychology).

I felt a bit nervous as I knocked on the door of Bell's[1] house in the main reservation town of Browning. Although I had spent some time driving around the reservation with her as she visited elderly and shut-in people in her role as a community health worker, her abrupt and somewhat gruff demeanor still had me a bit on edge. Added to that was the fact that I had never eaten with a Blackfeet family before, and I did not know what to expect. After we sat down, what I saw from my place of honor at the table was heaping piles of meat and potatoes and a salad consisting largely of iceberg lettuce. What I heard was "we don't have salad all the time—I made it because you were coming." I was surprised and a bit disconcerted (although I kept this to myself). I was on the reservation that summer of 1992 to determine if there was a chronic disease-related issue that I might be able to examine for my dissertation research, and I knew that this would likely involve research on nutrition and foodways. Yet how was I to study Blackfeet food habits if they were going to change them because I was present? As I munched on substantial portions of boiled rib meat, boiled potatoes, and salad, I also heard lots of questions from Bell and her grown kids about how I usually ate. I felt eyes on me, watching to see if I helped myself to seconds and what I chose to eat more of. My initial nervousness persisted, although for somewhat different reasons. Honestly, I am not a paranoid person. What I experienced, without understanding it at the time, was the discomfiture of the observer being observed.

These are experiences I have had the opportunity to repeat again and again during my many years of working in this community, studying health and food habits, and of eating in this particular household and others. The Blackfeet, or at least some of them, have been studying my food habits, and studying me studying their food habits, for years. In 1995–1996 I lived on the reservation for a year while I conducted my dissertation research, which was informed by the preliminary data gathering I did during that initial visit in 1992. I returned every year through 2007 for periods from a few days to a couple of months to do follow-up or additional projects. I discuss this work in more detail in the following sections.

In the field, we often eat with those whose foodways or nutritional intakes we are attempting to understand—and often in household settings. Yet there are dynamics in this very interaction, and in the expectations surrounding it, that may well alter the eating patterns and food choices of either or both parties and have impacts on the kind of data we gather. In this chapter, I tease apart some of the dynamics of this experience and explore ramifications of this bidirectional observation experienced by anthropologists of food and nutrition in the context of eating. But first I will outline where the Blackfeet live today and how that came to be.

BACKGROUND AND HISTORY

The Blackfeet Reservation, home of the people who refer to themselves officially as the Blackfeet Indian Nation or Blackfeet Tribe, includes approximately 1.5 million acres (6,070 km²) in northern Montana where the Great Plains meet the Rocky Mountain front (Figure 13.1). It is tucked up against Glacier National Park on the west and the international border with Canada on the

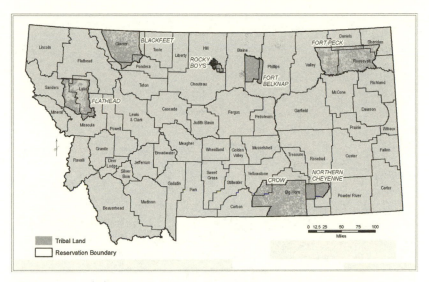

13.1. Montana tribal areas. (MAP COURTESY OF MONTANA DEPARTMENT OF COMMERCE, CENSUS AND ECONOMIC INFORMATION CENTER, HTTP://WWW.CEIC.MT.GOV/GRAPHICS/DATA_MAPS/TRIBAL. GIF, ACCESSED APRIL 19, 2009)

north. The climate is characterized by wide temperature fluctuations and average annual precipitation of fifteen inches. In the past decade or so, rainfall has been even sparser. These dry conditions support extensive grasslands and, near the mountain front, some timber (Figure 13.2). The growing season is short and does not easily support agriculture, although some wheat is grown on the eastern reservation and nearby with the aid of irrigation. Primarily, the grasslands of the reservation provide fodder for grazing cattle and horses.

When I conducted my dissertation research in 1995–1996, the tribal enrollment was approximately 14,600 members, of whom some 8,000 were living on the reservation (Blackfeet Enrollment Department, unpublished data, 1995). The reservation population is actually larger than this number reflects, since it also includes people who identify themselves as Blackfeet but who do not meet enrollment criteria, as well as members of other Indian nations and non-Indians. In 1990 the total reservation population was 8,488 (U.S. Census 1992). The proximity of Glacier National Park also affects the composition of some reservation communities, at least on a seasonal basis, as people from off-reservation take summer jobs in, or simply travel to, the park. The greatest concentration of residents is in and around the town of Browning, estimated population 1,220 in 1996 (Montana State University Local Government Center, personal communication, 1996). There are also several smaller communities, but the reservation is mostly rural. It is 100 miles

13.2. Reservation land with a view toward Glacier National Park. (PHOTO BY SUSAN L. JOHNSTON)

(160 km) on mostly two-lane roads over the mountains to Kalispell, the nearest city, and an easier 120 miles (193 km) across the plains to Great Falls, a major commercial center. Both have international airports. Amtrak runs through the reservation and has stations there. This railway line was originally laid by the Great Northern Railroad in the heyday of rail transportation and provided access to Glacier National Park for travelers from Chicago and the Pacific Northwest.

The Blackfeet, who are actually the South Piegan or, in the Blackfoot language, Amskaapipikani (see Frantz and Russell [1995] for orthography used here) are closely related to several other Native nations, the Blood (Kainaa), Northern Blackfoot (Siksika), and North Peigan (Apatohsipikani), who reside in what is now Canada. All of these groups share the same Algonquin language. In common (English) speech, the U.S. Blackfeet call themselves "Blackfeet." Most Blackfeet speak English as their first language, a legacy of intensive efforts on the part of the government to assimilate Indians at particular historic junctures. Most significant to language loss were the requirements by many boarding schools, mission schools, and the early day schools both on and off the reservation that students leave all aspects of their culture behind; often they were even beaten for speaking "Indian." This affected particularly those who were of school age from the 1920s on. Some people in the oldest generation still living are fluent Blackfoot speakers, and today there are efforts to increase knowledge of the native language in the community, including Blackfoot language-immersion schools and classes at the tribal community college.

During the first two-thirds of the 1800s the Blackfeet were a dominant force on the northwestern plains (Ewers 1958). Along with their allies, the Gros Ventres (Atsina) and Sarsi, the three divisions of the Blackfoot Nation controlled access to the resources of a large area including what is now southern Alberta and western Saskatchewan in Canada, as well as Montana. Horses became a part of Blackfeet life around the 1730s or 1740s, when they gradually made their way north from Mexico by raid and trade, replacing dogs as beasts of burden and providing the spark for a major increase in mobility. Blackfeet skill at horsemanship and their elaborate material culture related to the horse have been well documented (e.g., Ewers 1955). Buffalo were the mainstay of the diet and provided the resources for many of the objects used in everyday life (lodging, clothing, cookware, etc.). The importance of this animal to the Blackfeet and other Plains nations cannot be overestimated. American buffalo are actually more properly called "bison" (their scientific name is *Bison bison*), as they are in a different genus from the true buffalo, which are Asian and African animals of the genera *Bubalus* or *Syncerus*. However, the Blackfeet, and many North Americans generally, call these animals buffalo, and I will continue to do so in this chapter. Plants also were significant sources of food and had important roles in ceremony and medicine (Hellson and Gadd 1974; Johnston 1960).

The dependence on buffalo and other game and on plant resources required a high degree of mobility and the pursuit of a yearly round of subsistence-oriented activities (Ewers 1958). The social relationships and structure of the nation were centered on this cycle, as the size of social groups, ranging from small bands to the entire nation, depended on the time of year and availability of resources. Ceremonial life also followed an annual cycle, with events that involved the entire group, such as the Sun Dance or medicine lodge, taking place when all of the bands gathered together for the early summer buffalo hunt. Buffalo tongues were an important sacred food in the ceremony and had to be in plentiful supply. The holding of this event was precipitated by the solemn vow of a woman to the Creator to serve as "medicine woman" in the ceremony in return for the healing or safety of a relative. After such a pledge was made, the bands were notified and arrangements made for the conduct of the ceremony that year. The site for each ceremony was chosen by tribal leaders based on its ability to afford protection against enemies as well as proximity to buffalo with good availability of grass for grazing (Dempsey 1986). In late "buffalo days," the Sweetgrass Hills were a favorite location for the Piegan sun dance, but it was held at various places in their vast range in the historical period (Ewers 1955).

By the early 1850s, the Blackfeet began to be subjected to a series of treaties with territorial and U.S. governments that gradually whittled away at the original large territory used by the tribe until the reservation reached its present size in 1896 (Ewers 1958). White settlers desired Blackfeet land for raising cattle and agricultural pursuits. Tribal life became increasingly focused on trading posts like Fort Benton, the location of the government Indian agent responsible for distribution of treaty-promised goods and services. Sporadic violent confrontations between whites and Blackfeet occurred, as did periodic epidemics of diseases, like smallpox, that caused many deaths. In January 1870 the infamous massacre of Heavy Runner's band by Colonel E. M. Baker of the United States Cavalry, in which women and children were among the killed and captured, occurred on the Marias River. This effectively ended the active Blackfeet resistance to settlement of their lands.

Throughout this time the government agents encouraged the Blackfeet to become farmers or ranchers, telling them that the buffalo were decreasing in numbers (Ewers 1958). Treaties with the United States had promised goods and services in exchange for land; this included farm equipment, seed, and annuity goods (e.g., foodstuffs, clothing, dishes, cookware, knives). Farming efforts proceeded in fits and starts, hampered by weather, insect infestations, and inadequate support from the government agents (Forbes 1936). Most Blackfeet preferred to try to continue their traditional hunting way of life, albeit over limited territory (Ewers 1958). Nonetheless, the buffalo numbers dwindled as fur traders continued to urge Indians to bring in hides for trade, government authorities killed animals outside the reservation in order to limit Indian mobility to the areas where buffalo remained, and white hide hunters killed buffalo for profit (Denman 1968; Ewers 1958). The Blackfeet were able to hunt buffalo until the "starvation winter" of 1883–1884. That year, none could be found, other game was scarce, the weather was severe, agricultural and stock production inadequate, and government rations were not forthcoming. One-quarter or more of the Blackfeet starved near the government agency (Ewers 1958; Grinnell 1962).

Thenceforth, the dependence of the Blackfeet on the federal government for rations and other services was sealed. About 2,000 people survived the 1883–1884 winter, and most of them settled within a few miles of the agency, many in lodges ("tipis") and some in log cabins (Ewers 1958). Rations for a family were picked up weekly at the agency by the head of household, whose ration ticket was punched and name checked off a roll. Rations included a specified quantity of meat (beef from government herds raised on the reservation and butchered at the slaughterhouse each Friday), flour, bacon, coffee, beans, sugar, soda, salt, and tobacco per "ration" (i.e., per person per day). Meat was the staple dietary item, as it had been in hunting days, with a pound and a half

(0.68 kg) of beef allotted per ration. The other food items listed above were standard provisions supplied by the U.S. government wherever it had treaty obligations with Indians and reflected the kinds of foods eaten generally on the frontier at that time—foods that did not readily spoil. (I daresay they also reflected the government's desire to "civilize" the Indians, i.e., to make them more like the farmers who surrounded them.) These kinds of foods were first provided as gifts to the Blackfeet by the government negotiators at the signing of the 1855 treaty (Ewers 1958). At that time, most of the Blackfeet had no idea how to prepare or eat foods like rice, flour, and coffee and found some of them unpalatable. However, by 1884, they had become accustomed to them and had little choice of foods because of their limited mobility and dependence on the government agency.

By 1890, cattle were being issued to some Blackfeet in an effort to help them turn to ranching as a livelihood (Ewers 1958). While farming had raised little interest, and is a highly chancy enterprise in this particular climate, herding cattle was similar to caring for horses, which had long been a part of the Blackfeet lifeway, so many families took to this new venture. By 1896 there were 500 registered brands, and the Blackfeet were shipping quite a few prime beef steers to Chicago.

From the mid-1880s to the turn of the century more Blackfeet built log homes and spread out through the valleys of the reservation to raise cattle and horses and grow some vegetables and grain (Ewers 1958). However, this promising trend at the end of the nineteenth century did not persist through the twentieth century. That period was marked by a series of advances and setbacks in the ranching/farming economy, sometimes because of local or regional factors such as severe weather and drought, sometimes because of national economic forces or governmental policies. The U.S. government instituted land allotment in 1907 (with changes in 1918), which ended up dividing some tribal lands among individuals in ways that ultimately allowed the lands to be bought by non-Indians. Impoverishment was rife in the early part of the century (Ewers 1958; McFee 1962).

World War II probably had the greatest impact on changing Blackfeet life of any event in the twentieth century. Many young Blackfeet women and men joined the armed services or moved to the cities to join in the defense effort, the first major migration of Blackfeet from the reservation (McFee 1962). These individuals learned a range of trades never before available to them, and many never returned to the reservation. Those who did brought back new ideas and lifestyles. It was around the late forties and fifties that a migration of people from the rural parts of the reservation to the town of Browning began, possibly in response to the declining rural economy (Blackfeet Land Department, personal communication). Browning had become a relatively prosperous community after World War II because of the influx of capital. More people came to town from the rural areas to visit and do business, returning home at the end of the day (Denman 1968). The movement to resettle was given a boost in 1964 when a terrible spring flood from high mountain runoff and broken dams caused a lot of property damage and some loss of life (Blackfeet Land Department, personal communication). Another factor was a series of bad winters in the sixties, including one in which there was snow until June. Calves were lost and cattle prices were low, putting ranchers out of business and forcing them to move into town. People who migrated sought employment in tribal or other governmental programs, in tourism, or in other seasonal labor industries or ended up on welfare programs. Fortunately, much economic development and job creation took place through the Great Society and other federal programs and policies in the 1960s and 1970s (Lopach et al. 1990). However, by 1979 there was still a high percentage (29.2 percent) of Blackfeet families living below the poverty level.

In subsequent decades, life on the reservation, although seemingly isolated, has continued to be affected by the larger political and economic realities in the region and country. For example, tribal programs suffered under the budgetary constrictions of the Reagan years in the 1980s (Trosper 1996). Economically, life today remains difficult for many. Mean household income of Indians on the reservation was $17,933 in 1990. In 1995 there was 41 percent unemployment among Blackfeet (Bureau of Indian Affairs [BIA] 1995). Poverty and unemployment are still high in this decade. The major employers on the reservation are the Blackfeet Nation, school districts, and federal agencies such as the Bureau of Indian Affairs and the Indian Health Service.

Today, the town of Browning has a number of small businesses, some of them Indian-owned, that employ Blackfeet workers. Yet there are far fewer businesses in this town now than there were forty or fifty years ago, according to a number of informants. One can see the remains of former businesses in boarded-up gas stations and shops. Where once there were several food stores, including two larger markets, now there is only one (Figure 13.3). Recently, the Ben Franklin variety store in this shopping center went out of business, as did a long-time restaurant that served typical Western food. Since I have been visiting this community, a couple of national fast-food chains have built restaurants in Browning and the gas stations have enhanced their fast-food offerings.

BLACKFEET FOODWAYS TODAY

This larger history of change in political economy framed the research focus for my dissertation, which was health and lifestyle change among Blackfeet women. I wanted to understand what had changed in the lifeways of women

13.3. Lone reservation supermarket and local restaurant, ca. 1996. (PHOTO BY SUSAN L. JOHNSTON)

during the twentieth century that could explain particular chronic disease patterns that had only appeared in the decades just before my study (what we refer to as a "health transition"). Specifically, Indian women in the northern plains area had a higher rate of lung cancer deaths than did other U.S. women, and a rate equal to that of Indian men in that area (an anomalous finding). I thought that I could contribute to our understanding of this epidemiological observation as an anthropologist through an in-depth examination in one population, the kind of work we do so well. From what I could ascertain, Blackfeet women seemed to share this pattern, although with the smaller numbers of "cases" in one population it is harder to see the patterns than when looking at numbers for seven or fifteen reservations. Furthermore, cancer (of all types) had become a leading cause of death for the Blackfeet in the two decades before the 1990s; for Blackfeet women, breast cancer predominated. Also, diabetes and coronary heart disease had increased greatly since 1960. All of these conditions have dietary and/or nutritional components, so studying food choice and nutritional status was central to this investigation. During my 1992 visit, which lasted one month, I talked with people about what most concerned them about health on the reservation, and I talked a lot with the tribal health director. Community members often mentioned cancer at the top of their lists, as well as diabetes. The health director was quite concerned about rising cancer rates. So we agreed that my study should focus on some aspect of that problem. When I designed

13.4. Crowd at the annual Browning powwow (North American Indian Days). (PHOTO BY SUSAN L. JOHNSTON)

the study, I broadened it because so many chronic diseases are affected by some of the same risk factors, such as particular aspects of diet and nutrition.

With the assistance of several Blackfeet women, I conducted a community-wide survey in 1995–1996 of a probability sample of 150 women, ages eighteen to ninety-three, who were enrolled tribal members. The survey covered the areas mentioned above in addition to demographic data and detailed information about reproductive and health histories and childhood and present-day household environments. I also did in-depth life-history interviews with several women who had been diagnosed with lung or breast cancer and talked with employees of various tribal and federal programs as well as other informants. As a biocultural anthropologist, I obtained data not only through interview and measurement but also through participant observation, including eating in various contexts, including people's homes and public events such as powwows (Figure 13.4).

After that year-long research experience, I returned to the reservation at least once a year through 2007, for different lengths of time depending on the reason for the visit. During these trips I gathered additional data, met with tribal officials, disseminated findings of the research, and engaged in a second

13.5. Assorted food dishes at a potluck. (PHOTO BY SUSAN L. JOHNSTON)

project working with the community to develop a culturally competent diet assessment tool for evaluating diet-related chronic disease risk. Each time, I visited with Bell and usually with other contacts and friends as well. Food was always a central part of these occasions (Figure 13.5).

In casual conversation with Blackfeet people, diet is one of the aspects of life most frequently mentioned as having changed over the years. The major transformation in the 1800s occurred when buffalo no longer were available as the key dietary resource; some people's focus goes back to those changes brought by reservation confinement in the late 1800s (they do not personally remember this, obviously, but it is a collective historic memory of a culturally significant event). Less apparent, and less often discussed, perhaps because meat continues to be the most culturally valued dietary component, was the limitation on the availability of natural plant resources resulting from restricted population movements with reservation confinement. This restriction was compounded by changes in plant ecology with increased cattle grazing and farming into this century.

During the lifetimes of the women in my study there were less catastrophic, but still considerable, alterations in how and what people ate. Over the twentieth century, as automobile transportation became a greater reality, access to markets off the reservation played an increasingly larger role in food sources. Simultaneously, the home gardens that were widespread in the early twentieth century, providing food to many families in the rural areas, declined greatly with the large shift of population to Browning. Home gardens typically provided foods such as potatoes, carrots, rutabaga, green beans, corn, beets, spinach, peas, and lettuce. Some of these vegetables could be canned or stored in the root cellar for winter use. One woman in the study, born in 1924, described a diet typical for women of her generation at the evening meal—meat, potatoes, and homegrown vegetables—and said, "We ate well for poor people." Contrast this with women who were born in the 1960s or 1970s, when the food source was not a home garden but rather a store in Browning or off-reservation: the response was more often that vegetables were eaten "when available" or "once a week." Given the time period and the distance to major commercial centers, coupled with my own knowledge of Montana dating from the 1970s, I would venture that few of these vegetables were fresh (with the exception of potatoes and other root crops). Today, the one supermarket on the reservation, in Browning, has a fair selection of fresh vegetables and fruits, but many people say they cannot afford them.

Hands down, meat is the most culturally important dietary item to the Blackfeet. This is a long-standing phenomenon, as suggested earlier. To many Blackfeet, a meal is not complete unless there is meat. A sign of being poor is having to eat macaroni and tomatoes (plain macaroni pasta mixed with canned tomatoes) without meat; this might occur at the end of the month if one receives food stamps or commodities. The Blackfeet Commodities Program is a state-administered food assistance program for low-income families that is funded and federally administered by the U.S. Department of Agriculture through its Food Distribution Program on Indian Reservations. It provides a variety of USDA-approved foods directly to people, cost-free, on a monthly basis. These programs exist on a number of Indian reservations in the United States. Although people commonly think of this as "government surplus," for the most part the foods currently supplied are not surplus. Examples of foods available in 1995–1996 included canned fruits and vegetables, canned meat, cereals, dried beans, rice, flour, macaroni, and other dried goods. The director had plans to bring in refrigerators with the idea of providing some fresh foods, although this was still in process when I last spoke to him several years ago. People who receive commodities cannot also receive food stamps in the same month.

The meat consumed today is primarily store-bought and therefore feedlot-fattened beef, although some people consume their own grass-fed cattle. Traditionally, fat is also highly valued, probably because of its one-time survival import (fat is more calorie-dense than protein or carbohydrate). In today's diet, fat is automatically consumed at a rather high level with the store-bought beef, in contrast to the relatively lean traditional diet of wild game. Interestingly, although there have been some episodic efforts to support a tribal buffalo herd, this meat is not widely eaten or popular. Bell told me she did not like the taste of it; I do not know how typical this view is. I do know that people really like beef. I have never heard any opinions that have unfavorably compared today's buffalo to those of the past; it seems more that it is just not on most people's cognitive map in today's world. One does not often see buffalo in local stores, and when it is sold, it tends to be expensive relative to cheaper cuts of beef. However, among some of the more traditional Blackfeet, access to buffalo meat is valued. For example, when buffalo stray out of Yellowstone National Park (some 300 miles [480 km] south of the reservation) and are shot before they can roam onto nearby private property, the carcasses are distributed for free among Montana's Indian nations. I know of some Blackfeet who have relished the ability to access this resource for meat and for the hides.

Meat is customarily boiled, often fried, and occasionally roasted. Very recently, since the 1990s study, game meat seems to be on the increase in popularity, although "dry meat" (dried meat, sometimes smoked) has always been valued, even during years when less wild game was consumed overall. Organ meats such as kidney, tripe, "many-fold" (one of the bovine stomachs), and tongue are still popular among the more traditional and some older people. Potatoes are important, often boiled with the meat. Potatoes were mentioned by the oldest women in my study as something available to them in their childhood (this would have been the early 1900s), but they were clearly not part of the earliest treaty annuities paid to the Indians in the 1850s. Stews and soups, made with meat and a starch such as rice or macaroni and sometimes containing tomatoes, are prominent. Rice was first introduced to the Blackfeet in 1855 as one of the "gifts" at the time of that major treaty, and it became a regular annuity item thereafter, along with flour, coffee, sugar, and pilot bread. Root vegetables such as carrot, turnip, and rutabaga may appear in stews. Green vegetables and fruits are not consumed at high rates, although their consumption may be increasing with greater awareness of chronic disease risk. Fresh versions of these are not always an affordable choice. The major exception to this is wild berries and cherries such as sarvisberries (serviceberries) and chokecherries, which are a traditional food that many people pick in the summer months near the mountains. A food called berry soup is made from sarvisberries and meat broth (formerly buffalo, now usually beef), thickened with flour and sweetened with sugar, and is served at certain festive or somber ceremonial events such as those that celebrate a new building or program or honor a deceased relative. Sugar is consumed frequently, and sweet beverages (particularly "pop"—the regional term for sweet carbonated drinks) are imbibed at a high rate among younger people and even among a significant proportion of older ones. My friend Bell drank several cans of Coca-Cola daily into her sixties. I think her reasons for doing so were typical for older women who drink this beverage, and perhaps for many younger ones as well. The beverage provides stimulation, and it has become a habit (not implying any sense of addiction). "Coke" is not an inexpensive beverage, and relatively poor people purchase it just as they might also buy cigarettes. For Bell, this was not a substitute for "real" food or a status marker of any sort, nor have I gotten that impression about Blackfeet intake of "pop" in general.

As implied above, processed and fast foods are readily available and enjoyed by many people on a regular basis. While there are culturally unique or "traditional" foods and foodways among the Blackfeet, part of the Blackfeet diet reflects the food choices of the larger U.S. population.

THE BIDIRECTIONAL GAZE

As participant observers, anthropologists want to eat as the Other (a term used sometimes to reflect the dynamics in the research relationship) eats, as a way of understanding local foodways—how people usually eat in that society or community. Sounds simple, right? However, it turns out things may be a bit more complicated than we expect. Although often we eat foods as they are eaten locally, because that is the custom and reflects available resources, sometimes the local person may alter the food or meal in some fashion because of the presence of the researcher. For example, she might prepare a "special" food (perhaps more valued) to honor her guest, or a food that matches her idea of what the anthropologist eats at home, or a meal that is like what she thinks the anthropologist expects her to be eating ("healthier," more "traditional," etc.). In these situations, the anthropologist has been interpreted by the Other, which affects what both parties eat.

In the meal vignette I related at the beginning of the chapter, and in others like it that I have experienced during subsequent years, the local person is also eating this same food and sharing in the altered diet. In this case, she is eating as (she believes) the anthropologist usually eats, at least in part. In an effort to please me, Bell prepared a non-typical food, green salad, for a supposedly typical local meal. Serving an atypical food may also be a move to mask a food practice about which the host may feel some embarrassment in front of a nutritional "expert"—for example, because green vegetables are a rare meal item in usual practice.

Obviously, in this kind of situation, the conditions a researcher is studying have been altered. Is the anthropologist really eating as the local person usually eats? Or as the anthropologist usually eats? Or as the local person *thinks* the anthropologist eats? Or, finally, as the local person believes the anthropologist would *like* to see her eat (e.g., more "traditionally" or "healthier")? In fact, it may be that the anthropologist is fed a meal that reflects special foods or preparation, foods that are valued but seldom served in everyday life, or foods that are known to be "traditional"—the local person is reinforcing the role of Other, shaping a meal that she thinks the anthropologist wants her to be eating. Bell often accomplished one or another of these variations when I visited. Sometimes she would serve green vegetables or fruit, things that are not part of her family's typical diet, because she wanted to please me or use my being there as an opportunity to serve something different—that is, healthy or special in their eyes—to her family. Sometimes she served a dish that is more "traditional," reflecting old customs, to honor me or to teach me something. Once I visited her over the Fourth of July holiday while she and her family were camping out by a dam in the general area of the reservation where she grew up. She had decided to prepare many-fold for her relatives and for me to try for the first time. That was the only time I saw her make that food. Of course, she watched closely while I ate it. Like tripe, it seemed kind of rubbery to me and had a mild flavor. I indicated that I thought it was fine—although I did not take a big second helping! This seemed to satisfy Bell. The other eaters, all relatives of some degree, seemed to enjoy this dish, although the children did not eat it. Sometimes Bell made Indian tacos, a special meal that takes a lot of preparation, because she knew I liked it. An Indian taco is actually a pan-Indian food consisting of a large disk of fried bread (that is the time-consuming part) smothered in chili (beans and ground beef) and topped with tomatoes, lettuce, onions, and hot sauce. I once made the mistake of eating two of these; ever after, if I only ate one, I was considered to be under-eating. The thing is as big as a dinner plate, for Pete's sake!

It is a truism to say that we alter the conditions of our own observations simply by being present; of course, we may also be altering the accuracy of our interpretations, depending on our level of consciousness about this. We seem to be gazing at a shifting focus, one that certainly cannot be taken for granted as representative of everyday existence when an anthropologist is not around.

There is another dynamic I wish to explore, that of the researcher as the focus of study. In the situation just described, when we are sometimes eating what the Other thinks we would usually eat or what we would want them to eat, the conditions of the experiment of which *we* are the subject have also been altered. We have been interpreted, accurately or not. This may be based on stereotypes held by the Other about people of our national or professional background or on actual observations of us as we eat with them. As surely as we note carefully all that we can of our surroundings and experiences while eating, we also are scrutinized. Note was taken of the scraps of meat fat left on my plate (a behavior not typical for this community, as alluded to earlier); the first couple of times I did this, Bell commented on it, saying such things as "Don't you eat fat?" or "That's the best part." If my plate was otherwise empty, even as the last bite was going into my mouth, I was prompted to eat more or told I had hardly eaten anything. In good ethnographic fashion, observations were supplemented with interviewing. I was asked how I liked a dish I had never tried before, after I had been watched to see how I reacted to the new food. I was often asked questions about my usual eating patterns: How do you eat at home? Do you eat like this at home? Do you eat meat at home? How much meat do you eat at home? Do you eat macaroni and tomatoes at home? It was easy to wonder just who was doing the study. Obviously, we both were.

Being the focus of study in this way affects how we behave and how we think about our research. Beyond whatever discomfort or self-consciousness we do or do not feel about being watched at the table or in the food market, we may find ourselves behaving differently than we customarily would at home, or even differently than we would expect ourselves to typically act in a field setting, because we are being watched. I found myself eating a lot more meat, for example, than I usually would, even though there were other food options. I was somehow living up to expectations. However, I still could not get myself to eat the fat scraps on my plate.

More importantly, awareness of the bidirectional gaze may affect what we learn as researchers. It can become difficult at times to tease apart the various layers and directions of dietary influence, a problem if one's goal is to gather accurate, firsthand information about dietary customs. And it can be challenging to keep observing when one is aware of being observed or while answering questions; it shifts one's attention away from the task at hand. Data are changed; data go missing.

Clearly, it would be best not to rely solely on observational data gathered while eating with the Other in a household meal setting. As nutritional anthropologists, we have a number of other strategies and techniques we can use to help us learn about foodways to supplement what we observe in household encounters. Also, time may ameliorate some of the initial divergences from typical patterns. In my own work, I have noticed that familiarity has led to a return to usual patterns. Over the years that I ate with this particular Blackfeet family, they appeared to stop trying to represent their eating habits as other than what they were when I was not around. They sometimes made a special meal because I was there, but they readily stated that fact. However, they continued to interview me periodically about my own food habits at home and watched to see what and how much I ate—so the bidirectional scrutiny continued.

Perhaps most profoundly, being simultaneously the observer and the observed teaches a lesson in humility by bringing to the fore the effect we have on the Other and that the Other has on us—making it difficult for us to hide behind the notion that the Other is somehow separate from us, an objectified reality to be studied. There is a blurring of roles and boundaries here that is extraordinary; the reality is simultaneously subjective and objective. So much for the Other as a concept! Ultimately, anthropologists of food and nutrition engaged in participant observation must ask, answer, and address the consequences of the question, "Who is eating whose food?"

NOTE

1. Not her real name.

REFERENCES

Bureau of Indian Affairs (BIA)
1995   Indian Service Population and Labor Force Estimates. Online data from U.S. Department of the Interior, BIA. http://www.doi.gov/bia/laborforce/1995IndianLaborForceReport.pdf, accessed June 2, 1998.

Dempsey, Hugh A.
1986   The Blackfoot Indians. In *Native Peoples: The Canadian Experience*, ed. R. B. Morrison and C. R. Wilson, 404–435. McClelland and Stewart, Toronto.

Denman, Clayton Charlton
1968   Cultural Change among the Blackfeet Indians of Montana. Ph.D. dissertation. Department of Anthropology, University of California, Berkeley.

Ewers, John C.
1955   *The Horse in Blackfoot Indian Culture, with Comparative Material from Other Western Tribes*. Bulletin 159, Bureau of American Ethnology. Smithsonian Institution, Washington, DC.
1958   *The Blackfeet: Raiders on the Northwestern Plains*. University of Oklahoma Press, Norman.

Forbes, Charles G.
1936   History of the Blackfeet Indians until 1907. Master's thesis. Department of History, University of Oklahoma, Norman.

Frantz, Donald G., and Norma Jean Russell
1995   *Blackfoot Dictionary of Stems, Roots, and Affixes*, 2nd ed. University of Toronto Press, Toronto.

Grinnell, George Bird
1962   *Blackfoot Lodge Tales: The Story of a Prairie People*. University of Nebraska Press Bison Books, Lincoln.

Hellson, J. C., and M. Gadd
  1974   Ethnobotany of the Blackfoot Indians. *Canadian Ethnology Service Paper No. 19*. National Museums of Canada, Ottawa.

Johnston, A.
  1960   Uses of Native Plants by the Blackfoot Indians. *Alberta Historical Review* 8:8–13.

Lopach, James J., Margery Hunter Brown, and Richmond L. Clow
  1990   *Tribal Government Today: Politics on Montana Indian Reservations*. Westview Press, Boulder.

McFee, Malcolm
  1962   Modern Blackfeet: Contrasting Patterns of Differential Acculturation. Ph.D. dissertation. Department of Anthropology, Stanford University, Stanford, CA.

Trosper, R. L.
  1996   American Indian Poverty on Reservations, 1969–1989. In *Changing Numbers, Changing Needs: American Indian Demography and Public Health*, ed. G. D. Sandefur, R. R. Rindfuss, and B. Cohen, 172–195. National Academy Press, Washington, DC.

United States (U.S.) Census
  1992   1990 Census of Population and Housing, Summary Tape File 3 Comprehensive Report, Blackfeet Reservation, Montana, November 10, 1992. Processed by the Census and Economic Information Center, Montana Department of Commerce, Helena.

Beverages

CHAPTER FOURTEEN

Drinking Ethiopia

Ronald Reminick

Biographical sketch. Ron Reminick, a psychological anthropologist, earned his Ph.D. from the University of Chicago in 1973. He has conducted research in Jamaica, Brazil, India, Appalachia, and the inner city of Cleveland, Ohio. He has been studying about and researching in Ethiopia for more than forty years. His original fieldwork, conducted in Ethiopia during the late 1960s, focused on gender identity and ritual symbolism. His two-year Fulbright in the mid-1990s involved contributing to the M.A. program at Addis Ababa University, and with the assistance of his graduate students he conducted four major research projects. In 2005 with a Senior Scholar's Fulbright grant, Reminick advised on a social science curriculum and developed workshops on grant writing and research methods at Bahir Dar University. At present, Reminick is beginning research on tribal healers of the Western Ghats of southern India, with a general focus on cosmology and intention. He is working with two of his co-directors at Cleveland State University's Center on Healing Across Cultures to develop a cross-cultural study of traditional healing in South India, Belize, Ethiopia, and North American Appalachia.

ETHIOPIA: THE LAND AND THE FOOD RESOURCES

Forty million years ago the earth in the Horn of Eastern Africa cleaved and allowed lava, steam, and bedrock to burst to the surface. The gradual process of lava and volcanic rock oozing to the surface built up the highlands, ranging in elevation from 6,000 to more than 15,000 feet (1,800 to 4,500 meters). When this process ceased, it left a rich wide-ranging plateau suitable for highly productive farming. Ethiopia today is about the size of Texas and New Mexico combined. In Ethiopia for millennia the ancestors of humanity have hunted game and gathered fruits, nuts, roots, and edible vegetation. This was the original way of life of our ancestors. Recent finds by paleoanthropologists have found evidence of humanity's ancestors as old as 5 million years, which strongly suggests that the northern Awash River Valley of the Ethiopian Great Rift, now a hot dry desert, is the homeland of us all.

About 7,000 years ago, Semitic peoples from the Arabian Peninsula crossed the Straits of Bab el Mandeb and settled in the highlands, often called Abyssinia. They brought with them many of the cultigens that have become the diet of the Abyssinian peoples. Among these peoples were the Agau. They made major contributions to highland food products. The genius of ancestral Agau culture is primarily responsible for central highland Ethiopia ranking as one of the world's important centers of the origin of cultivated plants, along with China and India.

Although the Agau adopted elements of Sudanic agriculture from the pre-Nilotes to the west, they continually experimented with wild plants and developed new cultigens that now make up the bulk of the Ethiopian agricultural complex. These include cereal grains such as *eleusine*, or finger millet (*Eleusine coracana*), which spread widely through East and South Africa and to India, and *t'eff* (*Eragrostis abyssinica*), which spread to a limited extent into the eastern Sudan. Barley and wheat are also popular, but they were, by and large, developed in South Arabia. The root crop *ensete* (*Ensete edulis*), or false banana, is the staple in southwest Ethiopia, especially among the Gurage people. Both the leaves and the oil pressed from the seeds of garden cress (*Lepidum sativum*) are consumed. The Agau also developed condiments including coffee (*Coffea arabica*); fenugreek (*Trigonella foenumgraecum*); *ch'at* or *qat*, also called Arab tea (*Catha edulis*), which is a mild alkaloid stimulant; and vegetable mustard (*Brassica carinata*).

We must also credit the Agau for developing oil and dye plants such as castor (*Ricinus communie*), nug (*Guizotia abyssinica*), and safflower (*Carthamus tinctorius*), used both for its oil and as a dye. Cattle, sheep, goats, and the ubiquitous chicken were likely obtained from the Nubians and pre-Nilotes approximately 5,000 years ago, along with donkeys and horses that they later bred to produce the sure-footed mule. These cultigens and domestic animals provide the basis for Ethiopian cuisine, which in modern times has been supplemented by foods imported from all over the world.

Frederick Simoons (1960) itemizes the highland food plants in contemporary Ethiopia, including ensete, t'eff, wheat, barley, sorghum, finger millet, pearl millet, oats, rye, maize, lentils and other legumes, and root crops, including the potato and squash. Also included are the fruit trees yielding olive and fig. Although Ethiopia has a wide-ranging and varied food-resource base that I will review, I am happy to narrow my focus, at the request of the editors, to the specific beverages consumed and the meanings and social contexts of drinking that occur on the Abyssinian highland plateau.

A COMMENT ON THE CULTURALLY SYMBOLIC SIGNIFICANCE OF FOOD AND DRINK

Humans do not eat only to stay alive. Commensality is an expression of relationship and solidarity. It is the sharing of a common gustatory and social experience. Eating together warms the channels of communication and reinforces existing relationships and fosters belongingness (Cargill 2007). People eat together to express nurturance, especially of hosts to guests. The symbolic value of food and its consumption is intensified on important holidays. People eat particular foods to reinforce their cultural identity. Culturally symbolic foods offer a modality of identification with the family and with a people's ethnicity (Long 2003; Lupton 2005). The ingestion of symbolically significant foods offers a sense of an identity shared with an entity larger than the self. Symbolic foods offer the one who eats them a sense of power, however subtle it may be. Ingestion of the wafer and the wine in the Catholic ritual is the symbolic ingestion of the body and blood of Christ. In several New Guinea tribal cultures the ingestion of human flesh imbues the eater with the power of the person who recently died or, often, an enemy who has just been killed. Among the Sambia of New Guinea (Herdt 1987) boys' ingestion of the semen of warrior men is believed to make boys powerful men. Lifting a glass of fine wine in consonance with a rich cheese on a fine cracker is more than a tasty appetizer; it identifies the consumer with a particular aspect of culture and class. Vegans and vegetarians are not only eating cultigens to stay healthy but they are also expressing a particular ideology about health, animal sanctity, vibrant living, and spiritual sophistication.

Feasting in highland Ethiopia is certainly an integral institution of the culture. But fasting may be the most important aspect of Amhara Christianity. If a person decides not to fast, one's family is not obligated to provide memorial feasts in their name. Fasting also protects one from the devil and provides better chances of getting into heaven (Levine 1965:233). The Amhara peasant fasts

14.1. Reminick journaling in the mountains. (PHOTO BY RONALD REMINICK)

about 165 days each year, and the clergy, about 250 days each year. Normally, on a fast day, one has nothing to eat or drink until midday. After midday milk, eggs, animal fat, beef, sheep, or chicken are forbidden. The peasant survives on pulses and cereal grains. After age fifteen, the eight-week Lenten fast must be observed.

A strictly forbidden food is pig. Pork is the food of unclean people. It is un-Christian to eat pork and one who does is despised. In the late 1960s, while doing fieldwork in the remote highlands, I was accused of harboring pork (Figure 14.1). I had two beautiful Shepherd/Collie dogs that I had gotten from the last Peace Corps director, who had returned home to the United States of America. I had a fairly large store of canned dog food bought in Addis Ababa. The peasantry was suspicious of what was in those cans; one old woman who was a coffee-party guest in my house suspected that pork was in the dog food. She would not believe otherwise because she could not see what the meat was like. She told the whole community about the suspicious cache of dog food, and so I was persuaded to publically dump the dog food into the garbage pit and feed my dogs scraps of people food, as is the custom in the highlands.

INJERA: THE MAINSTAY THIN PANCAKE-LIKE SOURDOUGH BREAD

Injera, like *berbere*, is made with elaborate care, for this is not only the bread component of the essential mainstay of Ethiopian (Abyssinian) cuisine but has

14.2. Asqala pouring batter for sourdough flat bread. (PHOTO BY RONALD REMINICK)

symbolic significance as part of Ethiopia's national dish and cultural identity. The primary ingredient is t'eff, the seed of a grass (*Eragrostis teff*) with a light and delicate taste. Where unavailable, as in the higher reaches of the Ethiopian highlands, wheat or barley is used. The batter is fermented and then poured onto a hot pan in a thin stream starting at the outside and spiraling in, from left to right, to the center (Figure 14.2). It is then cooled slightly and the pan covered with its lid. The cooked injera should have bubbles on the top like a pancake or crepe cooked on one side, and it will rise from the edge of the pan and be easily removed from the pan and onto the *mesob*, or basket table.

BERBERE: THE MAINSTAY SAUCE IN ETHIOPIAN CUISINE

The major ingredient in *berbere* is red or cayenne pepper (*Capsicum annuum longum*), which is normally dried in the sun and pounded/ground and mixed with some or all of a number of spices and plants (some of which I believe have no English names), such as red shallots, garlic, ginger, fenugreek, Bishop's weed, black cumin, cardamom, cinnamon, turmeric, nutmeg, cloves, black pepper, salt, *kebebe sine*, and *hidar filfile*.

The preparation is elaborate and must be carried out with care and attention to detail. After all, it is a culturally significant, symbolically salient ingredient. First, the wife or maidservant takes sun-dried peppers with their stalks removed. They are pounded into powder. Then she pounds together red shallots and garlic, and this mixture is added to the pepper. She sprinkles water on the mixture and keeps it covered for two or three days. It is then put in the sun to dry. Now she peels and chops fresh ginger and lets it dry in the sun. As it dries, she roasts the fenugreek on her injera baking pan, as with the rest of the spices. As my friend Ma'aza said: "We heat the pepper and mix with the other spices. Now, I add salt. It is time to take it to the flour mill and have the mill man grind it to a very fine mixture, or, if he is closed we will ask Lemlem, our maidservant, to use our home grinding stone. We will then mix the immediately usable portion with warm water into a thick paste to mix later with the food! It will be good!" Chicken, mutton, or beef can be added to the sauce. A variety of vegetables, with or without berbere, may be added as a side dish.

JOURNEY INTO THE HIGHLANDS

My first fieldwork in Ethiopia commenced in 1967. I wished to visit the remote highland district of Manz, a fascinating land written about by Donald Levine (1965). Leaving my wife, two-year-old son, and five-year-old daughter in the capital city of Addis Ababa, I set off with my research assistant and a guide to our proposed field site. We climbed into my Land Rover in Addis Ababa, starting at about 8,000 feet (2,400 meters) elevation, and followed the tarmac road north into the Amhara heartland, home of the peoples and culture that were the focus of my research. This road winds and curves along a sunny, rolling plateau decorated with a patchwork of cultivated land growing a variety of crops, such as t'eff, wheat, barley, beans, and hops.

After a few hours we reached the town of Debra Berhan, "City of Light," 85 miles (136 kilometers) distant from Addis Ababa and situated at an elevation of approximately 10,000 feet (3,000 meters). Beyond Debra Berhan the road continues to climb, becoming much steeper and with many winding grades. We climbed into a cold, wet, windswept, fog-shrouded, mountainous country, to an elevation of 11,500 feet (3,500 meters). The road here was hard-packed rock and gravel with steep drop-offs on one side. Some of these gorges are 3,200 feet (1,000 meters) deep, with sharp-sided gullies along the other side, forged by roadwork and the runoffs from rain.

Before we reached Mussolini Pass, a deep tunnel bored through nearly the top of a mountain by the Italians, where the road begins its steep, precipitous, and winding descent toward the town of Debra Sina (about 37 miles [60 kilometers] from Debra Berhan), we reached a turnoff in the road to the right, hardly noticeable unless one is looking for it and already knows its location. Appearing out of rain and fog was a rough-hewn sign, pointed at one end so as to simulate an arrow, with fading painted English letters spelling out "Molalie 76 km." At this point the road assumes a much steeper grade, and I shifted into four-wheel drive and low gear in order to gain greater stability with increased torque. Even though it was the end of the rainy season, the climb continued into charcoal gray, bone-chilling, wind-driven rain and fog and then down into high valleys, traversing narrow ridges along escarpments with frighteningly steep cliffs and precipices that opened into vast gorges on one or both sides of the road.

The trip appeared interminable, but finally the gorges retreated from the road, and after one last torturous winding climb we emerged out of the dark and cold into a brightly sun-warmed rolling highland plateau dotted with round mud and stone homesteads and surrounded by a colorful patchwork of cultivated land. This is the region of Manz, the homeland of the Amhara of Ethiopia. Several peasant farmers greeted us, wrapped in large white handspun and handwoven cloaks, topped with heavy woolen blanket wraps. The peasants encircled the vehicle with quiet suspicion and apprehensive curiosity. A few of the men shouldered carbines with bandoliers of cartridges slung over their shoulders. A "big man" asked us our business there. I learned later that he was the judge of the court in that district. My research assistant spoke (I had little command of Amharic at that time); he said we had documents for them to see. We had documents from the Ministry of Interior with a photo of the Emperor and the red seal of the government, papers from the Ministry of Foreign Affairs, and a letter of introduction from Haile Sellassie I University. We said we wanted to study the history of the Amhara people—the Amharic word for history, *tariq*, is a buzzword. The men became more interested. The Amhara are proud of their history. I said I had studied about this culture and had grown to love the country, and I wanted to learn more if they would permit us. They accepted this coolly, studying our faces. After several long moments of quiet, they invited us into the "hotel," a mud and stone house with a small bar and straw tables and stools with sleeping rooms in the rear. The "big man" ordered coffee and we conversed about my project.

COFFEE PARTIES AND CONVERSATIONS

It is said that Ethiopian coffee is some of the finest in the world. I saw recently on a television program an international coffee-tasting festival; the Yirgach'efe and Harar coffees of Ethiopia came out on top in a blind tasting. Coffee originated in Ethiopia, specifically in the southwestern Kaffa Province. There is a mythical story about the discovery of coffee: once upon a time a goatherd saw his goats eating the coffee cherries and the males became excited and hypersexual and began mating with the females. It did not take long for the peasant farmers to take heed and began experimenting with this fruit!

In Ethiopia, coffee is served in little cups that look like Chinese tea cups. In fact, I believe many of these cups actually came from China. The coffee can be drunk black, with sugar, or in some areas with a little pinch of salt. Once in a café in Addis Ababa I watched a man add countless teaspoons of sugar into his little cup of coffee. I leaned over to him and said, "Why don't you put a little coffee in your sugar!" He looked at me a bit quizzically with a faint smile and proceeded to drink his "coffee." If there is a coffee party in a home, you might find the hostess offering to put a leaf of *t'ena adam*, what we call rue, into your cup to add a bit of exotic flavor to the coffee.

No home life is complete without the daily coffee party, called *t'irt'ib* (Figure 14.3). On special occasions, such as the visit of an honored guest or a holiday, a special long, soft grass called *gwassa* is scattered on the floor. The coffee party is greatly enjoyed, especially by the hostess. One woman said: "It gives me great pleasure to serve my *t'irt'ibenya* [coffee-party members]. It gives me an opportunity to talk and to be sociable. And, it brings my *ch'elley* [female *zar* spirit] near to me!" Abyssinians, especially the Amhara, are habitual coffee drinkers. Ethiopians are reputedly the biggest coffee drinkers in the world. The term *sus* refers to that time of day when one goes to a friend's house or bar to drink and to socialize. The coffee party may occur from one to three times per day, depending on a person's free time. It may last from one to three hours. If one does not drink coffee at the accustomed time, he or she will feel all sorts of bodily ills and a mild sense of malaise because "the *wuqabi*[2] hasn't gotten his regular tribute." I heard many times that the headache caused by not drinking coffee for one day, what we might call caffeine withdrawal, is the punishment of the annoyed zar spirit who wants his daily recognition. This condition will last until the next coffee party. Belief in the zar spirit is widespread throughout northern Africa and parts of the Middle East. The zar is a form of ancestor spirit, and the belief associated with it goes back to time immemorial.

14.3. Amhara woman preparing coffee. (PHOTO BY RONALD REMINICK)

Throwing the dregs of one's cup out the door is also an offering to the zar spirit. In 1995 I was at a coffee party of a friend. The attendees were all educated businessmen and academics. At the end of the first cup I threw my dregs out the door and muttered "my wuqabi wants this," which caused uproarious laughter and joking. The zar spirit is something held very dear, although secretly, in the hearts of these Ethiopians.

Snacks are always served with coffee, both in the countryside and in cities and towns. Traditionally, there are a variety of snacks commonly offered to coffee-party guests. One is *dabo k'olo*, which are little toasted or fried bread balls that are tasty with or without a little salt, and another is *gubs* (toasted barley). Other toasted grains served are simply called *qolo* and are either barley or wheat. Chickpeas, called *shimbere* in Amharic, are served raw or boiled. A hot, crispy bread called *chechebsa* is also a favored snack item during coffee time. Raw, minced, and spiced beef called *kitfo* sometimes counted among the fare, or sometimes dried beef or lamb cut into long strips, called *qwanta*, is served. In

14.4. Rahel pouring coffee. (PHOTO BY RONALD REMINICK)

the capital of Addis Ababa a plethora of Italian-style pastry shops offer alternatives to the traditional fare.

No coffee party can end without having boiled the coffee three times, in other words, with each member having consumed three cups. First the green beans are washed, then roasted, and then ground or pounded. Water is poured into the flared top of the *jabana*, a small, black clay-spouted pitcher. Then the coffee is poured in and it is brought to a boil over a fire fueled with dung, wood, charcoal, or kerosene. The first coffee is strong and rich. Subsequent boilings do not use more coffee, so each subsequent cup is milder and the third coffee is thin and weak (Figure 14.4). It is said in the Amhara highlands that this is also the case with friendships, both amorous and marital relationships as well as more casual relationships. At first one has a strong and rich relationship. Then follow progressive degrees of indifference. And, finally, just as the thin and bitter coffee is thrown out, so must the relationship be dispensed with.

About eight months into my fieldwork, I once had to leave a coffee party after the first boiling because it was getting dark, I was about half a mile (one kilometer) away from my place, and I wanted to walk home before the hyenas began prowling. We had just completed a lively conversation about marriage during which my hostess had told me about their customs of arranged marriage and I had shared that we had the freedom to marry anyone we love. Kebebush sighed: "That sounds like heaven! To choose who you wish!" And then I added,

"And we stay with that person until the day we die." And Kebebush exclaimed: "That sounds like hell! What kind of country do you come from! You are between heaven and hell! What kind of life is that?" When I stood up to leave, Kebebush exclaimed: "What? You are leaving after one cup of coffee? That just isn't done! Is it good to make enemies of your friends? It is an insult to the host to act 'strange' [i.e., to ignore the custom have drinking three cups of coffee] in their house after being invited in." I stayed for awhile but begged in the name of God for her to excuse me. She knew it could get dangerous at night, and I was anxious as I thought of the 9 mm I had bought from my Land Rover mechanic, sitting uselessly at home.

Stories and conversations abound in "news," the term referring to gossip and news about what is going on in the community, and can take the form or talk, song, or jocularity. Topics of conversation range widely and can include even intimate matters. People speak of newcomers, family affairs, pregnancies, arguments between spouses, illicit relationships, impending marriage arrangements, illnesses, and the health of children, animals, and crops, as well as salacious joking, mild insults, and occasional arguments over money or litigation. In 1968, for example, Yeshimibiet ("Wife of a Thousand") was hosting a nice coffee party at her house and serving the distilled beverage, *qatiqala*; the local beer, *talla*; and toasted grains. Just then her husband came into the house. He had been plowing the fields, so there was dung between his toes, mud and bits of hay stuck to his legs, and he was covered in sweat. He sat down and, as is the ancient custom, she washed his feet. While carefully washing away the evidence of his labor, she exclaimed, "Now that's what makes my vagina water! To see my husband working hard to keep this family!"

Another example of the willingness to discuss openly intimate matters occurred during my first fieldwork season, in the late 1960s. For months I had been taking numerous field notes about land, plowing, seeding, watering, and crops, gathering a lot of material on agriculture. One afternoon at a lively coffee party, Almaz, a beautiful woman in her thirties, exclaimed that her friend had visited the previous night: "The moon was high and he was handsome and I let him into my house and he plowed my land so good and he let the seed spill and the water came." Prepared to add to my notes on agricultural practices, I was puzzled and queried: "Wait a minute! Who plows land at night?" The naïveté of my question brought forth howls of laughter and finger-pointing at me. It was then that I realized that not all those notes were about agriculture!

Salacious joking and metaphor are common once a coffee party gets going. At one wedding party, which began with a coffee ceremony, guests commented, with the young couple present, about whether the eighteen-year-old groom would be "warrior" enough to conquer his young bride and would the *ch'agula*, the white cloth placed under the bride's buttocks, catch the blood of the battle, for a true warrior sheds the blood of the enemy. It was at this party I learned the complex semantics of the term "enemy," which includes one who poses a challenge (see Reminick 1976, on ceremonial defloration).

Sometimes a darker mood can dampen the joviality. During my neighbor's coffee party in the mid-1990s, her husband came into the house drunk. He looked at his three-year-old daughter and muttered, "That girl is mixed!" This comment was meant to suggest that his wife had had sex with other men and that their semen had mixed with his to make the child. This brought forth yells of vituperation from the older men and women, mainly the women, admonishing him to be quiet and stop making a fool of himself. Anyone could see that that beautiful little girl looked just like him. He then sat down quietly and drank his coffee. The older women had put this inebriated man in his place.

OTHER HIGHLAND BEVERAGES

Tea

A variety of teas come from the lower elevations of the country. A good deal of tea also comes from India, just across the Arabian Sea; India has been connected to Ethiopia through trade routes for 1,000 years. Teas can be flavored with sugar, cinnamon, or cloves. Tea is a warm alternative to coffee and consumed on no specific occasion. Coffee has a greater spiritual significance, tied to the zar spirit, but tea is the preferred drink for the Muslim populations who do not live in this Amhara region. Unless the occasion is a more formal coffee ceremony with special ceremonial grass on the floor, incense, and special cups on a little ritual table, the guest may often be offered a choice of coffee or tea.

For me, tea bring to mind the fourteen-hour excursion my students and I made to the pilgrimage site of the tomb of Shek Hussein, a Muslim Sufi healer who lived in the thirteenth century and is known to have performed miraculous cures. Muslims and people of other faiths traveled here from all over the country for healing and revitalization. On the way, I was anticipating seeing a large river, a tributary of the great Wabe Shebele, which courses eastward into Somalia, a tributary that cascades over an escarpment into a valley 3,200 feet (1,000 meters) below. It normally feeds a lake from which the inhabitants take their water. Much to our chagrin, like many rivers affected by a growing drought, this one was dry and the lake was a shrinking pond. People used this pond as a source of drinking water, to water their animals, and to do their laundry.

One morning we had a breakfast of camel meat and a good deal of tea. I knew the teas here had been boiling since dawn and the water was good.

Then we descended into the valley to see some caverns where monks lived and prayed. On the way back up, which took the better part of an hour, I became progressively more ill. By early evening I was very sick: feverish, nauseous, and with my guts in an uproar, convulsing at both ends. Thanks to our rehydration salts, I was able to survive the trip back home, although one of my students had to drive. The American Embassy lab determined I had amoebiasis and girardiasis. Could it have been the camel meat? Then I realized it was the tea cup; it had been washed in that pond water; the boiling tea did not kill the germs on the cup.

Milk

Cow's milk is not a popular beverage but it is often what children drink while growing up. During my first fieldwork in Ethiopia in the late 1960s, our neighbors Almaz and her husband, Shebbie, had a healthy cow who had recently calved. We got a liter of milk every day for many months from Almaz's cow for my two-year-old son, Michael, and five-year-old daughter, Lisa, and my wife used it for cooking. We would scald the milk before using it.

One cold morning (during the wet season, sometimes frost would be on the ground in the mornings) in 1967, I went to visit neighbors who lived about half a mile (one kilometer) away. At 13,000 feet (4,000 meters) in elevation the chill took the heat right out of your bones! I arrived at the house of Fallaqa, hoping for a hot cup of tea with a cinnamon stick in it. I could drink a lot more tea than the strong coffee of the highlands. His wife exclaimed: "Oh, look at you so cold! You need some warm milk to make you comfortable!" I really do not know why she insisted on offering me milk. Was it because she was older than me and felt nurturing, like a mother? I responded that milk was not necessary; a cup of tea would be fine. She ignored my comment and ordered her grandson to bring the cow into the house.

Fallaqa's wife handed me a cow's horn. I peered into it and saw fleas jumping around in it. I deftly turned the horn upside down and then back again, but much to my consternation the fleas were still there! The one-horned cow was brought to where I was sitting on a low eucalyptus-wood chair covered with a sheepskin. The grandson steadied the horn cup under the udder while I held it and then he proceeded to squeeze the steaming milk into my horn cup. A guest is supposed to relish the offerings of the host and so I held the glass high and, with a flourish, drank the milk. We passed some minutes with casual conversation before my stomach began to churn and then my guts went into spasms. In no time at all that milk had traveled some twenty-five or thirty feet of gut and was demanding to get out! I excused myself and hurried to a small grove of bamboo where the blast, I hoped, could not be heard.

Beer

T'alla is the Amharic name for a popular fermented beverage, and no self-respecting homemaker would be caught without it. If one does run out, one only has to go into the neighborhood and look for a tin can sitting upside down on a stick outside a house. There you will find your t'alla. It is brewed in a large black clay jug with a narrow neck called a *gan*, which can weigh thirty to forty pounds (thirteen to eighteen kilograms) when empty. Into the *gan* one pours about five gallons (twenty liters) of water. Then the woman of the house grinds hops and leaves and puts them into about one gallon (five liters) of water; this container is put aside. On the third day she adds dried, ground, germinated wheat and bread broken into small pieces. On the fifth day, woody hops are pounded into a meal and combined with ground roasted barley or, if needed, wheat. The whole mix is poured into the *gan* and sealed. After six or seven days the brew is well fermented. The container is opened and the t'alla can be poured through a strainer and kept in a separate container or glass bottles until guests are ready to drink. T'alla is mildly alcoholic and has a slightly sour taste; it is welcomed on warm afternoons. In modern-day towns more Western-style beers can also be found. In fact, by the mid-twentieth century, during the time of Emperor Haile Sellassie I, the Saint George Brewery became one of the most lucrative businesses operating in the capital city, Addis Ababa (Bahru 1991).

T'ej

T'ej is a honey mead or hydromel served in attractive small, round-bellied, wide-mouthed bottles. It is made by mixing honey with water, adding cooked hops, and allowing it to ferment for about five days. Ullendorf (1960) notes that the bitter roots of *Rhamnus saddo* may be used as an alternative to hops, *Rhamnus pauciflorus*. The hops are then removed and the brew is allowed to stand a day or so. Then it is poured into a clean container and sealed. After about a week the mixture becomes stronger and subsequent drinks must be strained to remove the sediment that has collected. As with the other beverages, *t'ej* can be drunk at any type of social gathering, public or private. The unfermented honey drink is called *berz*. The preparation of t'ej and t'alla is entirely the work of women.

Richard Pankhurst has described the status of t'ej in medieval times up through the nineteenth century. Camp followers of the Emperor included women who carried honey for t'ej and jars of t'ej for the nobility. T'alla was for the soldiers. Pankhurst cites Almeida, who wrote that some 3,000 women served in this capacity, including "tapsters" who were kept quite busy satisfying the thirsts of the royalty and soldiery (Pankhurst 1992:68). "The drinking of *taj*, or honey wine, was . . . restricted to those of the highest rank" in the nine-

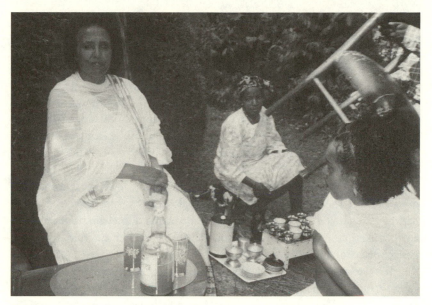

14.5. Women with t'ej. (PHOTO BY RONALD REMINICK)

teenth century and earlier (Pankhurst 1992:166). "The manufacture of *taj*, or mead, was . . . a royal monopoly," and King Sahla Sellase alone had "the right of preparing the much prized luxury" (Pankhurst 1992:175, quoting Harris 1844). Today, in the social gatherings that I have experienced, the beverage of choice among men of wealth and power is Johnny Walker Black Label Scotch whiskey.

Qatiqala

Qatiqala, also called *areke*, is a native distilled beverage. It is clear like vodka but has a distinctive aroma. It varies greatly in alcoholic content, but I estimate from experience that it normally runs 60 to 100-plus proof. It is common for any social gathering to begin with a drink of this beverage. It is the custom in the highlands for the guests never to drink from a full bottle before the host demonstrates that it is good. Throughout the centuries, poisonings are legendary in highland culture. When one wants to kill an enemy, he may poison the qatiqala because it disguises the poison. The whole party may be wiped out but that is okay if one's enemy will be among them! So the custom is for the host to open the full bottle, pour himself or herself a drink, and then wait a moment before declaring it good. Then everyone in the party exclaims, "Yes, it is good!" Often there will be a toast: *Lenya t'ena*!, which means, "To our health!" Then all drink as much as they wish. It is a beverage that lubricates conversation and enhances the food offerings.

YISMAW'S FEAST

It was the Christmas of 2005 in Ethiopia. This celebration is called Gaenna and occurs in January, according to the Julian Ethiopian calendar. My friend Yismaw is in his sixties and a retired high-ranking military officer. He has a large compound about two-thirds the size of a soccer field. Inside the compound is a circle of juniper trees, about thirteen feet (four meters) in diameter, bound together at the top so that the trees make an enclosure. It is his little private space. The compound is lavish with flowering bushes, coffee trees, an herb garden, and tall dense shrubbery that surrounds the celebration area, with an opening that served as an arched gateway into the inner sanctum. It was the perfect place for a Christmas party.

The celebrants arrived gradually beginning around noon. As guests continued to arrive, they were greeted with kisses on each cheek. Peremptory greeting kisses are three; highly valued and loved individuals get multiple kisses. A "big man" entered the compound. Some of his relatives fell to their knees, kissed his feet and hugged his knees, and he chucked them under the chin and raised them up.

Yismaw offered t'alla and qatiqala to his guests. To very special guests, he offered Johnny Walker Black Label Scotch whiskey and an assortment of European beers. As more guests arrived over the next hour or so, the maidservant Worqnesh (Amh. "You Are Gold") began the coffee ceremony. As the coffee was brewed, Yismaw's wife brought out popcorn to eat with the coffee. She also brought out several bottles of t'alla and exclaimed that it was Christmas t'alla, strained, clear, and very special. She handed the brew to guests with both hands, and the guests received it, half-rising from their seats and subtly inclining the head, taking the glass of brew with both hands, a gesture of respect and gratitude. Several minutes later, Yismaw brought out a large bottle of qatiqala. It was a new bottle and the guests anxiously awaited the pronouncement of its goodness. Yismaw opened the bottle and poured some into a tall shot glass and toasted the guests, *Lenya t'ena! Tiru nuew!* ("To our health! It is good!"). The guests saw that Yismaw looked fine after his drink, and then those who asked had their glasses filled.

Maybe an hour or two passed. I was not keeping track of the time, since the Johnny Walker was good, the t'alla was fine, and the qatiqala was powerful. A child of ten years made the rounds with a basin, a pitcher of warm water, and a bar of soap held in a rag. She poured water on the hands of each guest, who then washed with the soap, the basin catching the dirty water. Each guest used

14.6. Reminick and Yismaw with Johnny Walker Black Label Scotch whiskey. (PHOTO BY RONALD REMINICK)

the dry cloth or shook the excess water off their hands. In better restaurants, a hot, moist towel would be offered instead. There were basket tables (*mesob*) arranged around the compound with four or five guests seated at each. On a large, round pan on each basket table, the maidservants placed a freshly made, steaming-hot injera. The injera was then cut into strips, rolled, and placed at the edge of the pan. These pieces were torn apart and used to pick up mouthfuls of food. As in other societies where one eats with the hands, like India, only the right hand is used to pick up food. The left hand is used to take care of business at the other end of the alimentary canal.

Older children and the maidservants then served little piles of meat, cheese, legumes, and vegetables that had been prepared the day before and throughout the morning. The pepper sauce (*wat'*) and sheep meat and beef were dumped in the middle of the big injera; the sauce, normally spicy with a cayenne-pepper base, is an essential ingredient. A salty old woman named Etaferau quipped, "You know it's good when it burns twice!" The chicken stew—*doro wat'*, the national dish—is the *pièce de résistance* of the feast, and each serving was graced with a hard-boiled egg. There were also piles of pureed peas, chickpeas, and beans. Some foods were left unspiced for those whose stomachs have trouble with berbere. There was also a pile of a dry, tart cottage cheese, called *ayb*, which complemented the spiced foods nicely. A variety of salad greens added taste and color to the table. On a separate table, I saw a large tray piled with spit-roasted sheep kidneys, hearts, and livers and large lumps of mutton and beef fat. This was optional fare.

Relatives and friends expressed their intimacy by placing a mouthful of injera-wrapped food from their own basket table in the mouth of the receiver. A short time later, the receiver would take food wrapped in the flat bread from his or her own basket table and give the *gursha*[3] in reciprocation. This continued in a lazy non-ceremonious way throughout the hours of feasting. I certainly did not mind my wife, at this party, or my former Ethiopian girlfriend, or the pretty neighbor next door, or even my adoptive mother giving me gursha, but I found it distasteful when a man put his fingers into my mouth. One would think that a veteran ethnographer would be quite comfortable with any custom, but I believe there is a higher priority working here on a more primitive biological level. In 1995 while traveling with my M.A. students in the countryside, I had nine men giving me gursha, which significantly attenuated my appetite.

I used to eat everything on my plate at feasts, small or large, but I soon learned that if the host sees your plate is empty, more food will be piled on. This is fine when you still have room for more, but when you are "stuffed to the gills" and more food gets dumped on your new injera, how is one supposed to politely refuse? It is not good to refuse food. When I was new to the culture I would beg them not to put more food on my plate, but to no avail. Then I realized that I would have to leave food so that more would not be added. As time went by, I also learned that I could beg in the name of God for the host not to give me more food. Then in 2005, an English engineer friend I knew in the town of Bahir Dar taught me the foolproof thing to say when I positively could not eat another bite: *Imbertey yiggalebetal*!—literally, "My bellybutton has turned inside out!"

CONCLUSION

Although a people's ecology puts constraints on what natives can eat and drink (Harris 1985), Ethiopia is a land of diverse ecologies, cultures, and languages; approximately ninety languages are spoken within Ethiopia's boundaries. These ecologies include desert, riverine, highland plateau, montane, and urban lifeways. Each of these regions grows distinct species of crops and maintains domestic animals such as chickens, sheep, goats, and cattle. In the capital city of Addis Ababa, goods from all over the world can be accessed. This vertical ecology allows for a wide variety of crops to be grown, and the numerous market centers throughout the countryside provide nexuses for these goods to be accessed by the surrounding populations. This allows for a complex cuisine of foods and a variety of beverages that are enjoyed by the populace. In this chapter, I focused on the beverages and the social contexts in which they are drunk and what it means to imbibe them, providing a window through which the reader may glimpse the highland culture of Ethiopia.

NOTES

1. The apostrophe signifies an exploded consonant where the glottis closes the trachea and the sound is exploded out of the mouth.

2. Wuqabi is another name for a zar spirit, often used as a euphemism so as not to directly name it.

3. Gursha is a tip in a restaurant or a gift of appreciation, but most popularly it refers to putting a handful of food in another's mouth.

REFERENCES

Bahru, Zewde
    1991   *A History of Modern Ethiopia 1855–1991*. James Curry, Oxford, Ohio University Press, Athens, Ohio, and Addis Ababa University Press, Addis Ababa.

Cargill, Kima
    2007   Desire, Ritual, and Cuisine. *Psychoanalytic Review* 94:2.

Harris, Marvin
    1985   *The Sacred Cow and the Abominable Pig*. Simon and Schuster, New York.

Harris, William Cornwallis, Sir
    1844   *The Highlands of Ethiopia*. Winchester Publishing House, New York.

Herdt, Gilbert
    1987   *The Sambia: Ritual and Gender in New Guinea*. Holt, Rinehart, Winston, New York.

Levine, Donald
    1965   *Wax and Gold*. University of Chicago Press, Chicago.

Long, Lucy
    2003   Food as Symbol. In *Encyclopedia of Food and Culture*, ed. Solomon Katz, 376–377. Charles Scribner's Sons, New York.

Lupton, Deborah
    2005   Food and Emotion. In *The Taste Culture Reader,* ed. Carolyn Korsmeyer. Berg, New York.

Pankhurst, Richard
    1992   *A Social History of Ethiopia*. Red Sea Press, Trenton, NJ.

Reminick, Ronald A.
    1976   Symbolic Significance of Ceremonial Defloration among the Amhara of Ethiopia. *American Ethnologist* 3(4):751–763.

Simoons, Frederick
    1960   *Northwest Ethiopia: Peoples and Economy*. University of Wisconsin Press, Madison.

Ullendorf, Edward
    1960   *The Ethiopians*. Oxford University Press, London.

CHAPTER FIFTEEN

You Are What You Drink in Honduras

Joel Palka

Biographical sketch. Joel Palka is an associate professor at the University of Illinois, Chicago, where he holds a joint appointment with the Departments of Anthropology and Latin American and Latino Studies. He received his Ph.D. in 1995 from Vanderbilt University. Palka's research and teaching interests include the archaeology and history of Mesoamerica and the Caribbean, Classic Maya culture, Maya hieroglyphic writing and art, cultural evolution, social inequality, and settlement patterns. His current research covers ancient Maya social differentiation, settlement archaeology, and the collapse of Maya civilization, along with his new historical archaeology project in which he examines Lacandon Maya culture change in Guatemala and Chiapas during the seventeenth to the nineteenth centuries.

In the field, anthropologists learn to cope with and even eventually appreciate unusual food and drink. But they also experience "out of the ordinary" consumption etiquettes, behaviors, and ethics in those host communities as well. In most societies what is put into the body and how, when, and where the consumption of food or drink occurs communicate crucial information about the individual and his or her culture. Personal identity, ethnicity, perceptions of self, and how others perceive you are determined in part by what and how one eats or drinks. Moreover, it is important for anthropologists to be accepted by their hosts, to "fit" in their adoptive communities, and not to insult new friends. Being in a foreign country presents certain challenges to the visitor, and the adjustments regarding food and drink are among the most important and interesting field adaptations for anthropologists.

The culture of drinking is just as significant and symbolic as the social life of eating, yet there are relatively fewer anthropological studies of drink compared to food (Douglas 1987; Garine 2001:1–3). The biological importance of drinking is universally acknowledged and drinking is a common social activity, from initial encounters between people of different cultures to rendezvous with close friends. Many times people only interact through the medium of drink, especially alcoholic beverages in public settings. Importantly, earlier literature in the social sciences often treated moral issues regarding drinking alcohol (Pittman and Snyder 1962), but more recently, anthropological studies in general recognize the less negative social significance of drinking and intoxication. The consumption of alcohol is often tolerated, if not encouraged, and it is significant for social group cohesion in many cultures. The use of alcohol and the associated behaviors and contexts of drink are culturally determined, and they communicate information about the self and one's position in society (Garine 2001:5–7; Gonzalez Turmo 2001). Also, while drinking with acquaintances in a foreign land, you learn much about them, their culture, and eventually yourself. Furthermore, the sociability of drinking explains certain instances of alcohol consumption, its cultural contexts, and the specific use of alcohol (Douglas 1987; Eber 2000; Mandelbaum 1965; Partanen 1991; Patrick 1952), which will be revisited in the concluding section. In this chapter, I will concentrate on the symbolism of drinking and outsiders' adaptation to drinking alcohol in Honduras rather than discussing factors of morality, age, religion, socioeconomic status, and gender with reference to drink. These other topics are important as well, but they can be taken up on another occasion.

This narrative treats my experiences with local attitudes, beliefs, and behaviors with regard to drinking in small-town and rural Honduras while participating in a long-term archaeological excavation. In a period totaling one and a half years in the late 1980s, I lived with people who were mestizos or Ladinos (persons of mixed European, indigenous, and African ancestry who spoke Spanish, wore Western clothing, and generally followed Western customs); I worked with them every weekday and also spent many evenings and weekends in their company. Drinking alcohol, mostly a beer or two, in social situations was an important part of being a young man in this cultural setting, and it signified that a person had the resources and friends for drinking. My observations largely treat alcoholic beverages. I must clarify from the start that most young men in Honduras are not habitual drunkards, although alcoholism in the country can lead to health, social, and economic problems (Vittetoe 1995). These young men merely have interesting attitudes about drinking alcohol, including where it is consumed, who and what kinds of drinks are involved, and how much is ingested. Alcoholic drink is a common vehicle for festive occasions and social group formation in many cultures (Garine 2001:5–9), and Honduras is no different. While living there, I was exposed to local issues and perceptions of identity, friendship, and sociality as I drank with my friends. Since I already enjoyed cold beer at the end of a workday before arriving in Honduras and I was fully aware of the culture of drinking among archaeologists, I was presented with the perfect opportunity to become a loyal participant observer.

The people I spent time with were typically young men from local villages and small towns who ranged from about twenty to thirty years of age (I was around twenty-five at the time). This demographic profile highlights the fact that alcohol consumption in Honduras can be associated with men, youth, and "machismo." The men I got to know may or may not have represented the practices of their peers elsewhere in the country, but they were certainly common in rural and small-town western Honduras. These men were workers on an archaeological project (together with their friends and young male family members). Many of them had a high school education and a few had college degrees. They were from an area where international tourism was common because of the Classic Maya sites found throughout the region. Many of these young men had steady employment and relatively high earnings by nonurban standards in Honduras at the time. Manufactured spirits are not cheap in Honduras; thus, money had to be earned or borrowed to pay for drinking. These people were friendly, tolerant, generous, protective, honorable, and genuine, and it was easy to share stories, advice, jokes, and information on just about anything over drinks. What I had to get used to were the social contexts, the drinks themselves, and the language of drinking in addition to the excessive quantities of alcohol consumed on some occasions.

DRINKING CONTEXTS

I was surprised by the quantity of beer and rum consumed by young men I had recently met during my first month in Honduras. Dozens of empty beer bottles and open rum bottles frequently crowded the tables of my friends on Friday evenings, and sometimes with only two revelers present! More commonly, though, there were only a few beers shared among friends during lunches, breaks during the weekends, and even after breakfast. A high tolerance for alcohol was necessary to "go the distance" with them on select occasions, and outsiders usually did not have it, at first anyway. To make friends and gain mutual respect it was important to be able to drink a lot sometimes and hold your alcohol. Moreover, it was crucial to participate frequently in drinking in the afternoons or evenings, on the weekends, and during special occasions such as parties, fairs, and holidays. I remember bringing down two bottles of good whisky and drinking them in one sitting with very thankful, cheery friends before going out to listen to music over beers! And then on the following evening, we relaxed by playing guitar and sipping generous amounts of rum. For us, many evenings with our new friends would not have been the same without the alcohol flowing.

Local and foreign men who did not drink alcohol or drank very little were not entirely accepted by many of the young men I was acquainted with. They did not enter the same social circles. It was considered proper behavior and "macho" for men to drink alcohol during visits and important social events and not to act drunk or suffer from a hangover the following morning. The kinds of beer and rum drunk were also essential. There were two brands of beer available: one was for tourists and women and the other brand (whose name actually translates as "lifesaver" in English, an important point in itself!) was reserved for men because it was viewed as stronger, tastier, and "vitamin rich" (*muchas vitaminas*). Guatemalan rum was prized over other available liquors; the latter were described as "liquids for drunkards." Beer was the preferred substance during the social interactions and much of the time only one or two were consumed by each member of the group. Alcohol in general was always the main choice for these young men; drinks like sodas, water, or juices were not typically chosen during times for socializing. Drinks were also not horded or saved for later—they were consumed in their entirety on the spot.

Most of the drinking was done together in restaurants, bars, sidewalk beer stands (*cervezerías*), and hotel lobbies. The frequent dances in local towns were also scenes for drinking alcohol. Typically, the men met for several hours of drinking and visiting as friends came and went. It became a standing joke that the hours of our drinking episodes matched or exceeded those of our work shifts. Rounds of drinks were frequently bought, oftentimes when glasses or bottles were only half-finished, and it was expected that everyone buy drinks for the entire group. People who did not drink or freely purchase drinks were not invited into the group. Also, men who tended to share tales and jokes with the others, besides numerous drinks, were obviously sought out more frequently for social occasions. Drinking led to occasions of good conversation, jokes, and revelry; rarely were people belligerent, incoherent, silly, aggressive, or solitary. Because of the importance of socializing and storytelling while drinking, it was important for foreigners to gain fluency in the local language and in drinking speech. The communication of drinking was just as important as the social interaction and the company that one kept.

Drinking with friends was not often done in private, such as in homes, hotel rooms, or secluded areas. These gatherings were typically in public places where drinking was condoned (cantinas, beer stands near the street, restaurants, hotel lobbies, etc.) and where passersby could be invited to join the group. I did not hear of any private parties thrown by my friends that involved drinking. Furthermore, beer and liquor were not frequently purchased for private consumption; we did not acquire beer to take to our rooms or a house for a party, for instance. Foreigners were the only people who typically did this. Although it certainly was possible to acquire alcohol and drink it out of the public eye, it was more socially acceptable to consume alcohol in more public settings. This behavior can be partially explained as social control: tempers could be kept in check more easily and anyone could see that people were drinking but not getting totally inebriated, which was not acceptable. However, I believe this is also explained by the desire to maintain a public meeting place where acquaintances could drop by for a drink was for socializing and sharing alcohol. This observation also helps explain some of the contexts for drinking in Honduras that are surprising to foreigners, such as the beer tents located in parks, on street corners, and at entrances to theaters and even churches.

DRINKING LANGUAGE

The interesting linguistic terms surrounding drinking alcohol were meant to be descriptive or symbolic of the act, and of course were also highly amusing (see Gutmann 2007:173–195). For instance, there were terms used strictly for invitations to drink alcohol or to describe the act. Words like *chupar* ("suck [with force]") and *tragar* ("swallow [with force]") were used often for dramatic effect instead of the less frequently used term *beber* ("drink"), for example—much like "slam down" or "guzzle" are used instead of "imbibe" in English. Descriptive phrases like "let's go take/intake some cold ones" (*tomar unas frías*) or "let's get drunk" (*nos embolamos*) were occasionally employed as well. Friends also used humorous symbolic language among themselves to describe the act of drinking, such as *tomando vitaminas* ("taking vitamins") and *chupando como un bebe* ("drinking like a [suckling] baby [nursing a bottle]"). If you knew these terms and their correct usage as a foreigner and repeated them, you became part of the group and respected by local drinkers. It also allowed the speakers to be more familiar with each other, which was important in these social contexts. "How about a beer?" (*¿Quieres una cerveza?*) just did not have the same effect and was viewed as formal, unless a nickname or insult in jest with a trusted friend was added.

The language of drink was used to describe people and words and, thus, helped define insiders versus outsiders with the group of young male drinkers. The in-group was usually described as "drinkers," "drink sharers," or people who buy drinks for one another. Descriptive terms for persons who took consuming alcohol a bit too far or drank too much for the men's liking included "beer is pleasing to him" (*le gusta la cerveza*), "he is a drunk" (*es un bolo*), and—my favorite—he does "much sucking/drinking" (*mucha chupa*). Others included "he does not drink" (*no toma nada*) or the sarcastic "he is Evangelico" (*es un evangélico*), implying that a person refusing a drink was acting like a member of a Protestant church that avoided alcohol. The people who did not drink at all or drank too much were mostly avoided during social occasions in public.

Interestingly, container shapes were occasionally invoked by my local friends to describe people's bodies. They stated that young men have builds like solid, strong brown beer bottles, which contain fortifying substances. Older or heavier men had midsections like the large bulging bottles of Central American rum—the liquid whose overuse was responsible for this condition. Young women had hourglass shapes like Coke bottles; my friends would point to a woman and say *pura Coca-Cola* ("purely [like] a Coke [bottle]"). In Honduras at this time sodas sold "to go" were served in plastic bags (*en la bolsa*) with straws since bottles had to be returned for deposit. On one occasion a local friend pointed to a round woman nearby and said *pura Coca-Cola* while smiling. I and my college friends were puzzled by this remark, but the other local men sported huge grins. The reason for their smiles became obvious with the anticipated punch line *pero en la bolsa* ("but [like Coke] to go in a bag").

It was obvious from the beginning that public occasions for drinking were not tainted by inappropriate language. Rarely were embarrassing and hurtful comments ever exchanged between my local friends. Swearing was not common, even though foreigners were taught obscenities on a weekly basis. It is possible that out of respect, our friends refrained from colorful language or arguments in our presence. However, strong language was indeed exchanged from time to time, but the typical mood of the interaction was warm, friendly, and conversational rather than bawdy or belligerent.

DRINKING IDENTITY

I knew that I had been accepted into the local cadre of drinkers after individuals described me as sharing drinks by buying rounds when it was my turn and holding my alcohol without becoming belligerent or sick. Because I was able to drink with them and communicate in many social situations, I made lifelong friends. They were able to learn a lot about me and life in the United States, and I was able acclimate to my new surroundings, learn about Hondurans, appreciate their lives and their country, and become proficient in Spanish. Their perception of me as a rich foreigner who bought drinks for everyone did not enter the picture most of the time, at least after they got to know me. My new friends earned a decent living and they bought drinks just as much as I did, if not more. This practice was a matter of pride for them since I was a newcomer to their country and had to be welcomed and educated in their customs.

There were many things to be learned about drinking behavior and the people involved in these social occasions. These activities and behaviors were considered to be *cosas de bolos*, or whimsically classified as "the things that only drunks know." Examples of this specialized knowledge enjoyed by my drinking comrades were things like knowing how to open the twist cap on a sealed rum bottle by merely running the bottle quickly down the forearm. Another trick they knew was how to "remove the devil" (*sacar el diablo*) from an empty bottle of spirits, which was done by heating it up using friction from rubbing it on one's pants for several minutes and then putting a lighted match inside, which produced a whirling, whistling extremely hot blue flame that shot out of the bottle.

After learning the behaviors and language of drinking, I was always welcomed into the groups of young men. Additionally, I was respected for drinking local liquid home remedies for my upset stomach or hangovers. (It was the only thing that worked many times!) I was also renowned and respected for trying and liking home-brewed corn beer, or *chicha*. One local medicinal cocktail for stomach aliments consisted of water, an extract from an unidentified root, and a little rum. It was the bitterest concoction that I ever have tasted in my life. It actually cured my stomach within a few hours and reinforced my new friends' view of me as being one of them. I found the corn chicha good at any temperature, especially cooled in the shade, and my acquired taste for this brew had the same socially bolstering effect among my drinking peers. Some fellow students from the United States refused to drink the Honduran home remedies or beer with our hosts. When they made the important personal decision not to drink, they lost the opportunity to socialize with the locals who drank and they were never completely accepted by them. Essentially, they did not do things as these young Honduran men did.

Furthermore, it should not be surprising that attitudes and stigmas regarding drinking alcohol are different in Honduras than in the United States. For one, large drinking parties organized by young people with the goal of inebriation are uncommon. In fact, what we label as underage drinking and out-of-control keg parties are not common social problems. Despite the fact that anyone can buy alcohol of any proof in Honduras, adolescents are not really known to drink alcohol, let alone be seen drunk in public. And typically, many older men with families are not habitual drinkers; they spend their time and money with their families. Most Honduran women do not drink much and they are never caught drinking in public (but they enjoy clandestine sips of beer in private). However, it is expected that women from the city or foreign countries, and prostitutes, should have a drink or two, but that is all. It is mainly socially acceptable for unmarried male high school graduates to drink large quantities of alcohol in public. This behavior highlights the gender divisions in regard to drinking alcohol in Honduras, which follows the male-centric, public alcohol consumption patterns of many other countries (Gutmann 2007:190; Heath 1995; but see Weismantel 2001:29).

DRINKING ENCOUNTERS

Examples of interactions while drinking in Honduras will clarify some of the issues discussed. These vignettes illustrate the importance of the social situations, language, contexts, and symbolic behaviors involved in drinking. These stories were shared with local friends and colleagues in the United States and were often told and retold in the context of drinking.

During my first week in Honduras, numerous new acquaintances invited me several times to go have "just one beer," or "maybe two." At first, I consistently declined, not wanting to violate local customs or informal social rules that I was as yet unaware of. When I saw other foreigners with the archaeology project drinking with local men, however, I "took the plunge" into a local cantina one day with new friends whose company I really enjoyed. I could not leave for several hours and, of course, numerous rounds of beers. Every time I said it was time for me to go or I stood up, I was coaxed or pulled back into my chair by my hosts, who insisted on buying more drinks (I had no money during this particular fiesta) so that we could become friends and they could teach me more Spanish. They explained to me that in Honduras men sit for hours with their close friends to talk and buy each other drinks. That night they explained local drinks and drinking customs to me, and I learned a lot in this one sitting. I must admit that my Spanish and my understanding of Honduran culture greatly improved over months of interaction with my friends in these social situations. Over time, drinking and visiting with my friends became enjoyable and on only one occasion did a misunderstanding end in a disagreement between two of my local friends.

Beer was widely available all over town. Hard liquor was more difficult to obtain. Rum was sold in some stores, many of which closed early, or in a few select bars. Since anything stronger than beer was frequently associated with drunks, private consumption, and excessive drinking, liquor was not as desirable or visible. However, one night we learned that there were special, clandestine liquor dispensaries, or mini-bars, in town. A local friend took a few of us foreign guests to an unmarked structure that turned out to be the home of an acquaintance who sold strong, locally made liquor—essentially, moonshine. The owner let us in discretely and quickly (he was always open, even at 1:00 AM!), and we were seated in an undecorated room with one table before a small cabinet. Our friend requested drinks for everyone and the owner quietly unlocked the liquor chest and carefully measured shots of the tasteless, but extremely potent, concoction for us. He then quickly locked the cabinet and closely watched us as he immediately collected the money we owed. Drinking this substance in this social and physical context often had different outcomes, probably violent, compared to the open, cheerful interactions in cantinas over beers.

In another instance, a friend and I each brought a gallon of Canadian whisky to share with our Honduran friends. We seized the opportunity to introduce them to this foreign drink one night before the local town fair. Our intention was to measure a few shots and then be on our way. But we soon learned that frequently the local custom is to share all drinks available in one sitting rather than save bottles for six months, as we intended to do. This behavior may be related to resource redistribution, but the complete consumption of drinks on hand is also culturally determined and social in nature.

ALCOHOLIC DRINK: A SOCIAL LUBRICANT

Several points can be made about drinking in Honduras from an anthropological view. Cross-culturally, drinking is the prime lubricant for social interaction. It is most frequently done in groups rather than individually (Heath 1995). Drinking among peers is also prevalent in many societies (Orcutt 1991). Through drink, friends meet, economic interactions are initiated or finalized, and people gather for festivals and good times. Drinking in a group emphasizes the collection of individuals as a primary reference group or a gathering of individuals interconnected by social, economic, or kinship ties; drinking facilitates social interaction and is a way of expressing solidarity (Heath 1962:33). The initial stimulating effects of alcohol (what is called "good cheer" in pub talk) certainly are useful for generating joyful social intercourse. Increased camaraderie is achieved since alcohol lowers inhibitions and activates feelings of exaltation.

On an individual level, meeting with my Honduran friends over drinks definitely allowed me to get to know them, learn Spanish, and appreciate their company, lives, and country. The moments set aside for drinking provided informal social situations where we could share resources, stories, advice, and good times. The collection of friends in good cheer while in social settings enabled us to get to know one another more quickly and personally. Even if we only consumed one or two beers, the importance of sharing them and the effects of even minimal amounts of alcohol were enough to break down personal, language, and cultural barriers. My Spanish language skills improved immensely following hours of "fluid" conversation with my friends, and we joked that even non-Spanish speakers became uninhibitedly fluent by evening's end. Some of the local men even surprised us with rudimentary, but clear, English as the night wore on.

In my experience, it usually was not what was drunk that was interesting but when, how much, and with whom. Young men were the social drinkers who enjoyed ample amounts of beer and hard liquor in the evening. But many times one was expected to share a beer or two when encountering friends at just about any time of the day. As outsiders, we had to learn to adjust to different patterns of drinking alcohol and new social mores if we were to be accepted into specific social sectors of Honduran society. Drinking in these contexts took getting used to, but the real challenge and joy of discovery was in making new friends and gaining an understanding of their views of the proper contexts for social life during specific kinds of interaction.

It is obvious that select individuals participate in drinking alcohol in Honduras and that there are social and economic explanations for this patterned behavior. Drinking in small groups in public is tied to age, gender, and socioeconomic standing. Thus, having enough "disposable income" to engage in drinking and showing it in public are only part of the explanation. In European and Mesoamerican societies public consumption of alcohol has been the purview of men throughout history (Cantarero Abad 2001). This attitude reflects the norms of a patrilineal society, in which men hold the positions of political power and authority and are the heads of households and the major income earners. Drinking alcohol and consuming large amounts of it are connected to strength, masculinity, male camaraderie, leadership, and national identity (Cantarero Abad 2001:153–155).

What is also interesting in this case study is the language of drinking and the contexts in which language and symbolism are utilized. Terms for labeling drinkers versus non-drinkers and social drinkers versus drunks are important for people to contextualize and categorize drinking activities and actors. The drinking vernacular and symbolism, besides the social settings of drinking in Honduras, may be an important contribution of the analysis of drinking for the anthropological study of foods and consumption. While the study of eating has produced significant results for the understanding of social identity and the contexts of human interaction, the observations of the use of language, the social categories of people and symbols utilized during food consumption are underreported. (Categories of "eaters" versus "non-eaters" are usually not options!) Furthermore, people in Honduras were not classified, for instance, as someone who "does not share tortillas" and social categories typically did not result from which foods were consumed. Additionally, while I shared many drinks with my friends on many different occasions, we rarely participated in meals together, if ever. What the men drank and how much of it provided important signals for who they were and for how they were viewed by others. Thus, the study of the culture of drink and drinking can lead to additional insights into human behavior that cannot be found in the examination of food use alone.

Some scholars have elaborated on the social contexts of drinking and the importance of intoxication in drinking behavior (Douglas 1987; Partanen 1991). In the views of "integrated drinking" and the "sociability of drinking" (Doughty 1979; Partanen 1991:199–228; Simmons 1962:37–38), drinking is often a pursuit of specific social groups and not single individuals or members of a society as a whole. In this paradigm the public nature of drinking is crucial and select social segments, such as young men in rural Honduras, get together for social interaction and consume alcoholic beverages. The use of alcohol and its overuse, as the case may be, are frequently critical to one's identity, socioeconomic status, and place in society. The effects of intoxication are also central as the alcohol becomes a social lubricant enhancing the interaction and modifying the behavior of the people in the group in a desired fashion. When foreigners learn this sociability of drinking and the embedded behaviors, language, symbols, and contexts, they better comprehend and appreciate the lifeways of their hosts.

REFERENCES

Cantarero Abad, Luis
    2001   Gender and Drink in Aragon, Spain. In *Drinking: Anthropological Approaches*, ed. Igor and Valerie de Garine, 144–157. Berghahn Books, New York.

Douglas, Mary (editor)
    1987   *Constructive Drinking*. Cambridge University Press, Cambridge.

Doughty, Paul L.
    1979   The Social Uses of Alcoholic Beverages in a Peruvian Community. In *Beliefs, Behaviors, and Alcoholic Beverages: A Cross-Cultural Survey*, ed. Mac Marshall, 64–80. University of Michigan Press, Ann Arbor.

Eber, Christine E.
    2000   *Women and Alcohol in a Highland Maya Town: Water of Hope, Water of Sorrow*. University of Texas Press, Austin.

Garine, Igor de
    2001   For a Pluridisciplinary Approach to Drinking. In *Drinking: Anthropological Approaches*, ed. Igor and Valerie de Garine, 1–10. Berghahn Books, New York.

Gonzalez Turmo, Isabel

2001 Drinking: An Almost Silent Language. In *Drinking: Anthropological Approaches*, ed. Igor and Valerie de Garine, 130–143. Berghahn Books, New York.

Guttman, Matthew C.

2007 *The Meanings of Macho: Being a Man in Mexico City (10th Anniversary Edition)*. University of California Press, Berkeley.

Heath, Dwight B.

1995 An Anthropological View of Alcohol and Culture in International Perspective. In *International Handbook on Alcohol and Culture*, ed. Dwight B. Heath, 328–347. Greenwood Press, Westport, CT.

1962 Drinking Patterns of the Bolivian Camba. In *Society, Culture, and Drinking Patterns*, ed. David J. Pittman and Charles R. Snyder, 22–36. John Wiley and Sons, New York.

Mandelbaum, David G.

1965 Alcohol and Culture. *Current Anthropology* 6(3):281–294.

Orcutt, James D.

1991 The Social Integration of Beers and Peers: Situational Contingencies in Drinking and Intoxication. In *Society, Culture, and Drinking Patterns Reexamined*, ed. David J. Pittman and Helene Raskin White, 198–218. Rutgers Center of Alcohol Studies, New Brunswick, NJ.

Partanen, Juha

1991 *Sociability and Intoxication: Alcohol and Drinking in Kenya, Africa, and the Modern World*, vol. 39. The Finnish Foundation for Alcohol Studies, Helsinki.

Patrick, Clarence H.

1952 *Alcohol, Culture, and Society*. Duke University Press, Durham, NC.

Pittman, David J., and Charles R. Snyder (editors)

1962 *Society, Culture, and Drinking Patterns*. John Wiley and Sons, New York.

Simmons, Ozzie G.

1962 Ambivalence and the Learning of Drinking Behavior in a Peruvian Community. In *Society, Culture, and Drinking Patterns*, ed. David J. Pittman and Charles R. Snyder, 37–47. John Wiley and Sons, New York.

Vittetoe Bustillo, Kenneth W.

1995 Honduras. In *International Handbook on Alcohol and Culture*, ed. Dwight B. Heath, 110–116. Greenwood Press, Westport, CT.

Weismantel, Mary

2001 *Cholas and Pishtacos: Stories of Race and Sex in the Andes*. University of Chicago Press, Chicago.

SECTION V

The Last Course

Edibles and Ethnic Boundaries, Globalization and Guinea Pigs

Miriam S. Chaiken

After seeing a title like *Adventures in Eating*, many casual browsers might imagine this book to be part of the growing genre of media aimed at shocking and disgusting the U.S. public. Television shows depict "ordinary" people engaging in mock battles, testing their mettle in unfamiliar settings, and ingesting revolting objects in a quest to titillate, horrify, and amuse viewers. Many shows that are billed as travel adventures actually focus on the weird and kinky behaviors and customs of the cultures they examine. In all of these cases they objectify the people they depict and trivialize the cultures they examine—precisely the opposite of what anthropologists seek to do, and precisely opposite the focus of this book.

As the core principle of our discipline, anthropologists embrace the concept of cultural relativism; our goal is to understand another culture on its own terms rather than to impose our judgments of normalcy on others. While we do not always achieve this ideal, it has been the core goal of our field for more than 100 years, coming from the founding father of American anthropology, Franz Boas. Boas's challenge to us was to be systematic in our examinations of other cultures, to meticulously document cultural traits and history, and to find grounds of commonality among different cultural groups. Most of the

277

articles in this book have that quest for cross-cultural understanding as the central theme. Reminick, Palka, Zycherman, and Chaiken all reflect on the ways shared meals reveal and reinforce social relations and how offers of hospitality to the "outsider" anthropologist signal a measure of acceptance by the members of the communities we study. In the latter two cases, these offers raise challenges to our anthropological goal of cultural relativism, as our own enculturated values leave us hard-pressed to entirely surrender the food rules that can be both ingrained and purposeful, such as Zycherman's struggle to retain her kosher practices.

Our discussions of the uses of foods that are unfamiliar, and even challenging to us, show the difficulty of maintaining our cultural relativism in novel settings. Food has always had power beyond being a mere source of sustenance; it has enormous symbolic value in every society. The choices of what is deemed edible obviously vary from culture to culture, and more importantly, who is allowed to eat together has even greater significance. We see the importance of this when the "rules" of dining commensality are challenged, such as when the brave young African American students quietly took their seats at a Woolworth's lunch counter in the segregated South of Greensboro, North Carolina, in 1960. We see the importance of these boundaries when Hindus of different castes, Muslims, and Christians defied conventions and demeaning ideas of ritual pollution and had communal "eat-ins" in Kerala, India, to rebel against the caste system and hierarchy (Franke and Chasin 1994). Food and eating have often been contested terrain as cultures clash, define themselves, and erect the boundaries that define in- and out-group identities (see Barth 1969 for the classic discussion of this issue). Conversely, the choice to share in another's culinary traditions marks an erosion of the us-them dichotomy, as with Rachel Black's invitation to share the Italian family's dinner, the first sign of her acceptance as a member of the family.

Many of the chapters in this book deal specifically with the anthropologists' quests to overcome their naturally and culturally ingrained food preferences and prejudices as they tried to fit in among the communities they study. Learning a new language, trying to navigate the subtleties of customs, and knowing one's proper place are often challenges that anthropologists face; but the challenges of what we face on our plates or in our bowls can be even more significant. Some of our tales are deadly serious and others are more lighthearted, but they all share insights into how authors confronted their own biases and also the ways in which our eating practices were perceived by the people we study.

In a number of chapters in this volume, the struggles that the authors report reflect the critical concept of liminality, as they examine items on the threshold between two bounded, culturally defined categories. This concept has been the center of many anthropological investigations of ritual and rites of passage (Turner 1969) as well as perceptions of food in culture (Douglas 1966), and the tension that liminal states and luminal items engenders has been well documented. Lohmann questions whether a partially incubated egg is an egg or a bird; Haines asks if something labeled a rat can also be categorized as food; and Goldstein and Chaiken wonder whether we can train ourselves to see creatures that we view as pets (guinea pigs and dogs) as also being food.

People from outside our discipline have sometimes criticized us for purporting to know about another culture while not being a member of it, but our fascination about the people we study is often reciprocated. While we are examining, analyzing, and discussing their behaviors and food choices, our "informants" do the same with us as they check to see how far we can and will go to fit in and embrace the new culture we are studying. Johnston's description of the bidirectional gaze aptly summarizes this reciprocal curiosity and data collection. What does he think of guinea pig? Will she eat termites? Can she think of this rat as a source of meat? Do I need to serve vegetables because that is what the white lady eats? Can you believe she does not eat meat? Meanwhile, the anthropologists ask, Should I really have cleaned my plate; am I being rude? Is it an egg or a little chicken? Can I hide the chicken head under the noodles so they do not know that I cannot eat this? These are examples of the mental dialogs we have carried on with ourselves and those I imagine went through the minds of the people we studied.

In the end, our testing of our food boundaries allows us to develop our skills as anthropologists and often results in our profound reflection on who we are with regard to our profession, gender, or even national identity. This self-reflection sometimes makes us stronger as individuals and more accepted in the eyes of the communities where we work, as Cattell and Goldstein gain macho brownie points for relishing termites and guinea pigs, respectively. Conversely, Sammells describes herself as being humbled by her difficulties with simple agricultural chores, and Marte grapples with the dietary restrictions she must follow that are in direct conflict with her own culture's proscriptions for what is good to eat. In other cases these food challenges help us reflect on and encode our own core values, such as Aimers's principled opposition to whale hunting and Zycherman's need to maintain her heritage through observing the rules of kosher diets. We learn about ourselves through the disquiet of these cross-cultural challenges. In the end, we become better anthropologists, and possibly better people, for having grappled with this struggle.

The other key theme that is pervasive in this book is the issue of globalization—a topic that reaches far beyond the field of anthropology and, indeed, affects everyone, everywhere. The process of globalization is well manifested in studies of food, beginning with the Columbian exchange half a millennium ago to contemporary political dimensions of food production, consumption, and access. As one author debates the ethics of whaling by indigenous and multinational fishermen, Black examines the ways the Slow Food movement seeks to counter the homogenization and "McDonaldization" of food. As Sammells discusses the authentic versus the stereotypic presentation of foods for tourists in Bolivia, McBrinn shows her quest as a tourist to eat the forbidden fruit durian, which was the subject of much global food lore, and Marte describes the challenges faced when she is unable to consume the foods that her informants idealize. Many chapters touch on the loss of traditional foodways or the ways in which local people become increasingly incorporated into global food patterns and processes, from Johnston's discussion of the historic loss of the Plains horse and buffalo culture to the shift away from freeze-dried potatoes to more consumption of bread. These shifts away from traditional diets often result in declining nutritional status and other health consequences caused by the "mismatch" between one's genetic heritage and one's current lifestyle. The negative dietary consequences of these changes have been widely documented, but less often noted is the corresponding loss of important cultural traditions of food sharing, hospitality, and cultural norms about community identity.

In many respects the study of food provides the perfect grounds for examining the processes of globalization and the positive and negative consequences of global exchange of food and ideas about food. These chapters highlight those issues and provide food for thought about the pervasiveness of this unstoppable process.

REFERENCES

Barth, Fredrik
   1969   *Ethnic Groups and Boundaries: The Social Organization of Cultural Difference.* Little and Brown, New York.

Douglas, Mary
   1966   *Purity and Danger.* Routledge, London.

Franke, Richard, and Barbara H. Chasin
   1994   *Kerala: Radical Reform as Development in an Indian State.* Food First Books, Oakland, CA.

Turner, Victor
   1969   *The Ritual Process: Structure and Anti-Structure.* Aldine de Gruyter, New York.

*Page numbers in **bold face** indicate illustrations*

Abaluyia, 79–94; indigenous cuisine, 84–85, 90, 94n1. *See also* Indigenous peoples

Abyssinian, 244–247, 250. *See also* Amhara; Ethiopia

Addiction, 153–154, 158–159, 236, 250

Adobo seasonings, 154, 156–157. *See also* Spices

Agau, 244

Age, 11, 128, 129; aging, 82–83, 92, 223; generational differences, 11, 226–227, 264, 265, 269–270; and status, 83–84, 86, 91–92, 272; youth, 265, 269

Agouti paca. *See* Gibnut

Agriculture, 59, 70–71, 89, 102–103, 104, 106–110, **107**, 120n5, 184, 185, 198, 206, 208, 225, 248, 279; animal damage to, 45, 189–190, 228; changing forms of, 82, 84–85, 90–92, 149, 228–229, 233–234, 244–245; and gender, 104, 106, 253; plantations, 6

AIDS, 89, 92

Ají, 109. *See also* Spices

Alcohol, 8, 14–15, 38, 133, 186–187; and gender, 86, 265–266, 268, 269–270, 272; language of drinking, 266–269; private drinking, 267, 270–271; public drinking, 3, 14–15, 89, 186–187, 195, 256–258, 263–273. *See also various drinks by name*

Alcoholism, 265, 268, 273

Algonquin, 226. *See also* Blackfeet; Indigenous peoples

Allergies. *See* Food: allergies

Alpaca, 64. *See also* Llama

Alterity, 115–116, 216, 236–239

Amalwa, 86, 88, 89. *See also* Alcohol

Amazon forest, 172

Amhara, 245–246, 248–261, **251**. *See also* Ethiopia; Indigenous peoples

Anchovies, 136. *See also* Fish

Animal fat, 87, 168, 198–199, 209, 234–235, 237–238, 246, 260. *See also* Meat

Animal husbandry. *See* Cattle: ranching; Chicken; Gibnut; Guinea pig

Animal rights movements, 73–74, 245

Anthropologists: commensality among; 1–5, 63–64, 67–68, 183; fitting in, 30–31, 93–94, 170, 264; "native," 146, 155, 161–162, 201n1; as outsiders, 279; and privilege, 84, 160–161, 236. *See also* Method

Apple, 7, 62. *See also* Fruit

Arawak, 60. *See also* Indigenous peoples

Archaeology, 64, 94n1, 115; and commensality, 2, 12, 43–45, 53–54, 67, 270–271; of foods, 46, 68; projects, 1, 43, 47, 59, 127, 167, 170, 263–264. *See also* Guinea Pig: archaeology; Maya: archaeology

Areke. *See* Qatiqala

Argentina, 14, 23, 45, 53, 203–219; cuisine, 203–206, 209–210, 214–216

Asabano, 11–12, 21–41

Asado, 204, 210–219. *See also* Meat

Asparagus, 140, 194. *See also* Vegetables

Atsina. *See* Gros Ventres

Australia, 32, 170, 175, 176

Avocado, 133, 138, 140, **157**. *See also* Fruit; Vegetables

Aymara, 60, 102, 105–110, 114–117. *See also* Indigenous peoples

Azuki bean paste, 168. *See also* Beans; Legumes

Banana, 43–45, 80, 84, 85, 136, 149, 189. *See also* Fruit

Barbeque. *See* Asado

Barley, 244, 245, 247, 248, 251, 256. *See also* Grains

Beans, 84, 85, 88, 92, 137, 149, 151–152, 154–158, 228, 234, 237, 248, 259; green beans, 234. *See also* Azuki bean paste; Fava beans; Legumes

Beaver, 73

Beef. *See* Cattle: as meat

Beer, 1, 14–15, 88, 168–169, 186–187, 253, 256, 258, 264–272. *See also* Alcohol; Amalwa

Bees, 84. *See also* Insects

Beet, 234. *See also* Tubers; Vegetables

Beetles, 84. *See also* Insects

Belize, 2, 12, 22, 43–55, **48**, 59, 243

Berbere, 246, 248, 259

Beverages, 109, 195, 260, 264. *See also various drinks by name and type*

Birds, 189; hunting, 26, 84, 86. *See also* Hunting; Meat

Birthday celebrations, 186, 192, 209, 215

Bishop's weed, 248. *See also* Spices

Bison. *See* Buffalo

Blackfeet, 14, 223–239; history, 224–230; Reservation, 224–225, **225**, 228. *See also* Indigenous peoples

Bloch, Maurice, 24, 30

Blood (as food), 26–27, 86, 186, 210. *See also* Organ meats

Boas, Franz, 169, 277

Bolivia, 12, 43, 45, 51, 59, 69, 101–120, 203; cuisine, 101, 103, 111, 113, 119; touristic cuisine, 118–119, 280

Bouillon, 87, 151–157, 159. *See also* Spices

Boundaries, social, 10, 31, 34, 113–115; between anthropologists and informants, 23–25, 29–31, 34, 37–38, 40, 49, 160–161, 169–170, 237–238, 278–279

Brain (meat), 67–68, 114. *See also* Organ meats

Brazil, 6, 12, 45, 176, 243

Bread, 86, 114, 116, 120n4, 121n17, 193, 214, 215, 237, 251, 256, 280; comparisons to, 22; pilot bread, 235. *See also* Grains; Injera; Sago

Breastfeeding, 91, 92

Buddhism, 168, 169. *See also* Religion

Buffalo (American), 227–228, 233, 235, 280. *See also* Meat; Water Buffalo

Bugs. *See* Insects

Bukusu, 86, 89–90. *See also* Luyia

Butter, 22, 86

Cabbage, 128, 213. *See also* Vegetables

Cake, 88, 154. *See also* Dessert

Camel, 254. *See also* Meat

Campari, 195. *See also* Alcohol

Canada, 44, 73, 119, 192, 194, 224–227, 271; cuisine, 2, 52–53; educational institutions, 43, 167; food aversions, 12. *See also* North Atlantic

Cañahua, 116, 121n17. *See also* Grains

Cancer, 231–232

Candy, 7, 139. *See also* Dessert

Canned foods, 36, 37, 74, 109, 152–155, 185, 193, 234, 246

Cannibalism, 12, 31, 34–35, 245; and folklore, 34; of pets, 35, 114

Carachi, 109. *See also* Fish

Cardamom, 248. *See also* Spices

Caribbean, 6, 145–161, cuisine, 45, 149

Carrots, 103, 193, 209, 234, 235. *See also* Vegetables

Cassava, 60, 80, 84, 86, 89, 91, 114, 132. *See also* Tubers

Castor, 244

Cat, 185; as meat, 65, 75. *See also* Meat

Catfish, 128. *See also* Fish

Cattle, 84, 149, 244, 260; as meat, 11, 14, 27, 23, 49, 53, 88, 89, 102, 103, 109, 113, 115, 116, 172, 193, 203–219, **211**, 223–224, 228–229, 235, 238, 246, 248, 251; as beast of burden, 106, 188; meat as symbol, 204, 205; ranching, 172, 205, 225, 229–230, 233, 234; veal, 192, 200. *See also* Asado; Meat

Cayenne (spice), 248, 259. *See also* Spices

Celery, 193. *See also* Vegetables

Cell phones, 5, 83, 90, 212

Ceviche, 60, 67, 75. *See also* Fish; Seafood

Ch'at. *See* Qat

Chai. *See* Tea

Chairo, 102, 103, 111. *See also* Chuño

Chapattis, 86

Chapulines. *See* Grasshoppers

Charq'e. *See* Jerky

Cheese, 15, 109, 110, 128, 193, 213, 215–216, 245, 259; comparisons to, 133, 134, 139

Cherry, 198, 235. *See also* Fruit

Chewong, 132. *See also* Indigenous peoples

Chicha, 269. *See also* Alcohol

Chicken, 85, 92, 149, 184, 244, 260; animal husbandry, 185, 215; buffalo wings, 6; feet, 52, 183; heads, 52, 182–183, 279; as meat, 13, 49, 53, 84, 85, 93, 109, 115, 156, 183, 185, 187, 198, 200, 213, 215, 217, 246, 248, 259; "tastes like chicken," 55, 68, 72, 75. *See also* Meat

Chickpea, 251, 259. *See also* Legumes

Chicory, 198

Children, 12, 84, 91, 106, 121n8, 189, 228, 245, 253, 254, 258–259; feeding, 12, **27**, 84, 88, 92–93, 107–109, **108**, 116, 121n9, 128, 195, 212, 237, 255; feeding in schools, 170; and pets, 64, **66**; and play, 27–28; and food allergies, 160; and food taboos, 32, 34; and hunger, 181; teaching, 81, 83, 85, 86, 245

Chili (dish), 237

Chili (peppers), 2, 26, 60, 62, 85, 136, 248; *see also* Ají; Cayenne; Locoto; Spices

China, 43, 71, 74, 86, 244, 250; cuisine, 5–6, 65, 136, 153–154, 196

Chocolate, 6, 7, 133, 168; as beverage, 6, 151, 154, 200. *See also* Beverages

Chokeberry, 235. *See also* Fruit

Chorizo. *See* Meat, sausages

Christianity, 84, 190, 245–246, 278; Christmas, 5, 92, 192, 199–201, 258–259; conversion, 11, 21, 32, 34; Easter, 151; evangelical, 89, 268; and food, 6, 11, 34, 36, 86, 89, 199–201, 245–246, 278; and gender, 11, 21, 86; missionaries, 86, 94n1. *See also* Religion

Chuño, 8, 12–13, 101–120, **108**, 280; Bolivian identity, 106; cooking, 105, 120n3; distinct from potatoes, 12, 103, 105, 111, 113, 118; folklore, 102; fresca, 105; making, 103–105; nutrition, 116; in restaurants, 110, 112, 117, 119; in tour books, 110–111, 117. *See also* Chairo; Tubers

Cilantro, 151, 156. *See also* Spices

Cinnamon, 26, 36, 151, 248, 254, 255. *See also* Spices

Citrus fruit, 206. *See also* Fruit

Class, 149–150, 156, 159, 160–161, 263; and food, 7–8, 105–106, 114–117, 119, 129, 152–153, 245, 264–265, 272; and restaurants, 168; and travel, 7–8

Cloves, 151, 248, 254. *See also* Spices

Coca-cola, 6, 236, 268. *See also* Metacommodities; Soda

Coconut, 136, 146, 149. *See also* Spices

Coffee, 15, 26, 36, 38, 140, 147, **148**, 151, 154–155, 158, 185, 195, 235, 244, 250; as global commodity, 6, 36, 228–229; coffee party, 246, 250–254, 258–260; folklore, 250; preparing, 148–149, **251, 252**, 252–253; and Starbucks, 6; *zar* spirits, 14, 250–251, 254, 261n2. *See also* Beverages

Collards, 80. *See also* Vegetables

Colonialism: British in Africa, 82, 83–84, 85, 86, 87, 91, 94n1, 95n3, 128; British Empire, 1, 6, 15n3; Spanish in Caribbean, 6, 149; Spanish in Latin America, 6, 60–61, 102–103, 116, 205, 216, 263; Portuguese in Africa, 85; Portuguese in the Americas, 60, 85

Columbian exchange, 6, 84–85, 102, 104, 279–280

Commensality, 23–25, 28–29, 30–31, 38, 50–52, 194–196, 245, 261n3, 264, 278, 280; and anthropologists, 11–13, 22–25, **27**, 28–29, 38, 107–110, 192–194, 223–224, 237, 249–250, 260, 266, 269–271. *See also* Anthropologists: commensality among

Conch, 45. *See also* Seafood

Cookbooks, 6–7, 200, 209

Cookies, 26, 36, 87, 116, 195; as metaphor, 29. *See also* Dessert

Cooking oil, 26, 62

Cooking. *See* Food: preparing

Corn. *See* Maize

Cornish game hen, 68. *See also* Meat

Costa Rica, 101

Cowboys, 27. *See also* Gauchos

Cowpeas, 84. *See also* Legumes; Vegetables

Cuisine, 7; African, 196; crossing national boundaries, 196; household, 6; innovation, 93–94; Latino, 8, 153, 188; local, 127, 198; multicultural cosmopolitanism, 5–7, 13–14, 73–74, 136–137, 153–154, 196; national, 117; regional, 119, 192–193, 194, 196, 198, 209; touristic, 110–119. *See also* Judaism; *various nations and regions by name*

Cultural relativism, 169, 177, 277–278. *See also* Method

Cumin, 248. *See also* Spices

Custard pie, 37–38. *See also* Dessert

Cuy. *See* Guinea pig

Death, 9, 35, 83, 92, 134, 146, 149, 206, 228, 231; rituals, 9, 30, 83, 88–89, 93, 235

Deer, 172, 198

Denmark, 174. *See also* North Atlantic

Dessert, 114, 137, 154, 193. *See also various desserts by name*

Development projects, 46, 70–71

Diabetes, 156, 231

Disease, 11, 50, 82, 83, 149, 187, 228; diet-related, 149, 154, 217, 224, 230–233, 235; food-borne, 14, 254–255. *See also* AIDS; Cancer; Diabetes; Heart Disease

DNA. *See* Genetics

Dog, 27, 35, 62, 172, 227; as meat, 13, 35, 65, 115, 128, 173, 181, 186–188, 190, 279;

as pet, 35, 43, 187, 210, 246, 279. *See also* Meat

Dolphins, 171, 172, 175. *See also* Seafood

Dominican Republic, 146, 149–150, 152–153, 155; communities in New York City, 145–161; cuisine, 147–150, **148**, 155

Donkey, 244

Douglas, Mary, 27, 113, 114, 264, 273, 279

Drought, 82, 91, 105, 229, 254

Durian, 8, 13, 25, 127–140, 145, 280; and animals, 131–132; as aphrodisiac, 133; buying, 137–138; export, 130, 139; in folklore, 131, 132; harvesting, 130–131, 132; "King of Fruits," 131–132, 133–134, 135; and kinship, 132; markets, 132–133, 137; odor, 137–140; as symbol, 135; taste, 138–139, 140; in tour books, 135; Western dislike for, 134–135, 138–139; varieties, 129–130, 137. *See also* Fruit

Economics: cash economies, 12; downturns, 206–207, 212, 214; and food, 24, 87–88, 116, 119, 198–199, 210, 214, 272–273; global, 6–7, 81–82, 90–91, 94n1, 116, 128; household, 71, 203; markets, 12, 30–31, 46, 74, 132, 208; migration, 150, 229–230; non-monetary indicators, 12, 87–88; subsistence, 81, 83, 85, 176, 184, 186, 227. *See also* Class; Poverty; Wealth

Ecuador, 45, 73

Educational institutions, 80–81, 83, 85, 121n8, 226–227, 230; adult education, 212; and anthropology, 5, 64, 101, 146, 167–168, 181–182, 203, 223, 249; and etiquette, 3–5, 86; and food, 63, 86, 170, 195; and missions, 86, 94, 226–227; and status, 91, 265, 270. *See also* Children: teaching

Eggs: chicken, 62, 92, 102, 109, 200, 213, 215, 246, 259; fertilized, 11, 21, 23, 26–28, 30, 32, 38–39, 52, 279; rotten egg smell, 134; turkey, 21, 24, 26–28, 30, 31, **39**, 39–40; thousand-year-old, 128

Emjombola, 80. *See also* Fruit

Empanadas, 213, 215–216, 218

Ensete, 244, 245. *See also* Tubers

Environment, 128, 129, 171, 260; and agriculture, 206, 225, 229; changes in, 82; and pastoralism, 116, 225, 229; and food, 104–105, 121n7, 199

Environmentalism, 7, 13, 23, 46, 171, 172, 175

Eskimo, 176. *See also* Indigenous peoples

Ethiopia, 14, 243–261; cuisine, 244–246

Etiquette, 13, 148, 172–173; of accepting unfamiliar foods, 3–5, 8–9, 38, 47, 54, 263; of eating, 13, 107, 146, 193–194, 258–259, 260

Famine. *See* Hunger

Farming. *See* Agriculture

Fast food, 11, 73, 153, 196, 230, 236. *See also* McDonald's

Fasting, 245–246

Fava beans, 121n17. *See also* Beans; Vegetables

Feasting, 47, 51–54, 62, 74, 88–89, 186–187, 245–246, 258–260; theories of, 9, 30, 51–52, 245

Feminism, 160

Fenugreek, 244, 248. *See also* Spices

Fermentation, 134, 153, 169, 247, 256. *See also* Rotting

Festivals, 114, 198, 233; and guinea pigs, 60–62, **61**

Feuding. *See* Violence

Fiambre, 51, 53, 105, 106–110, **108**

Fieldnotes. *See* Method

Fig, 245. *See also* Fruit

Finger millet. *See* Millet

Fish, 36, 60, 68, 83, 84, 120n5, 128, 134, 136, 152, 172, 173, 185, 188, 209. *See also* Meat; *various types of fish by name*

Food: and acquired tastes, 4, 12–13, 113, 127, 139–140; advertising, 159; and authenticity, 110–111, 112, 115–117, 119, 236–237, 280; classifications, 26, 112–119, 128–129, 133, 140, 186, 272; in comics, 73; as commodities, 6, 75, 86, 128, 216, 234; as form of communication, 9–10, 52, 182–183, 263–264; and disgust, 4, 8–12, 15, 22, 30, 31, 34–35, 38, 45, 49–50, 114–115, 127–128, 134–135, 137–139, 216, 277; and gender, 11, 12, 14, 27, 32–35, 52, 84–86, 88–89, 90, 92–93, 109, 128–129, 151, 156, 186–188, 192, 200–201, 204, 214–215, 218, 260; and identity, 31, 38, 47, 65–67, 146, 147, 169–170, 216, 245, 264, 272, 279; as indigenous, 65–67, 112, 116–117; in

magazines, 36–37, 114, 118, 200; mealtimes, 50–51, 148, 209; as metaphor, 252; in movies, 55n3; in newspapers, 47, 65–67, 170; pollution, 186, 278; preparing, 28, 45, 62, 90, 92, 104–105, 128, 134–135, 159, 186–187, 192, 199–201, 210–211, 214; presentations of, 36–38, 51, 54–55, 92–93, 118, 214–215; refusing, 8–9, 13, 22–25, 27, 31, 38, 50–52, 80, 111, 114, 121n9, 146, 148–149, 155–159, 161, 169–170, 177, 183, 187–188, 193–194, 253, 269, 279; seasonality, 7, 104–105, 194, 227; serving, 107–109, 192; and shock, 1, 8, 169, 277; and status, 25, 31, 52, 53–54, 81, 84, 92–93, 109, 117–118, 192, 256–260; storage, 102, 104–105, 185, 188, 234; stories about, 3–5, 25–26, 112, 117–118, 270; on television, 6–7, 118, 277; in tour books, 7, 110–111, 113, 117, 121n11, 135

Food aid, 152, 228, 234–235

Food allergies, 11, 13, 145–161, 184–185, 279

Food and Drug Administration (FDA), 153

Food taboos, 11, 13–14, 21, 22–23, 38, 112, 113–115, 118, 121n12, 172, 190, 204, 246, 278, 279; of anthropologists, 49–50, 181–190, 204–205, 213, 219; and gender, 32–35, 38

Fox, 72, 75

France, 7, 192, 194. *See also* North Atlantic

Fruit, 7, 64, 87, 132, 133–134, 136, 140, 206, 210, 234, 237. *See also various types of fruit by name*

Funerals. *See* Death: rituals

Garbanzo. *See* Chickpea

Garden cress, 244. *See also* Vegetables

Garlic, 138, 139, 140, 151, 156, 188, 248. *See also* Spices; Vegetables

Gathering (wild foods), 84, 85, 86, 132, 227

Gauchos, 205, 210; as symbol, 205. *See also* Cowboys

Gender, 82–86, 88–89, 91–92, 264, 268, 270, 272; and fieldwork, 145, 148, 161, 243, 279; and travel, 7, 91–92, 208; and work, 82–86, 91–92, 195–196, 200–201, 218. *See also* Agriculture: and gender; Food: and gender; Food taboos: and gender; Meat: and gender

Genetics: animal, 171; human, 32, 280

Gibnut, 43–55; animal husbandry, 46; biology, 45–46; as meat, 12, 22, 43, 45–50, **49**, 53–55; compared to rat, 12, 22, 47, 49–50, 54–55, 279; as symbol, 47. *See also* Meat

Gift, 12, 44, 47, 51–54, 75, 89, 200; of drink, 88–90, 91, 257–258, 268–269, 270–271; of food, 9, 13, 25, 39, 44–45, 47, 51–53, 75, 80–81, 88–90, 92–93, 133, 229, 235, 260, 261n3; obligation to accept, 4–5, 47, 51–54, 146–147, 148–149, 155, 157, 159, 161, 193, 253, 255; obligation to give, 54, 92, 266; refusing to give, 30, 89–90

Gin, 1–4, **4**, 15n2, 187. *See also* Alcohol

Ginger, 36, 171, 248. *See also* Spices

Globalization, 6, 15n6, 36, 81–82, 85, 116, 172–173, 197–198, 208; and changes in diet, 5–9, 32–34, 36–38, 81, 86–87, 89–93, 116–118, 152–153, 198, 233, 279–280; and homogenization, 6, 14, 197–198, 280

Goat, 69, 84, 85, 244, 250, 260; as meat, 80. *See also* Meat

Grains. *See* Barley; Bread; Cañahua; Grits; Hops; Injera; Maize; Millet; Oats; Obusara; Pasta; Pit'u; Quinua; Rice; Rye; Sorghum; T'eff; Wheat

Grappa, 194. *See also* Alcohol

Grasshoppers, 2–4, **3**, **4**, 145. *See also* Insects

Greece, 204

Greenpeace, 171, 172, 174, 176–177. *See also* Non-Governmental Organizations

Grits, 80. *See also* Grains

Grocery stores, 150–151, 155, 158, 168, 185, 187, 193, 194, 230. *See also* Supermarkets

Gros Ventres, 227. *See also* Indigenous peoples

Groundnuts. *See* Peanuts

Grouper, 185. *See also* Fish

Guatemala, 43, 263, 266

Guinea pig, 60; animal husbandry, 12, 46, 64, **65**, 69–72, **70**, 73–74; archaeology, 12, 62, 68–70, 72; export, 68, 71–72, 73–75; in festivals, 60–62, **61**, 74; folktales, 72; meat, 12, 35, 49, 55, 60–62, **63**, 64–69, 103, 109, 116, 118, 279; in newspapers, 65–67, 71; as offering, 60–62, **61**; as pets, 64, **66**, 70, 75n1; preparations, 62, 67; compared to rat, 60, 73; as symbol, 73, **73**, **74**. *See also* Meat

Haiti, 149

Hawaii, 111

Health, 128–129, 155, 204, 258, 265; and classifications of food, 133; and cooking, 151–152; and fieldwork, 181, 223; healing practices, 227, 254; influences of diet, 12, 14, 116, 153–154, 158–160, 209–210, 213–214, 230–232, 234–237, 280; and nutritious food, 12, 68, 81, 88, 116, 170, 197, 213–214, 216–217, 245; standards for food, 8. *See also* Disease; Food allergies; Medicine

Heart (meat), 260. *See also* Organ meats

Heart disease, 217, 231

Herbs. *See* Spices

High fructose corn syrup, 154, 155. *See also* Sweeteners

Hinduism, 172, 278. *See also* Religion

Honduras, 14–15, 264–273

Honey, 86, 153, 256. *See also* Spices; Sweeteners

Hops, 248, 256. *See also* Grains; Spices

Horse, 114, 225, 227, 229, 244, 280; as meat, 114, 128, 171. *See also* Meat

Hospitality. *See* Commensality; Gift

Hotels, 2, 88, 115, 249–250, 266, 267

Huacatay, 62. *See also* Spices

Human evolution, 244

Humor, 13, 14, 60, 64, 113, 156, 168, 210, 253–254, 265, 266–269, 271–272

Humoral concepts of health, 133, 140

Hunger, 30, 34, 67, 109–110, 214; chronic, 90, 181, 203, 212; famine, 87, 90–91, 206, 212, 228; meat hunger, 187–188, 210, 217. *See also* Irish Potato Famine

Hunting, 131, 171–177, 234–235, 279; poaching, 46, 55n1; and status, 52, 54; subsistence, 21, 26–27, 84–86, 127, 188–190, 227–228, 244. *See also* Birds: hunting; Meat

Hyena, 252

Ice cream, 103, 137, 139, 155. *See also* Dessert

Iceland, 174, 176

Inca, **61**, 60–62, 72, 102

India, 84, 86, 172, 243, 244, 254, 259, 278; cuisine, 6, 136, 196

Indian taco, 237

Indigenous peoples, 52, 60, 81, 102, 105, 115–117, 121n16, 132, 149, 173, 176,

190, 264, 280. *See also various indigenous groups by name*

Indonesia, 129–130, 132, **136**, 182

Injera, 246–248, **247**, 259, 260. *See also* Grains

Insects. *See* Bees; Beetles; Grasshoppers; Locusts; Meat; Moths; Sago grubs; Termites

International Rice Research Institute (IRRI), 183

International Whaling Commission (IWC), 170–171, 173–176, 177n1

Internet, 5, 83, 90, 132, 171, 191

Intestine (meat), 168, 186, 210, 235, 237. *See also* Organ meats

Inuit, 134. *See also* Indigenous peoples

Irish Potato Famine, 117

Isaño, 103, 107, 111, 113. *See also* Tubers

Islam, 254, 278. *See also* Religion

Ispi, 109. *See also* Fish

Italy, 7, 8, 14, 59, 129, 191–201, 249, 278; cuisine, 6, 8, 191, 193, 194, 196, 198–201, 252. *See also* North Atlantic

Jackfruit, 137. *See also* Fruit

Jamaica, 243

Japan, 13, 31, 167–177; cuisine, 68, 153, 168–169, 172, 196, 216

Jerky, 88, 102, 121n13, 188, 235, 251

Joking. *See* Humor

Judaism, 5, 219; cuisine, 183, 186, 204, 214, 278, 279; kosher diet, 186, 204, 214, 278, 279. *See also* Religion

Juice, 87, 136–137, 266

Jungle rat. *See* Gibnut

Kale, 80, 86. *See also* Vegetables

Kenya, 12, 49, 79–94, 128

Kidney, 62, 67, 235, 260. *See also* Organ meats

Kimchi, 128. *See also* Spices

Kinship, 81, 83–85, 88–90, 92, 132, 150, 155–158, 182–183, 208, 211–214, 216–218, 271; of anthropologists, 21, 27, 84, 110, 137–138, 154–158, 182–183, 191–194, 248, 255, 260, 278; anthropologists as "fictive" kin, 83, 84, 94, 101, 104–107, 121n8, 191–192, 255; via food, 9–10, 12, 30, 82, 84, 87–88, 89–90, 91, 92–93, 107–109, 214, 216–218

Kirkiña, 102. *See also* Spices

Kosher diet. *See* Judaism: kosher diet

Labor patterns, 6–7, 14, 82–83, 85–87, 91–92, 152, 158–159, 195, 200–201, 217–218, 225, 230, 266. *See also* Slavery

Lamb. *See* Sheep: meat

Language, 15, 60, 74, 82, 83, 94n1, 104, 109, 110, 153, 161, 167, 168, 175, 187, 194, 260, 273; about food, 7, 12, 22, 36, 49–51, 54–55, 60, 168, 198, 260; learning, 183, 187, 191, 194, 260, 265–269, 270–272, 278; loss, 226–227; revitalization, 226–227

Lard. *See* Animal fat

Lasagne, 198

Law, 13, 188–189, 198–199, 201, 249

Lechon. *See* Pig: lechon

Legumes, 85, 245, 259. *See also various beans, legumes, and vegetables by name*

Lemon, 213–214. *See also* Fruit

Lemongrass, 136. *See also* Spices

Lentil, 210, 213, 245. *See also* Legumes

Lettuce, 209, 224, 234, 237. *See also* Vegetables

Levi-Strauss, Claude, 113; "good to think," 55, 81, 112–117, 118

Lime leaves, 136. *See also* Spices

Lime, 2, 60, 62, 151, 213–214. *See also* Fruit

Liminality, 15, 24, 27, 38–40, 278–279

Liver, 62, 67–68, 121n9, 210, 260. *See also* Organ meats

Llajwa, 102. *See also* Spices

Llama, 64, 101, 172; export, 116; as meat, 13, 101, 102, 112–119, 121n13; as pet, 114; as symbol, 112, 115–116; taboos against, 114–115; in tourist restaurants, 115. *See also* Meat

Locavores, 7

Locoto, 102. *See also* Spices

Locusts, 82, 84. *See also* Insects

Luo, 86–87, 92. *See also* Indigenous peoples

Luyia. *See* Abaluyia

Lychee, 136. *See also* Fruit

Machismo, 188, 208, 265–266

Mackerel, 37, 186. *See also* Fish

Maize, 60, 62, 80, 85–88, 90–91, 103, 107, **108**, 114, **157**, 210, 215, 245; as drink, 151, 269; farming, 85–88, 90–91, 120n5,

132, 234, 245; oil, 151; popcorn, 2, 80, 258. *See also* Grains; High fructose corn syrup; Obusuma

Malaysia, 13, 127–132, 133, 135–139, **136**; cuisine, 136

Malnutrition, 23, 87, 91, 116, 203, 206, 217, 280. *See also* Hunger

Mango, 136, 149. *See also* Fruit

Mangosteen, 137. *See also* Fruit

Mangú, 149, 151

Manioc. *See* Cassava

Maragoli, 86, 89–90. *See also* Abaluyia; Indigenous peoples

Margarine, 87

Market economy. *See* Economics; Money

Marketplaces, 83, 85, 117, **197**; for animals, 69, 74, 85; for food, 46, 85, 137–138, 194–195; lack of, 185. *See also* Economics, markets; Grocery Stores; Supermarkets

Marriage, 9–10, 81, 83, 121n8, 133, 182–183, 191–192, 215, 252–254; arranged, 252–253; rituals, 30, 88, 93, 95n2, 135

Mate. *See* Beverages; Tea: herbal

Maya, 46, 47, 52, 167, 170, 263; archaeology, 1–2, 43, 46, 47, 167, 170, 263, 265

McDonald's, 6, 73, 117, 118, 196, 198, 280. *See also* Meta-commodities

Meat, 11–13, 31, 35, 49, 52–53, 85, 88, 90, 113–114, 128, 149, 151, 152, 156, 186–187, 193, 204, 210; canned, 36; cured, 199, **199**; dried, *see* Jerky; feet, 52, 182–183; and gender, 52, 54; heads, 13, 52, 68, 114, 182–183; live, 22, 79–80, 93; preserving, 188; raw, 168; roadkill, 47–48; sausages, 11, 45, 115, 193, 204, 210. *See also* Animal fat; Hunting; Organ meats; Pets: as food; *specific animal species by name*

Medicine, 36, 128, 133, 154, 227, 243, 269

Melanesia, 31, 36; cuisine, 23

Memory, 9–10, 40, 87–88, 145, 147, 149, 154, 233

Merienda. *See* Fiambre

Meta-commodities, 6, 216, 280. *See also* Coca-cola; McDonald's

Metallurgy, 85, 88, 102

Method: anthropological, 9–10, 12, 15, 26, 40, 83, 94n1, 114, 147–148, 155–159, 160, 192, 207–209, 212, 214–219, 231–233, 237–238, 253; archaeological, 68–72; and cooking, 199–201, 212, 215–216; and

discomfort, 8–9, 15, 24, 212, 279; and eating, 4–5, 9–10, 11–14, 24–25, 36–38, 40, 67–68, 108–109, 120n4, 148–149, 154, 204–205, 214, 218, 236–239; fieldnotes, 120n4, 147, 253; life histories, 83, 88–89, 232–233; long-term, 82, 161, 243; maps, 147, 155–156, 158; and objectivity, 11, 159; participant-observation, 12, 29–30, 67–68, 83, 104, 137, 147, 158–159, 199–201, 204–205, 209, 211–213, 218, 232, 236–238, 264–265; and nutrition, 233, 232–234; reflexivity, 26, 35, 160–161, 237–238; training in, 4–5, 9, 14, 181–182, 204. *See also* Cultural relativism

Mexico, 1–5, 6, 43, 45, 52, 227, 263

Mezcal, 1, 4, 15n1. *See also* Alcohol

Migration, 5, 10, 32, 82–86, 91–92, 95n4, 106, 145–147, 150, 155, 182, 196, **197**, 227, 228–229; and remittances, 92, 150, 228–229

Milk, 36, 62, 85, 86, 88, 90, 110, 128, 148, 195, 200, 204, 246, 255; evaporated, 151. *See also* Beverages

Millet, 80, 84, 85, 86, 114, 244, 245. *See also* Grains

Mintz, Sidney, 6, 9, 10, 12, 38, 112, 128, 129, 149, 152, 216

Missionaries. *See* Christianity

Modernization. *See* Globalization

Molasses, 139, 153. *See also* Spices; Sweeteners

Money, 111, 218, 253, 265; currency, 115; gifts of, 83, 91–93, 95n2; introduction of, 82, 86, 90; lack of, 85, 88, 91–93; remittances, 150. *See also* Economics; Poverty; Wealth

Monitor Lizard, 190. *See also* Meat

Monkey, 131, 189–190; as meat, 181, 190. *See also* Meat

Morality, 7, 13, 175–177, 264

Moths, 84. *See also* Insects

MSG, 145–147, 151, 154, 156–160; addiction, 153–154, 156–157; affect on humans, 145–147, 153–154, 159–160. *See also* Spices

Mule, 244

Multiculturalism, 5, 13–14, 196

Mushrooms, 93. *See also* Vegetables

Mustard, 244. *See also* Spices

Mutton. *See* Sheep: as meat

Nationalism, 62–64, 67, 73, 116–117, 205, 216, 246–247, 272

Netherlands, 175

New York City, 68, 145–161, 203, 215. *See also* United States

New Zealand, 175, 176

Nile Perch, 93. *See also* Fish

Non-Governmental Organizations (NGOs), 203, 212. *See also* Greenpeace; Sea Shepherd Conservation Society; Slow Food Movement; Slow Water

Noodles. *See* Pasta

North Atlantic, 5–9, 11–15, 15n6, 102, 112–114, 117–119, 121n16. *See also* Canada; Denmark; France; Italy; Norway; Spain; United Kingdom; United States

Norway, 174, 176. *See also* North Atlantic

Nubia, 244. *See also* Indigenous peoples

Nug, 244. *See also* Spices

Nutmeg, 148, 248. *See also* Spices

Nutrition, 13, 25, 30, 62, 87, 93, 113, 116–117, 129, 181, 185–186, 214, 223–224, 231–232, 236, 238–239, 280

Oats, 151, 154, 245. *See also* Grains

Obesity, 81, 87, 153, 214, 217

Obusara, 90, 91. *See also* Grains

Obusuma, 80, 85, 88, 91, 92–93

Oca, 103, 107, 113. *See also* Tubers

Ohnuki-Tierney, Emiko, 31, 216

Okra, 128. *See also* Vegetables

Olives, 120n2, 245; oil, 151. *See also* Fruit

Omutere, 80. *See also* Vegetables

Onion, 60, 62, 80, 86, 109, 156, 193, 209, 213, 237; comparisons to, 133, 138–139. *See also* Vegetables

Oranges, 134, 149. *See also* Fruit

Oregano, 151. *See also* Spices

Organ meats, 114, 186, 205, 215. *See also* Blood; *specific organs by name*

Other. *See* Alterity

Overeating, 25, 81, 193–194, 237, 260

Pachamama, 109

Panama, 46, 52

Pandanus, 28–29, **29**, 32, 36; preparation of sauce, 28–29. *See also* Fruit

Papaliza, 113. *See also* Tubers

Papaya, 136, **150**. *See also* Fruit

Papua New Guinea, 11, 21–41, 51, 245

Paraguay, 45

Passion Fruit, 136. *See also* Fruit

Pasta, 6, 14, 103, 107, 116, 136, 183, 186, 192–193, 198, 200, 234, 235, 238, 279; making, 200. *See also* Grains; Ramen

Pastries, 154, 168, 193, 252. *See also* Dessert

Peanuts, 80, 84, 85, 102; peanut butter, 168, 189. *See also* Legumes

Peas, 234, 259. *See also* Legumes; Vegetables

Peccary, 46. *See also* Meat

Pepper (black), 188, 248. *See also* Spices

Peppers, 85, **152**

Peru, 45, 59–75; cuisine, 59–60

Pets, 12, 27–28, 35, 43, 64, 66, **66**, 187; as food, 12, 35, 64–65, 114, 118, 187–188, 279. *See also* Meat

Philippines, 13–14, 129, 182–190; cuisine, 187–188

Photography, 36–37, 64, 67, 71–72, 104, 112, 121n7, 121n10, 132, 145, 148, 158, 159

Pig, 28, 67, 149, 172, 184; avoiding, 204, 246; bacon, 228; cured fat, 198–199; ham, 188, 200; lechon, 186; meat, 26, 49, 53, 62, 109, 172, 186, 188–189, 193; "pig bomb," 188–189; salami, 199, **199**; sausage, 193; wild, 131, 188–189. *See also* Meat

Pineapple, 136–137. *See also* Fruit

Pit'u, 116, 121n17. *See also* Beverages; Grains

Pizza, 154, 196; comparisons to, 29, **29**, 107

Plantain, 84, 103, 107. *See also* Fruit; Mangú

Poi, 111. *See also* Tubers

Poison, 257–258

Poma de Ayala, Guaman, 60, **61**. *See also* Indigenous peoples

Pomelo, 137. *See also* Fruit

Pork. *See* Pig

Portugal. *See* Colonialism: Portuguese in Africa; Colonialism: Portuguese in the Americas

Potato, 12, 62, 107, **108**, 109–114, 117, 119, 209, 210, 215, 223–224, 234, 235; chips, 6, 81, 153, 186; and colonialism, 60, 86, 102–103, 128, 245; "meat and potatoes," 80, 223–224; planting, 106–110, 234; in tour books, 75; varieties, 64, 102–104, 106, 117, 120n6. *See also* Chuño; Irish Potato Famine; Tubers; Tunta

Poverty, 121n16, 212; expressed through food, 114–117; and global economic systems, 82, 87, 90–93, 95n3, 207–208, 229–230; and nutrition, 214, 217, 234. *See also* Economics; Wealth

Pregnancy, 121n12, 128, 253

Processed foods, 114, 116, 152, 153–155, 160, 196, 198, 236

Prosecco, 195. *See also* Alcohol

Puerto Rico, 154

Pulutan, 186–188

Qat, 244. *See also* Beverages

Qatiqala, 253, 257–258. *See also* Alcohol

Quechua, 60. *See also* Indigenous peoples

Queen Elizabeth II, 1, 2, 47, 50

Quinine, 1, 2, 15n4

Quinua, 103, 107, 110, 116, 120n5, 121n17. *See also* Grains

Rabbit, 55, 65; comparison to, 69. *See also* Meat

Race, 66, 83–84, 119, 161; and food, 22, 31, 36, 80, 278, 279

Rambutan, 137. *See also* Fruit

Ramen, 153–154

Rat, 55n3. *See also* Gibnut: compared to rat; Guinea pig: compared to rat

Reciprocity. *See* Commensality; Gift

Red snapper, 185. *See also* Fish

Religion, 9, 11, 21, 32, 35, 82, 85, 109, 171, 227, 245, 264. *See also* Buddhism; Christianity; Hinduism; Islam; Judaism

Remolacha, 113. *See also* Tubers

Restaurants, 69–71, 73–75, 105, 150, 154–155, 171, 209, 230, **231**, 266, 267; anthropologists' experiences in, 2–3, 67–68, 105, 137, 147, 158, 168–169, 216; and class, 8, 105, 114; distinct cuisines of, 8, 110, 118–119, 121n13, 128, 153, 198; vs. home-cooked food, 128, 151, 191, 195–196, 198, 218, 259; multicultural cosmopolitanism, 5–8; touristic, 110–112, 115, 121n13–15

Rice, 36, 37, 87, 93, 103, 107, 114, 116, 117, 119, 136, 151, **157**, 158, 183, 185, 229, 234, 235; farming, 132, 149, 184, 188–190; pudding, 26, 31, 36; rice and beans, 149, 151; as symbol, 31, 216; wine vinegar, 188. *See also* Grains

Rotting, 128, 134

Rue (spice), 250. *See also* Spices

Rum, 265–266, 269, 270. *See also* Alcohol

Russia, 74, 174, 175, 213

Rutabaga, 234, 235. *See also* Tubers; Vegetables

Rye, 245. *See also* Grains

Safflower, 244. *See also* Spices

Sago: as bread, 23–24, 26, 30, **39**, 39–40, **40**; pudding, **37**

Sago grubs, 11, 22–23, **23**, 27, 29, 31, 36. *See also* Insects

Salad, 53, 62, 151, 193, 209, 213, 224, 236, 259. *See also* Vegetables

Salt, 2, 80, 86, 87, 90, 93, 107, 152–154, 185, 188, 228, 248, 250, 251; rehydration salts, 255. *See also* Spices

Sambal, 136

Samia, 82–90, 93–94. *See also* Abaluyia; Indigenous peoples

Samosas, 6, 86

San, 30, 188

Sancocho, 149, 151, 155, 156, **157**

Sanitation, 259; of food, 111, 155, 255, 259; of water, 135–136, 254–255

Sardines, 109. *See also* Fish

Sarsi, 227. *See also* Indigenous peoples

Sarvisberry (Serviceberry), 235. *See also* Fruit

Schools. *See* Educational institutions

Scorpions, 8. *See also* Meat

Sea Shepherd Conservation Society, 174, 175, 176–177, 177n2. *See also* Non-Governmental Organizations

Seafood, 36, 37, 84, 93, 109, 115, 120n5, 121n15, 128, 134, 136, 152, 172–173, 185, 187–188, 210. *See also* Meat; *specific types of seafood by name*

Sesame, 84, 88. *See also* Spices

Sex, 52, 81, 84, 110–111, 113, 128, 132, 245, 250, 252–254

Shallots, 248. *See also* Vegetables

Sheep, 84, 85, 149, 244; head, 114; liver, 121n9, 260; meat, 53, 102, 103, 109, 113, 115, 116, 171, 246, 248, 251, 259, 260. *See also* Meat

Shellfish, 184–185. *See also* Seafood

Shining Path (Sendero Luminoso), 67

Shrimp, 136

Singapore, 134, 135

Slavery, 6, 7, 85, 149

Slow Food Movement, 14, 196–198, 280. *See also* Non-Governmental Organizations

Slow Water, 191. *See also* Non-Governmental Organizations

Smoking. *See* Tobacco

Snacks, 6–7, 28, 80, 128, 151–152, 195, 212

Snail, 128. *See also* Meat

Snake, 128, 185. *See also* Meat

Soda, 12, 15n5, 87, 91, 109, 195, 228, 235–236, 266, 268; "Soda test," 12, 91. *See also* Beverages

Somalia, 254

Songhay, 9–10. *See also* Indigenous peoples

Sorghum, 80, 84, 85, 86, 88, 91, 245. *See also* Grains

Soup, 93, 103, 105, 107, 109, 128, 136, 151, 153, 155, 156, 182–183, 193, 210, 235; canned, 154; packages, 87, 152, 154. *See also* Bouillon; Chairo

South Africa, 79, 244

South Korea, 174

South Piegan. *See* Blackfeet

Soybean, 172, 206; natto, 169; soy sauce, 8, 187, 188. *See also* Legumes

Spain, 6, 191, 205; cuisine, 188; language, 104, 146, 148. *See also* Colonialism; North Atlantic

Spices, 149, 152. *See also specific spices by name*

Spicy food, 36, 102, **108**, 136, 139, 145, 237, 259

Spinach, 234. *See also* Vegetables

Sports, 73, 115, 121n10

Squash, 85, 185, 245. *See also* Vegetables

Squid, 187. *See also* Seafood

Squirrel, 46, 49. *See also* Meat

Star fruit, 136. *See also* Fruit

Stew, 62, 149, 152, 157, 158, 190, 193, 235, 259

Stoller, Paul, 9–10

Stomach (meat), 235, 237. *See also* Organ meats

Strawberry, 194–195. *See also* Fruit

Street food, 2–3, 80, 113, 115, 136–137, 150, 151, 153, 154, 209, 267

Sugar, 36, 87, 90, 92, 139, 145–149, 152–154, 160, 185, 228, 235; addiction to, 153–154, 156; agriculture of, 208, 212, 213; in beverages, 80, 86, 121n17,

148–149, 151, 158, 250, 254; farming, 206–207, 212; increasing consumption of, 12, 116, 228; and the Industrial Revolution, 6; market, 206–207. *See also* Spices; Sweeteners

Supermarkets, 5–7, 37, 150, 152, 154–155, 160, 171, 193, 194–195, 198, 209, 216–217, 230, **231**, 234. *See also* Grocery Stores; Markets

Swahili, 80, 83, 94n1

Sweet potato, 26, **27**, 28, 36, 60, 85, 88, 103, 107, 114

Sweeteners. *See* High fructose corn syrup; Honey; Molasses; Sugar

T'alla, 253, 256, 258. *See also* Alcohol

T'eff, 244, 245, 247, 248. *See also* Grains

T'ej, 256–257, **257**. *See also* Alcohol

Taboos. *See* Food taboos

Tagalog, 183, 187

Tagbanua, 188, 190. *See also* Indigenous peoples

Tamales, 213

Tapioca, 26. *See also* Cassava

Taro, 23, 26, 28, 36. *See also* Tubers

Tea, 36, 80, 86, 90, 128, 155, 158, 254–255; herbal, 116, 215, 121n17. *See also* Beverages; Qat

Telephone. *See* Cell phones

Television, 6, 90, 118, 156, 195–196, 250, 277

Tequila, 15n1. *See also* Alcohol

Termites, 12, 22, 79–81, 82, 83–84, 93–94, 279. *See also* Insects

Terrestrial phalanger, 26, 32, **33**. *See also* Meat

Thailand, 7, 129, 131, 134, 135; cuisine, 5–6, 136, 153, 196

Theft, 83, 86, 87

Tobacco, 159, 228, 236

Tomato, 7, 11, 80, 86, 102, 109, 140, 193, 209, 213, 234, 237, 238; comparisons to, 29. *See also* Fruit; Vegetables

Tortilla, 128; chips, 6; Mesoamerican, 109, 272; Bolivian, 109

Tourism, 1, 5, 59, 64–67, 101, 110–112, 116–120, 135–136, 175, 230, 265, 280; as distinct from anthropology, 5, 12, 119; food tourism, 7–8, 67, 136; tour books, 75, 110–111, 113, 116, 117, 121n10, 121n11, 135; touristic cuisine, 110–119.

See also Food: tour books; Restaurants: touristic

Trade, 83, 87, 227–228; of foodstuffs, 5–7, 32, 36, 39, 71, 73–75, 83, 85, 102, 115, 128, 151, 175, 188–189, 207, 228, 254

Tripe. *See* Intestine

Trout, 115, 121n15, 128. *See also* Fish

Tubers, 28, 30, 103, 107–109, 113, 149, 158, 234. *See also specific tubers by name*

Tuna, 173, 192, 213. *See also* Fish

Tunta, 105, 107, 110, 113, 117, 119, 120n3. *See also* Tubers

Tupi, 60. *See also* Indigenous peoples

Turkey, **28**, 39, 73, 114; as pet, 27–28. *See also* Eggs: turkey; Meat

Turmeric, 248. *See also* Spices

Turnip, 235. *See also* Tubers; Vegetables

Ugali. *See* Obusuma

Uganda, 83

Umami, 153

United Kingdom, 2, 6, 15n3, 43, 47, 59, 86, 176, cuisine, 53. *See also* Colonialism: British in Africa; Colonialism: British Empire; North Atlantic

United States, 105, 106, 120n1, 121n7, 145–161, 173–174, 175, 176, 181–182, 207, 219, **225**, 226–229, 243, 246, 268; comparisons to, 186, 206, 210, 214, 216–217, 269; as cosmopolitan, 8; cuisine, 5–8, 14–15, 15n6, 30, 80, 101–102, 113, 145–161, 172, 236; embassy, 246, 255; export to, 71–72, 74; food aid programs, 234; food aversions, 12, 14–15, 15n6, 22–23, 30, 38, 64–65, 70, 127, 140, 145–161, 168, 213, 277–278; missionaries, 86; privilege of citizenship, 83–84; symbols, 73; tourists, 59, 101–102, 111–114, 117–119. *See also* North Atlantic

Vanatinai islanders, 30. *See also* Indigenous peoples

Veal. *See* Cattle, veal

Veblen, Thorstein, 7–8

Veganism, 146, 245

Vegetables, 7, 11, 37, 53, 80, 85, 114, 132, 140, 185, 186, 193, 194, 209, 210, 215–216, 229, 234–237, 248, 259, 279. *See also specific vegetables by name*

Vegetarianism, 14, 23, 53, 114, 172, 203–219, 245, 279

Vietnam, cuisine, 65

Violence, 85, 103, 149, 176–177, 207, 208, 245, 266, 271; and the state, 188, 207, 228; warfare, 34, 51, 245; metaphorical, 73, 253–254. *See also* World War II

Vodka, 257. *See also* Alcohol

Warfare. *See* Violence

Wari', 32. *See also* Indigenous peoples

Water Buffalo, 188

Watermelon, 136. *See also* Fruit

Wealth, 8, 31, 81, 83–84, 87–88, 89–90, 91, 102, 119, 121n7, 186, 256–257

Weddings. *See* Marriage: rituals

Whale: conservation debates, 170–173, 175–177, 280; as divine, 171; historic consumption, 171; meat, 13, 37, 134, 169, 170–173, 279; taste, 171–172; watching, 175. *See also* Seafood

Wheat, 90, 103, 114, 121n17, 200, 225, 229, 244, 245, 247, 248, 251, 256; flour, 109, 200, 228–229, 234, 235. *See also* Bread; Grains; Pasta

Whisky, 257–258, **259**, 266, 271. *See also* Alcohol

Wilk, Richard, 46, 47, 50, 117

Wine, 1, 7, 133, 139, 193, 195, 198, 201, 245, 257; rice wine vinegar, 188. *See also* Alcohol

World War II, 7, 171, 184, 229–230, 249. *See also* Violence; Warfare

World Wildlife Fund (WWF), 170

Yams, 149

Yuca. *See* Cassava

Zapatistas, 5. *See also* Indigenous peoples

Zucchini, 185, 216. *See also* Vegetables

Zulu, 79. *See also* Indigenous peoples